• PASSWORDS •

Passwords

Philology, Security, Authentication

BRIAN LENNON

THE BELKNAP PRESS OF
HARVARD UNIVERSITY PRESS

Cambridge, Massachusetts
London, England
2018

Library of Congress Cataloging-in-Publication Data
Names: Lennon, Brian, 1971– author.
Title: Passwords : philology, security, authentication / Brian Lennon.
Description: Cambridge, Massachusetts : The Belknap Press of Harvard
University Press, 2018. | Includes bibliographical references and index.
Identifiers: LCCN 2017031078 | ISBN 9780674980761 (alk. paper)
Subjects: LCSH: Computers—Access control—Passwords. | Cryptography. |
Data encryption (Computer science) | Philology. | Electronic surveillance.
Classification: LCC QA76.9.A25 L485 2018 | DDC 005.8 / 24—dc23
LC record available at https://lccn.loc.gov/2017031078

Contents

Preface

Proclamations of a digital age, and of its imminent transformation of every aspect and way of life, are old news. We know this by now. Still, in an era of systemic—that is, regular and engineered—political, economic, and cultural crisis, we volunteer to forget what we know, at each lap in the cycle. One might want to think that cultural workers—writers, artists, scholars, educators, and others in the arts, communication, and culture industries—are less tempted by such presentism, since they are free to contemplate the past if they wish. But under the right conditions and in response to the correct incentives, those with the most apparent freedom to think are among the most eager to suspend their own freedom.

The more or less psychological aspects of such behavior are not my concern in this book. Their documentation, in such pretty good sellers as Nicholas Carr's *The Shallows: What the Internet Is Doing to Our Brains*, Eli Pariser's *The Filter Bubble: What the Internet Is Hiding from You*, Jaron Lanier's *You Are Not a Gadget: A Manifesto*, and Sherry Turkle's *Alone Together: Why We Expect More from Technology and Less from Each Other* has done little to redirect them.[1] That may be because such works are important yet unimportant, much as the convention that the house always wins is acknowledged by the thoughtful gambler, and then declared beside the point.

"Since the financial crisis," Gideon Lewis-Kraus recently wrote of the private equity bubble of our moment, so-called unicorn companies, "along with their more established public predecessors, have been seen by many Americans as the last redoubt of confidence and productivity in an otherwise uneven recovery."[2] The severity of the so-called Great Recession, the continued depression of lower- and middle-income wages and assets, and the dramatic increase in U.S. income inequality during an uneven recovery are facts. Few will sincerely object to Lewis-Kraus's characterization of the technology industry in the United States as the "last redoubt of confidence and productivity" in our economic era, at least in the public imagination. Those able to find work in that sector in the years since 2008 have enjoyed at least the appearance of prosperity, and that matters. Those who, plausibly or implausibly, have imagined themselves retraining for such work have enjoyed it more anxiously. (No less so, to be sure, for the questions of value it raised, in leading us to a moment when "people are using Facebook to showcase suicides, beatings and murder, in real time," when "Twitter is a hive of trolling and abuse that it seems unable to stop," and when "fake news, whether created for ideology or profit, runs rampant.")[3]

The desperation introduced by the real estate panic of 2008 helped to remove the last of the tarnish from the Silicon Valley venture culture that had inflated the dot-com bubble of 1997–2000, while predatory investors, abandoning the securitization of U.S. homeownership, moved on to attack higher education. At the college and university level in the United States, a vast wave of hype, which would last through late 2013, encouraged the force-feeding of automated and virtualized education in the form of Massive Open Online Courses (MOOCs). Profoundly regretting their own educations, for the tedium of which they accepted no personal blame, an emboldened new class of edtech consultants, freelance opinionistas, and university apparatchiks of all stripes promised to flip classrooms and remove sages from stages. Much talk and some actual legislation boosted symbolic and material support for the expansion of instruction in so-called STEM disciplines—more precisely, in anything, disciplined or undisciplined, that promised defined technical applications. Obligingly, the social sciences and the humanities discovered the word "digital," manufactured new troves of data and new tools for fooling with them, and otherwise bent themselves to broadcasting compliance. As always, they moved slowly. Even computer science departments, whose enrollments had exploded again, reversing a five-year decline, faced complaints about useless "theory." Bootcamp-style coding schools promptly appeared in every major U.S. city, training an expeditionary force of junior web developers to meet market demand or depress wages, depending on whom one asked. Taken together, these developments promised that educational reform, new labor efficiencies, and new intellectual synergies would effect economic stabilization through vocational retraining for the unemployed and underemployed middle classes.[4]

What, one might ask, did U.S. college and university students think of that? The answer is not much. Many, perhaps most, more or less glumly accepted the fate the opinionistas promised them: that is, of living with their parents into their thirties (their forties? evermore?) while things sorted themselves out. Some are among those who told the National Society of High School Scholars that their ideal future employers included Google, Apple, the Federal Bureau of Investigation, Microsoft, the Central Intelligence Agency, Amazon, the National Security Agency, Facebook, the U.S. Army, and J. P. Morgan Chase, in that order.[5] A smaller proportion, no doubt, joined what would come to be called the Occupy movements, or the movements that would come to be called Black Lives Matter, or otherwise laid the foundations of the new, notably uncompromising student militance that would erupt on the national stage in 2015.

And the professionals? Were free, freelance, or academic cultural workers slow to respond to the new dispensation? Certainly not in the case of the self-appointed edupreneurial class, to whose tablet screens, perched on coffeehouse tables, wireless keyboards relayed the new soothsayings. From some of the rest of us, polemics construing the events of 2008 as avoidable disasters, rather than mystified opportunities, also appeared promptly. U.S. anthropologist David Graeber's *Debt: The First 5000 Years* made a quick splash with a long view. French economist Thomas Piketty's *Capital in the Twenty-First Century* became a bestseller on both sides of the pond. U.S. filmmaker Astra Taylor's *The People's Platform: Taking Back Power and Culture in the Digital Age* focused the general economic diagnosis on issues in digital and network culture specifically. A new domain named "critical university studies," devoted to scrutinizing the autocannibalization of higher education, gained traction slowly, but is today the special focus of book publishing series supported by at least two prominent presses. In the study of literary media culture more narrowly and specifically, the advertisement of Annie McClanahan's *Dead Pledges: Debt, Crisis, and Twenty-First-Century Culture* as "the first book to explore the ways that U.S. culture—from novels and poems to photojournalism and horror movies—has responded to the collapse of the financialized consumer credit economy in 2008" is not inaccurate.[6]

· · · ·

I REGARD 2008 AS A PIVOTAL year—a transition in recent history or the historical present, as were the years 1989, 1991, and 2001. In reorienting the attention of cultural workers, and in demanding a response, such moments force shifts in intellectual history, though the visible effects of such shifts are often delayed. In this book I sometimes argue and I everywhere imply that nothing in the activities of cultural workers is unmarked by the economic trauma of 2008. But in defining what I see as our era of present history, in the United States, the year 2008 is but a second moment of trauma in relation to the events of 2001, which ensured that U.S. citizens and other taxpayers would be funding sadistically asymmetric material and ideological warfare, judicially legitimated and academically abetted military and police torture, and other, equally violent human and civil rights abuses for decades to come. Altogether, I think it is fair to say that the period since 2001 and including 2008, in the United States in particular, has been an era not of burgeoning "culture, creativity, and commerce," as one remarkably circumscribed cultural history of the last decade has it, but of brutality, bootlicking, and bank fraud—just to begin with.[7] While one might not want to say that *nothing* good can have emerged from the cultural change of the period in question, it would be infantile to deny that conditions for goodness have been unpropitious in the extreme, possibly as unpropitious as they have ever been in U.S. postwar history. (One wonders if those unmoved by unprecedented income inequality might be more impressed by a 2016 publication by the Centers for Disease Control and Prevention, a U.S. federal agency, reporting that U.S. suicide rates increased by 24 percent from 1999 to 2014, with markedly greater increases beginning in 2006.[8])

As I see it, the panic of 2008 added economic immiseration to the civic and political instability of the years following the U.S. national security crisis of 2001. In *A Curriculum of Fear: Homeland Security in US Public Schools,* Nicole Nguyen has chronicled its effects on the U.S. secondary education system, as the antiterrorism industry that emerged after 2001 found allies of convenience in educational policy wonks and school administrators to whom unfriendly legislators were applying the screws.[9] It was only after 2013, with exposure of the vastly expanded surveillance programs of the U.S. National Security Agency and its sibling and child agencies, that the role of security in post-2001 political and economic reformism aimed at the higher education system, among other domains, could be clearly suggested.[10] Today it is in no way far-fetched to speak of an "academic surveillance complex" whose operations are actively or passively aligned with new modes of authoritarianism.[11]

As it had through the Second World War and the Cold War that followed it, with a lull during the 1970s, STEM discipline boosterism served to justify and naturalize massive investment in weaponry of all kinds, not excluding both research and teaching as weaponizable endeavors. The latest wave of automated education was not merely a vehicle for pedagogical experimentation, but a subprocess of a general securitization of higher education whose products are homologous to and sometimes contiguous with new military and police tech—for example, in text-based biometric identification techniques like the typing pattern recognition system used by MOOC provider Coursera's Signature Track offering, itself merely a variation on one of many techniques developed by security agencies for monitoring internet communication by analyzing text patterns in real time. Each of the major disciplinary clusters that organize teaching and research in the United States, from secondary through higher education, was offered its own avenues to renewed complicity in military adventurism. Until the so-called revelations of 2013, for example, enthusiasts of the "digital humanities" movement that emerged promptly and by some accounts grew rapidly after 2001 were uncircumspect

regarding the legitimation and the opportunities that the vastly enlarged scale and activity of U.S. security agencies had afforded their work
in humanistic information retrieval and natural language processing.
Far from being new and unprecedented, this structural alignment of a
revived or resurgent philology with the activities, if not always or necessarily the goals of the surveillance state, serves to recall the long history
of literary humanists' active and open service to security agencies, beginning with the direction of First World War military cryptanalytic
service units by scholars of the works of William Shakespeare.

In providing us with some facts, the so-called revelations of 2013 now
afford us the opportunity to study the culture that supported the growth
of U.S. security agencies, in the years since 2001, and their role in the
post-2001 transformation of the U.S. university, among other domains.
Opportunities for such study will be configured differently for each of
the major divisions of research and teaching, and I have felt no desire,
need, or obligation, in writing this book, to pretend that I am in any way
or in the smallest part a social scientist, a natural scientist, an engineer,
or a vocational professional instead of what I am, a humanities-based
scholar and critic of post-1945 and contemporary culture. In the humanities disciplines, I suggest, and specifically in the literary humanities, it
will be in returning to the historical origins of philology and secular
humanism in the western hemisphere, to the divergence of philology
from and reconvergence with military cryptanalysis, in the epochs of
European and U.S. imperialism, and to the path that the computational
analysis of literary text in particular has followed in the United States,
from the mid-nineteenth century through the Cold War—none of these
being anything less than integral to the history of the so-called humanities as we know it—that we find our best opportunity to historicize the
recent past and draw some normative conclusions about it.

· · · ·

TODAY WE REGARD CRYPTOLOGY, the mathematical and technical
science of ciphers and codes, and philology, the humanistic study of
natural or human languages and documents, as separate domains of
activity. But the contiguity, even intimacy of these two domains is a
historical fact with an institutional history. From the earliest docu-

mented techniques for the statistical analysis of text and experiments with mechanized literary analysis, to electromechanical and electronic code-breaking and machine translation, early literary data processing, and the computational philology of late twentieth-century humanities computing and early twenty-first-century "digital humanities," what I call *cryptophilology* has flourished alongside imperial jingoism and war—and occasionally served them. In this book I argue that while computing's humanistic applications are every bit as historically important as its mathematical and technical origins, they are no less marked and no less constrained by the priorities of national security agencies and institutions devoted to both offensive signals intelligence and mass surveillance—and that our hope for human progress must be tempered by that, so far as even (or especially) in modern democracies, the proliferation of security institutions and the scale of their operations can be justified only by and through programmatically sustained insecurity.

This book is a specific, angular history of institutions, institutionality, and institutionalization—chiefly those associated with the university in its North American form. That makes it an academic book, to be sure, in more senses than one. Still, any reader who is not actively allergic to the university and is curious about the longer histories and historical contexts of those new applications of computing to cultural data that we've heard so much about in the last decade, from digitizing and indexing millions of books, photographs and paintings, and audio and video recordings to automated real-time analysis of the firehoses of textual, visual, and audio data (not to mention personally identifying information) exposed by social media platforms and services, should find something of interest in this book. Not unlike the phrase and concept "big data," albeit in more restricted contexts, the phrase and the concept "digital humanities," which appeared during the 2000s, now floats freely in both the academic humanities and cultural journalism as a descriptor of practices of computational analysis trained specifically on the cultural data of the arts and the entertainment industries, rather than natural- or physical-scientific data, social-scientific data, or financial and other business data. That even after more than a decade of energetic speculation, the phrase and the concept "digital humanities" still frustrates attempts at provisional definition, let alone precision, is a liability and a predicament for anyone who has come to realize that sustained shouting about novelty only deafens.

History offers some help here. We might begin by recalling that the first electromechanical and electronic computers were constructed for two quite different applications, one computational in the primary sense (automating the analysis of aerodynamic measurements, in the case of the Zuse Z3 in Berlin, or ballistics calculations, in the case of the ENIAC at the University of Pennsylvania), and another that was as textual as it was anything else (the manipulation of symbolic cipher systems used to encipher natural-language written text, by the Bombe and Colossus machines at Bletchley Park). Further, that machine translation or "MT," the earliest name for the operation performed for us today by a service like Google Translate, was the first undertaking with which wartime computers were tasked (or burdened) in postwar peacetime. And still further, that the very earliest work in literary data processing, as we know it today, was undertaken at the same moment, in the use of computer programs to compile concordances of canonical works of western theology and literature.

Andrew Kopec has argued that "for better or worse, through their fluidity the digital humanities reproduce the hallmarks of postindustrialism—flexibility, teamwork, and so on—and, in doing so, dream of training people to contribute in the increasingly compressed space-time of the global economy."[12] To this I would add that the phrase and concept "digital humanities" also serves to dissociate scholarship from its past, enabling it to continue uninterrupted and uninterrogated as something ostensibly new. Those who insist, today, that this phrase and concept stands for a set of practices crossing or linking several or many disciplines are for the most part quite mistaken, though possibly only through ignorance of its formation in and emergence from literary scholarship in particular (and perhaps also of similar but separate histories, such as those of "cliometrics" in historiography and logic programming in legal scholarship[13]). Though I grant the phrase and concept "digital humanities" due credit (and blame) for its inspecificity, my main focus, in the larger part of this book, is on the history of efforts to mechanically and electronically automate the interpretive analysis of text, rather than on the history of the remediation (that is, reproduction in other media) of printed text as such, including digitization. The modes of such analysis in which I am interested have their origins in, and still bear predominantly on, literary-critical and scholarly questions, from translation (an interpretive act, whether we like it or not) to the identification and verification of authorship and authorial identity, or typical and variant traits of literary and nonliterary genres and style. The most suitable designator of a genus of such projects is the phrase "computational philology."

I use the latter term to refer very broadly to an ensemble of contemporary scholarly practices whose representatives have largely welcomed the umbrella term "digital humanities," and whose predominantly quantitative-analytic approaches to literary research questions have been indispensable to the publicity the digital humanities movement received beginning in the late 2000s. Within such an ensemble, such domain- and subdomain-specific terms as "stylometry," "computational stylistics," "authorship attribution," and "authorship verification," among others, can be granted their own specificity; but that specificity ought not to be exaggerated. Indeed, the historical origins of such research practices suggest that they can sensibly be collectively termed *cryptophilology,* in at least two possible senses of the latter term (a more apposite term, in my view, than "e-philology"[14]). The first sense, in which "crypto" suggests secrecy or concealment of identity, would mark the accidentally or deliberately obfuscated historical relationship of ostensibly new techniques of automated analysis, within the contemporary humanities, to a much longer history of philology. A second sense, in which "crypto" is not a modifier but one part of a portmanteau word, marks the routine and uncontroversial historical intimacy of philology with cryptology established by shared, analogous, or homologous techniques for the relative frequency analysis of letters, words, and other units of written text. Where such analysis produces a message with a meaning whose secrecy and revelation through an automated computational procedure lend it authority, and whose context or occasion enjoins us to accept it as meaningful fact, whether that message be "Attack at dawn" or "James Joyce used more color words than T. S. Eliot," it is fundamentally cryptanalytic, treating a text as a cipher.[15]

. . . .

BY THE NINTH CENTURY, Quranic philology had established the methodological basis for an Arab Muslim science of cryptanalysis including sophisticated techniques for measuring and predictively extrapolating from measurements of letter and word frequencies in written Arabic. This is knowledge that did not emerge from Jewish or Christian theological textual practices at the same level of sophistication, as far as we know. And it is knowledge that did not begin to appear in Europe until the fourteenth century, with the emergence of diplomacy and diplomatic communication requiring secrecy, along with other historical conditions for the knowledge practice we now call diplomatics.

European cryptology as a state security practice emerged alongside the modern textual secularism of scholars like Lorenzo Valla, whom we associate with the birth of European historical humanism as a mode of life and work serving the modern state and finding itself at odds with the state, as well. The historical braid joining modern cryptology as a state security practice with modern philology as its literary other has never completely unraveled. The mechanization, mathematization, and computerization of cryptanalysis in the United States during the interwar period and the Second World War can be understood as the culmination of historical affinities between cryptology and an "axiomatic rationalism" that best represents the humanities' disciplinary other today, even if those affinities remained entangled virtually up to the war, and in other ways are not completely disentangled even now.

I have adopted the term "axiomatic rationalism" from Pieter A. Verburg's magisterial (and eccentric) study *Language and Its Functions: A Historico-Critical Study of Views Concerning the Functions of Language from the Pre-Humanistic Philology of Orleans to the Rationalistic Philology of Bopp*.[16] Verburg used the term to describe the subordination of language to mathematical and logical symbolization in the thought of Descartes, Hobbes, Locke, and Leibniz and their respective legacies, and he identified it as a historical condition for the emergence of Romanticism as a counterrationalist "language-based ideology" of "subservience to language," or a "lingualism," with the conflict between the two major modes being understood as complex, enduring, and insoluble.[17] In the age of imperialism, philology served and was served by state security with relish, as the booty of imperial conquest furnished scholars with one lost writing system after another, beginning with the Egyptian hieroglyphics. But the 1848 revolutions swept many of the European "black chambers" away, and when an imperial United States assembled its first cryptanalytic military intelligence service in 1917, it was recruiting its personnel from two seemingly unlikely places: Riverbank Laboratories, a private research foundation in Illinois whose staff included amateur scholars laboring to decipher Francis Bacon's ostensibly enciphered authorship of Shakespeare's plays; and university departments of English, especially at Chicago and Yale, where the Baconians' Stratfordian opponents in Shakespeare studies served on the faculty.

This genealogy of the philological origins of U.S. military cryptology, and of the sublation or archiving of those origins in probabilistic applications of electromechanical and electronic computing to text, has been outlined in the works of the historian David Kahn and the popular science writer Simon Singh, both very well-known and widely read outside academe. Kahn's version of that genealogy has been read closely, and productively corrected, by the far more obscure (and in one case largely unpublished) work of the literary scholars Shawn Rosenheim, Gerhard F. Strasser, and Henry Veggian. I have relied on the research of this unlikely quintumvirate, and on other chroniclers of the intimacies of Mars and Minerva like Carol S. Gruber and Robin W. Winks, in several portions of this book. Together, this work tells a story that anyone interested in the history of the university, and specifically of the humanities disciplines (and even more specifically literary criticism) in the United States, ought to know better. It goes unacknowledged in the canonical disciplinary history of philology in the United States, Gerald Graff's *Professing Literature: An Institutional History,* as well as in James Turner's both more recent and more ambitious *Philology: The Forgotten Origins of the Modern Humanities,* lauded as "the first history of Western humanistic learning as a connected whole ever published in English."[18] Left entirely undocumented in all of this work, from Kahn and Singh to Rosenheim, Strasser, Veggian, Gruber, and Winks to Graff and Turner, is the emergence of literary and linguistic computing as such, after the Second World War, as literary humanists went their own way and philology mutated into literary scholarship including both comparative literature and Anglophone textual criticism. The genealogies of cryptophilology, I suggest in this book, did and do not terminate then or there.

PASSWORDS

Passwords

Philology, Security, Authentication

The main philosophical tradition of thought about language in the West, Umberto Eco wrote before the turn of the millennium, is a "dream that has run now for almost two thousand years." It is a dream of perfectible representation—not the same as *perfect* representation—submerging what Eco called the "pedestrian" story of Genesis 10:5, which records that after the Flood the Gentile nations found themselves speaking different languages, beneath the dramatic and tragic account of Babel in Genesis 11:1, interpreted as a story of human punishment by a vengeful, if wise God.[1] Essentially, Eco implied, it was an *antiphilological* dream: the image of a perfected state in which historical time, and along with time, change—in language, in the history of language, in the order of things managed and maintained by language—might come to cease.

Philology is a secular countertradition to this main philosophical tradition—which is also secular, but more rationalist than historicist in its disposition, in ways that will leave these two traditions incompatible, even incommensurable. But that is not to say unconfused, or unconfusable. Insofar as we might describe that main tradition—it is a cultural tradition, not merely a philosophical one—as a tradition that either presumes or attempts to establish a certain *security* in the face of time and change and their confusions, including linguistic and attendant ordinal confusion, we might say also that philology's characteristic practices and operations, which are so often practices of *authentication,* are incompatible with the history, the historicity, and the historiography for which philology stands or stands in.[2]

Is there any word in the domain of the humanities that means so much—and so little—to so many of us as this word, "philology"? Ancient Greek *philologia*, from *philos,* love, and *logos,* word, articulation, or reason, carried connotations including volubility, talkativeness, love of argument or reasoning, learned conversation, or literature (*philologos*), and in Hellenistic Greek, love of argument (in contrast with *philosophos,* love of wisdom). Latin *philologia* retained many of the Greek meanings, and *philology* entered the English language via Middle French *philologie,* with the earliest occurrence (1522) provided by the venerable *Oxford English Dictionary* carrying the broad, ancient meaning "love of learning and literature, branch of knowledge dealing with literature, literary or classical scholarship." Nineteenth-century British usage narrowed *philology* to an association with historical linguistics as a science of language, while twentieth-century United States usage revived the older, broader meaning before diffusing it nearly completely.

In declaring "philology" a *password,* I draw on a little book titled *Mots de passe* published in 2000 by the French radical Jean Baudrillard. The organizing conceit of this intellectual memoir-in-lexicon juxtaposes what I will call the philologically figurative connotation of "le mot de passe," "password," and some equivalents in other languages with the technical denotation also invoked by the book's title.[3] The technical denotation of "le mot de passe" / "password" is its everyday sense, raised to a difficult public awareness over the last half decade by a series of unprecedented, highly publicized password and other personal data breaches aimed at so-called web 2.0 and social media services mostly based in the United States but operating on networks imagined as worlded or worlding space.[4] It was this series of attacks, accompanied by increasingly severe admonition of "lusers" by those in the know, that finally introduced a counter-discourse at odds with the wave of enthusiasm for consumer utility or cloud computing that a new generation of

IT pundits and consultants rode to power in the late 2000s, as the survivors of the dot-com crash reorganized their data service operations.[5] The "Year of Security" has taught us a lesson that, to be sure, was always there to be learned, which is that since the very beginning of the long march of component miniaturization that brought us the personal computer in the late 1970s, a password provides effective security only to the extent that it is *not* a word; or, to put it more (or less) concretely, when it can no longer be found in a dictionary, that chain of signifiers stable or sliding as the case may be. As an elementary assault on password security, so-called dictionary attacks, which submit the entries in a dictionary to an authentication mechanism, ensure that the strongest password is a pseudorandom assemblage of characters, impossible for a human being to guess and so impossible for a human being to remember, requiring storage in a local electronic password safe or, ideally, physically secured—for example, recorded on a piece of paper placed in a safe secured by a combination lock and bolted to the floor, as information security becomes physical security becomes information security once again.

The technical function of the password is to thwart time in the name of security: to verify, by means of an invariant linguistic signature, that for the purpose of access to resources, I am the same user I was yesterday. The password permits me, the user possessing it, to pass, and serves as a pass or key, a promise that nothing has changed. Contrariwise, we might say that the philological connotation of *password* marks a commitment to the recognition, even the embrace of time, of time's passing rather than my passing—or else precisely my passing, in another sense again, that of time's passing over and through me: of an irreducible insecurity. A word, Baudrillard insists in *Mots de passe,* is temporal, a metaphorization that bears or passes ideas, exerting form on thought in passing away. That words thus "have a life of their own and, hence, are mortal is evident to anyone who does not claim to possess a definitive form of thought, with ambitions to edify. And this is my own case."[6]

* * * *

WE MIGHT SAY THAT Baudrillard thus points to a historic conflict between two dispositions: to a schism with both real and imagined power through which secular historical or historicizing humanism, orienting itself in and by time, opposes an antiphilological, technocratic endeavor to mitigate time.

To be sure, a structure can be built over that great divide, masking its incommensurability. The relation of a strong password, taken as a signifier, to its signified is technically arbitrary. Imposed for the occasion, it is no less purely relational than any signature, since its function is not to *be* but to differ. A strong password is of course also conventionally or historically arbitrary, in the sense that it is chosen at a particular place and time, is subject to degradation in time, and requires renewal if it is to continue to perform its function: that is, to differ. Yet such change is itself technical in character, a reconstruction of structural difference against temporal deferral, intended to preserve the security of the immutable that authentication provides, defends, and presumes or requires all at once. One changes one's password to preempt its degradation in time, as storage follows use, exposure threatens storage, brute force computational attack follows exposure, and identity masquerade follows a successful attack. Even where it is a strong password and thus nothing like a word at all, the password suffers the passing that time imposes on language, and which literary language perhaps merely accents with constructed polysemy. As infosec professionals have always known, but ordinary "lusers" are only now coming to understand, the strongest password serves as a one-way function, easy to formulate but difficult to invert, at least within the limit of the computing power available at a given moment.

I have honored Baudrillard by describing him as a "radical." That is because his thought represents a sustained refusal of the unilateral concept of communication derived from information theory, which inscribed the telematic trigram *encoder/transmitter → message → decoder/receiver* onto what he described as the reversible bilateral ambivalence of human symbolic exchange: "Symbolic exchange is the strategic site where all the modalities of value flow together towards what I would term a blind zone, in which everything is called into question again. The symbolic here does not have the usual sense of 'imaginary,' nor the sense given to it by Lacan. It is symbolic exchange as anthropology understands it. Whereas value always has a unidirectional sense, whereas it passes from one point to another according to a system of equivalence, in symbolic exchange the terms are reversible."[7]

In Baudrillard's thought, the informatic or cybernetic semioticization of the media, its atemporal, indeed time-repellent hypercirculation of hyperlegible signs, can be grasped as a simulation of such reversibility in feedback, the autoimmune integration of reciprocity and exteriority designed to forestall any compromise (human or otherwise) of abstract systemic integrity.[8] Baudrillard never succumbed to the French fascination by cybernetics recently explored at some length by Lydia Liu, John Johnston, and Bernard Dionysius Geoghegan, among others;[9] indeed, for all the intellectually violent dynamism of his both saturnine and mercurial oeuvre, Baudrillard seems quite consistently to have opposed the stakes of that fascination, counterposing to it an antipositivism derived from largely (not exclusively) progressive elements of the historical legacy of ethnology, including philology. In this light, the value of Baudrillard's work lies in its rejection of any forcing of thought into the form of what Geoghegan has called "crypto-intelligence"[10]—and what we could with less indirection also call knowledge conditioned by (and on) security.

· · · ·

J. FREDERIK M. ARENAS OPENS HIS history of the Western concept of security with the admission that "to study the history of concepts seems the innocent pastime of philological hobbyists." The retraction that follows ("At least in the case of the concept of 'security' that judgment might prove to be a misunderstanding") might be said to serve as a placing of philology under erasure, insofar as the insecurity of words that marks their historicity is identified as a border zone needing as much critical interrogation as observation—or, to put it in terms of the strife of faculties, as that which security studies must disavow, at least temporarily, to construct itself as a discipline.[11]

Distinguishing two phases in the etymological, philosophical, and ideological history of security, Arenas suggests that the polysemy of classical Latin *securitas,* denoting the "freedom from care" of the pax romana but also used by the Romans with a second, negative connotation (carelessness, negligence, complacency), was attenuated by the narrower early Christian usage associated with faith and contrasted with *dubitatio*. Subsequently, Arenas suggests, the narrower early Christian usage would be displaced in theology, at least, by the medieval Latin *certitudo*. But the modern concept of security emerged with Hobbes, mediated by Hobbes's translation of Thucydides's *History of the Peloponnesian War*. Retaining nothing of the ambivalence of Roman *securitas*, Arenas argues, Thucydides, the chronicler of the Athenian empire and its civil war, employs the word and concept *asphaleia* "immovability" (derived from the verb *sphallô*, associated with wrestling and used metaphorically to describe the stability of an institution) as a substantive for the Athenian state threatened by civil war. Hobbes's induction from a "Thucydidean anthropology" to a Lucretian "mathematical foundation independent of party strife," Arenas concludes, represents an attempt to mediate modern secularization by stabilizing the meaning of a concept, expressed metaphorically in the consensus of subjection to the state as a guarantor of punishment for violations of law.[12]

· · · ·

THOUGH WE ASSOCIATE INFORMATION SECURITY with the technical and technological history of modern telecommunications, it was a central administrative concern of the states of the ancient world, arguably coeval with the origin of writing itself.[13] It can also be argued that something historically unprecedented inheres in the acceleration and integration made possible by digital computing, in relation to security as to anything else. Indeed, one assessment has emphasized the "unprecedented civilian deployment of security tools and technologies" in the information societies of the historical present.[14]

Electronic information security depends on the authentication of identities and data, a procedure marked by a single antinomian principle and set of concepts associated with it.[15] A thinking infosec professional operates on the assumption that every new security enhancement produces a new security risk by presenting attackers with new means and opportunities for technically (and nontechnically) compromising any given system or class of systems. "If a person can trust keeping belongings in a locked compartment," as Pieter Wisse puts it, "then it is the key that should be of concern."[16] The physical security perimeters of massive early mainframe computers, material installations removable, in material space, to a material distance from any given attacker, had been obviated by the 1970s by two mundane elements of personal computing, network connectivity and the portability effected by component miniaturization.

But electronic information security also rests on a concept of availability inflected by the relative immateriality of data and its elementary reproducibility, which under everyday conditions leaves data remarkably persistent.[17] Under such conditions, there is nothing to compromise when no information has been stored or transmitted at all, and perfect security can be ensured only by not recording or transmitting in the first place.[18] As many a Facebook user now discovers anew, every few months, the confidentiality of data in storage or transmission will always be undermined by its availability to someone, even if that someone is a single user.

Electronic authentication regulates access to data that is already available in this sense. An authentication mechanism manages the identities of users, granting access to resources with different levels of privilege codified for classes of identities and granting different mixtures of rights to resource ownership and access.[19] While in larger networks there is no meaningful limit to the hierarchical differentiation of this matrix of privilege (even the most basic versions of the Unix-type multiuser permissions schemes still in use permit many permutations), the clear differentiation and assignation of interactive roles is unavoidable, and as a first step always separate the administrators of a given system from the users on whose behalf they manage services. Usually, administrators manage services for the system's proprietor, in liaison with a telecommunications carrier that links the system to others outside its domain. Any relationship to a given system is marked by its interiority or exteriority, in this sense, and relation—in some ways, the very possibility of relation—with an outsider is considered an attack.[20]

So-called Tempest standards for electromagnetic shielding, developed to defend equipment from the close-range radiation emission attacks directed against electromechanical cipher machines, mark the first recognition of the intrinsic hazard of availability in computing systems. Networking over telephone lines, introduced with the U.S. Air

Force SAGE (Semi-Automatic Ground Environment) air defense system in the late 1950s, brought with it the threat of "man in the middle" interception, and the time-sharing systems of the early 1960s are generally understood to have forced what Jeffrey R. Yost calls a sea change in computer security. Though the multiplexing of dumb terminals attached to mainframes allocating processing cycles, memory, and data storage to multiple simultaneous users was far more efficient and convenient (for some) than the manual and batch processing systems preceding them, their multiple differentiated levels of access proved incompatible with military document classification and clearance protocols.[21]

Accompanied by rapid growth in software complexity, it was the widespread adoption of time-sharing systems that brought the computer security problem to historical maturity, with the work of David Elliott Bell and Leonard J. LaPadula on a multiuser, multilevel security model for the U.S. Department of Defense marking the emergence of computer security as a distinct research area.[22] From that point on, those employed to protect information security and those attempting to compromise it would be locked in the dialectic marked by the iconography of white, black, and gray hats today.[23] The later 1970s would bring the first preassembled commercial personal computers, removable storage media, Bulletin Board Systems (BBSs) run on public telephone networks, and software viruses, along with the emergence of a hacker group youth subculture. By the 1980s, computer security was a topic of popular culture (in such films, for example, as 1983's *War Games*) and public awareness, especially following the Morris Internet worm of 1988 (a "watershed event for Internet security") and the formation of the first U.S. Computer Emergency Response Team (CERT). The 1990s has been called the "contagion period" of early public Internet use, with the Netscape browser incorporating RSA and SSL public key algorithms to provide for encrypted commercial transactions on the one hand, and the emergence of new forms of both advertising and criminality (spam e-mail, spyware, denial of service and distributed denial of service [DDoS] attacks on websites, launched by virus-infected botnets of Internet-connected home and business PCs) on the other, in turn spurring the development of commercial firewall software, virtual private network (VPN) services, and authentication products like RSA SecurID.[24]

* * * *

IF COMPUTER USER AUTHENTICATION has employed software-based encryption almost from the very start, that is no reason to abstract it from the material and intellectual history of modern authentication techniques beginning with currency watermarking and culminating in the automated biometric techniques of today.[25] Unlike serial manual or batch processing conventions for computer programming, in which sets of instructions were processed serially (initially, in a strict division of labor, by human computer operators who submitted instructions, initiated processing, and returned the results), time-sharing systems are interactive, permitting multiple authorized users both direct and limited access to apportioned computing resources. The Compatible Time Sharing System designed at the Massachusetts Institute of Technology in 1961 assigned each user a username linked to storage space for personal files accessed using a stored plaintext passcode, as did the Unics (Unix) systems developed at Bell Labs later in the 1960s. Richard E. Smith observes that users of such systems, often students, promptly began probing the multiplexing architecture of the new time-sharing systems—and the hacker was born.[26] From that point forward, as Smith puts it, access authentication evolved under attack, in a dynamic illustration of what we might have to call the law of the insecurity of security, which ensures that the possibility of masquerade can never be eliminated entirely, given that no new security mechanism "ever meets all the security objectives for which it was designed,"[27] while every advance in security techniques offers new exploits to potential attackers.[28] When the Titan system at Cambridge University, followed by the Unix systems, added cryptographic hashing to protect stored password files from theft by users with unauthorized access, attackers shifted their efforts to the interception of passwords using key sniffing and logging software that records keystrokes, and a new round of competition ensued. The endurance of this social and technical dialectic suggests on the one hand that perfect information security is effectively a metaphysical concept, transcending any worldly implementation—and on the other that the practical usability of any system simply and irreducibly requires a measure of trust, that form of security that can never be consummated beyond all limit of possible loss or violation.

. . . .

As Smith describes it, an authentication mechanism performs identification before granting access, relying on a "base secret" possessed by the user and serving as a distinguishing characteristic.[29] In practice, many such characteristics are straightforwardly cultural, so that it makes sense to speak of some forms of authentication as cultural rituals. Cultural authentication involves base secrets that are not arbitrary, often not frequently or easily changed, and subject to exposure (one's mother's so-called maiden name, for example—which in a society in which many married women do not take their partners' names, or who divorce at a rate higher than a few percent, is a very weak secret indeed). What we call shibboleths, or recognizable marks of communal membership ascertained through tests, are perhaps the best example— from the shibboleth incident narrated in the Old Testament book of Judges, in which the base secret is the difference between local dialects,[30] to the twenty-first century academic resource-sharing system that takes its name from the biblical story.[31]

In contrast with cultural authentication, pseudorandom authentication, relying on a secret such as a pseudorandom numeric or mixed alphabetic and numeric code, is more secure insofar as it is not a secret shared by one's cultural or social group, but something assigned to one as an individual, personally possessed, often physically, and requiring interception or capture in order to compromise (for example, a credit card number). But the arbitrary character of pseudorandom passcodes makes them difficult to remember, and they need to be synchronized in advance in order to be useful.[32] Arguably, the folkloric scenario in which a password is uttered to the guard at a city gate combines elements of cultural and pseudorandom authentication, with the answer to the challenge being neither easily guessed by unauthorized strangers, nor granting unconditional access—instead serving merely supplementing visual identification.[33]

The folktale of Ali Baba and the forty thieves, in which a password alone suffices, through the intermediation of some mechanism that opens a door, to grant access to the cave, is in fact closer to the single-factor unattended authentication on which most consumer computing systems still rely today. Technically conceived, the thieves' cave is protected by an "unattended, password-controlled lock . . . an unexplained and probably magical device that mechanically responded to the spoken words" *Sésame, ouvre-toi.*[34] As a magically mechanical authentication system, what guards the cave resembles a combination lock or a computing access mechanism in that anyone who possesses the secret, regardless of intent or disposition in relation to what it secures, can masquerade as its authorized user. That is to say that what such a system authenticates is the password itself, not the user possessing or providing it.

• • • •

AS THE OLDEST AND STILL MOST widespread form of electronic authentication, a password system identifies each user with a username and tests for the user's distinguishing characteristic, possession of a (secret) password. In most designs, this is accomplished by comparing user input with a stored system record synchronized with the user at the time that an authorized account was established. For this reason, the earliest technical attacks on password systems were directed at that stored record itself. This is precisely why what we call *words*—the lexemes of a particular human language and writing system, marked by statistical unit frequency patterns of various kinds (letters, digraphs, trigraphs) that computers can analyze quickly and efficiently—make the weakest and thus least suitable passwords. Taking advantage of the difficulty of memorizing random information, and the tendency for users to select actual (often personally meaningful) words as passwords, so-called dictionary attacks simply submit all the entries in a compiled dictionary to an authentication mechanism.[35] Encryption or hashing of passwords adds little security to any password found in a dictionary if an attacker is able to generate cryptographic hashes of dictionary words themselves (in other words, to hash the entire dictionary) and compare these hashes with the hash signatures in a password record file.[36]

Rooted in widespread consumer and enterprise ignorance when it comes to how authentication mechanisms operate and how they can be compromised, poor judgment in selecting passwords is now considered a security threat of the highest order, with the intractability of the problem spurring many recent commentators to declare password authentication fundamentally broken.[37] Recommendations initially formulated in the late 1980s, according to which passwords should include mixed lower- and uppercase letters, digits, and punctuation, are no more consistently implemented today than they were thirty years ago; underlying such "classical" password selection rules, Smith notes, is an ideal of perfect security in which "the password must be impossible to remember and never written down." In what Smith calls the "rather bizarre duality of security tools and attack tools,"[38] the defensive software that screens user passwords to evaluate their strength is converted into password "cracking" malware. Proactive password evaluation, Smith notes, "occasionally produces an 'arms race' between the user community and the people responsible for password enforcement. The users keep finding shortcuts and mnemonics while password software designers keep tightening up the constraints on acceptable passwords." At its vanishing point, practical password security actively impairs usability: "Without extensive training, people would not know how to construct legal passwords and would have trouble understanding why their personal choices were rejected. Under such circumstances, a user community is more likely to accept machine-generated passwords, since the draconian rules make a mockery of the concept of personal choice." Unable to memorize automatically generated pseudorandom passwords, and prompted frequently to change them, users resort to measures that expose them to high levels of risk, such as keeping a written copy of the password nearby (under their mouse pads, for example).[39] The future of authentication thus appears, for now at least, to lie in multiple-factor authentication making use of biometric techniques and physical tokens such as electronic smart cards and keys—a development that may bring the linguistic, even literary history of account-based electronic access control to an end.

• • • •

IN THE TECHNICAL LITERATURE ON PASSWORD authentication, the linguistic and literary history of the password begins with the so-called shibboleth incident. Judges 12 contains an account of a battle between Gileadites and Ephraimites, at one point during which the retreating Ephraimites, attempting to cross a river in Gileadite territory, were challenged by the Gileadites to identify themselves by pronouncing the word שבלת (*shibboleth*). With the suggestion that the Ephraimites' pronunciation, סבלת (*sibboleth*), substituting ס *samekh* for ש *shin*, gave them away, we are told that the Gileadites slaughtered forty-two thousand Ephraimites on the spot:

> And capture did Gilead the fords of the Jordan against Ephraim.
> And when the fugitives of Ephraim would say,
> "Let me cross,"
> the men of Gilead would say to him,
> "An Ephraimite are you?"
> And he would say, "No,"
> And they would say to him,
> "Say, pray, 'shibboleth',"
> and he would say "sibboleth,"
> And he could not accomplish to say it thus,
> and they would seize him and slaughter him at the fords of the Jordan.
> And fall at that time from Ephraim did forty-two thousand.[40]

This first password in Western literature appears in nineteen places in the Hebrew Bible in all and in sixteen places in the Old Testament.[41] *Shibboleth* is understood to have had two different denotations in biblical Hebrew: the first, ear of grain or corn ("olive branch" has also been proposed), is the most common, while the second, flood or torrent of water in a stream, appears unambiguously in only two of the sixteen appearances of *shibboleth* in the Old Testament. While this second, less common meaning is more plainly related to the context of the shibboleth story, it is not unambiguously clear which of the two meanings the word is meant to carry in context, though in many similar legends the password's meaning as a word is contextually significant.[42]

The *Oxford English Dictionary* offers three denotations for "shibboleth" dating to the seventeenth century: (1) "a word used as a test for detecting foreigners," linked to the testing function described in the biblical story; (2) "a peculiarity of pronunciation or accent indicative of a person's origin," denoting an identifying distinction in itself; and (3) "a catchword or formula adopted by a party or sect, by which their adherents or followers may be discerned, or those not their followers may be excluded."[43] The latter is closer to the contemporary journalistic sense in which, for example, the phrase "family values" might be described as a shibboleth. Recent work in sociolinguistics and the sociology of language has treated shibboleths as elements of "everyday verbal behavior"[44] including phonological elements of computer-mediated written communication,[45] or returned to the word's scriptural origins—arguing, for example, that Australian government language proficiency tests should be understood as "weapons in the tradition of the Shibboleth test," less performance tests than means of detection and identification in border control.[46] In folklore studies, "shibboleth" is given the wider nineteenth-century sense of the second definition, which also encompasses the extralinguistic ("a custom, habit, mode of dress, or the like, which distinguishes a particular class or set of persons").[47] Jennifer Michael, for example, distinguishes between "exclusion shibboleths" designed to prevent access by outsiders and "inclusion shibboleths" including indoctrination rituals that make joining a community possible with effort.[48]

Pack Carnes, meanwhile, suggests that we call a large body of similar legends "neck legends," from apocryphal stories about testing for the aristocratic pronunciation of the word "moi" during the French Revolution. Such stories, Carnes notes, are numerous; often involve warfare; and tend not to depict reliable tests or to involve great difficulty for the speaker being tested, rather representing difficulties that a nonnative speaker is assumed by caricature to have with a particular, putatively native language in a specific context; and almost always depict failure to pass.[49] More or less frequently cited examples include English use of the place-name "Chichester Church" to identify Danes during the St. Brice's Day massacre of 1002;[50] Sicilian use of the phrase "ceci e ciceri" to identify the French during the rebellion of 1282;[51] use of a phrase in Frisian to identify the Dutch during the Battle of Warns in 1345;[52] use of the phrase "bread and cheese" to identify the Flemish during Wat Tyler's peasants' revolt in 1381;[53] use of regional variations in the pronunciation of the English words "cow" and "bear," in 1850s Bleeding Kansas;[54] the phrase "setze jutges mengen fetge d'un jutjat" (sixteen judges from a court eat the liver of a hanged man) used to identify Castilian immigrants in Catalonia;[55] and an abundance of anecdotes from the Second World War[56] and subsequent conflicts, including the pronunciation of Levantine Arabic *bandora* (tomato), used by the Phalangists to identify Palestinians in the 1970s and 1980s, and of Sinhala *baldiya* (bucket), used by Sinhalese to identify Tamils during the first year of the Sri Lankan civil war.[57]

• • • •

WITH THE EXCEPTION OF DAVID MARCUS, who insists that we take the shibboleth incident as satire,[58] much of the philological scholarship on Judges 12:6 itself is narrowly technical in character, seeking to secure and authenticate the derivation and etymological history of *shibboleth*. Where that debate is drawn toward the interpretation of the story told in Judges 12:6, it tends to divide on the question of whether *shibboleth* serves or does not serve as a password in something close to the technical sense: that is, the question of whether the denotation of *shibboleth*, whether it be "ear of grain, corn" or "flood, torrent of water in a stream," has any meaning in and for the story at all or whether the shibboleth story depicts purely cultural authentication, a "test-word episode"[59] that turns on its pronunciation in different Hebrew dialects.[60] George Foot Moore, for example, argued that "any other word beginning with *sh* would have served as well," and that contemporary readers have construed *shibboleth* as a password only because the Greek of the Septuagint "had no way of reproducing the distinction of sounds represented."[61] From this perspective, the meaning of *shibboleth* is irrelevant to the story, because the story depicts a test of pronunciation of the initial sibilant written either as שׁ or as ס in the Gileadite and Ephraimite dialects: the initial sibilant of *shibboleth* is, in other words, "the point of the test, and . . . inability to pronounce it like the Gileadites was the Ephraimite problem."[62] Judean scribes, it is argued, represented this phonetic difference by deliberately choosing ס to represent the nonrepresentable phonetic difference of the Ephraimite pronunciation of a Gileadite spirant.[63]

But by the same token, *shibboleth* can be imagined as a password in a figurative sense, one more expansively than restrictively or technically philological. Just to the extent that its denotation is insignificant—to the extent that it functions merely to test for a phonological differential characteristic that the Judean scribes were unable to represent in writing—the shibboleth is a mark of passing or a trace of that difference, the "insignificant arbitrary mark" of a "secret without secrecy": its resistance to translation, including translations of the text of Judges 12, is not the resistance of secret meaning, but of the "cut of the non-signifying difference."[64] Marcus takes this approach in another direction, and to something of an extreme, rejecting the idea of dialectal difference and thus all of the more traditional restrictively philological debate along with it. Marcus concludes that the shibboleth story is a Judean satire written to ridicule the Ephraimites, the dominant tribe, "as ignorant nincompoops who cannot even repeat a test-word spoken by the Gileadites' guards."[65]

• • • •

IN ADDITION TO THE SHIBBOLETH STORY in Judges 12, the technical literature on password authentication has embraced a second literary antecedent: the tale of Ali Baba and the forty thieves.[66] Here, too, we are dealing with another foundational artifact of Western literary history, insofar as a ninth-century fragment of *Alf Layla* or *Thousand Nights,* the collection of tales to which Antoine Galland (1646–1715) would add the tale "Ali Baba et les quarante voleurs" in the eighteenth century, was the oldest known surviving artifact of an Arabic paper book.[67] Imagined by Tzvetan Todorov as an "extreme example" of the literary "a-psychologism" of the *Nights* as a whole, populated by "narrative-men" who "illustrate" nothing but are subservient to the action,[68] the tale describes a magical cave whose opening is unsealed by the pronouncement "Sésame, ouvre-toi" ("Open, Sesame!").

Here, too, philological scholarship has sought to authenticate a password: in this case, "sésame." Supposing that Galland worked from Hanna Diab's written Arabic, and that the word at issue was thus the Arabic *simsim,* F. E. Peiser suggested it was a duplication of *shem* "name," the Hebrew word for God that appears in Leviticus 24:11, or else a cabbalistic invocation, the Talmudic *shem-shemayim* "name of heaven."[69] This, Paul Haupt subsequently declared, was fanciful: *simsim* need not mean "sesame" in the cave, Kasim's attempting the names of other grains notwithstanding. *Simsim,* Haupt suggested, might instead represent modern Arabic pronunciation of an older word meaning "stopper, shutter, barrier."[70] But Haupt also noted parallel locutions in similar tales in Chinese, modern Greek, and German,[71] suggesting that something more (or less) than linguistic genealogies was at stake.

· · · ·

INCORPORATED THUS INTO THE TECHNICAL LITERATURE on authentication and on information security more generally, as precedents for technical operations that the philological scholarship devoted to them both mimics and complicates, such literary artifacts occupy a site where technical history crosses literary history and the history of philology, as the practice of the verification of written sources as historical and human, rather than divine. Following the work and the example of Edward W. Said, late twentieth and early twenty-first century returns to philology have sought to salvage the secular historical humanism of modern philology by extricating it at least partly from its imbrication with the scholarly Orientalism of the European empires and its transmogrified afterlife in the applied social science of a new postwar U.S. security state.[72] It is understandable that such revisionist concepts of philology have often resisted its associations with scientism, positivism, and the charisma of authority[73] in a way that might be taken as conflating, for better or for worse, the security of truth with the security of the state. And yet, it is precisely in retaining a reasonable valuation of reason itself, of reasoned inquiry, and of science if not of scientism, that such work has often also been able to insist, suggestively, that such conflation is not merely an act of the will or imagination, either. Seth Lerer's glib yet piquant collation of the philological impulse with a charismatic-authoritarian egoic need for security has put some of his interlocutors on the defensive for a good reason, even if their counter-critiques are also reasonable.[74] To make headway here, we need to move beyond disputes rooted in intellectual dispositions and their conflicts, to the material institutional context in which such dispositions are formed. Henry Veggian has traced a line of transmission from the Franco-Prussian War to the French Bureau du Chiffre and the literary-critical origins of U.S. military cryptology—that is, from nineteenth-century German philology to literary criticism as we know it today, by way of modern military intelligence. Far from being outlandish in character, the relationship between military intelligence and literary scholarship, Veggian has observed, is perfectly mundane, marking philological practices that would escape philology in a mathematization sponsored by the security state, as philology was dispersed into other sciences.[75] The latest chapter in this story, which has drawn a corps of new "digital" humanists to symbolically and symbologically serve the surveillance state produced by the security crisis of 2001, has yet to be told.

2

Cryptophilology, I

To read the meticulous but unworldly accounts of their own practices published by "digital humanities" enthusiasts today, one might never suppose that the historical origins of computational philology as practiced in the Euro-Atlantic world today lie in eighth- and ninth-century Abbasid caliphal administrative, military, and intellectual culture, recorded in languages that a supermajority of such scholars tend not to know, in documents they have no reason to work with, collected in archives they have no reason to visit. In this respect, at least, such research as practiced today has abandoned the both worldly and grand intellectual ambitions of those historical philological traditions on which it has otherwise drawn a great deal, if only technically and procedurally. Symptomatically perhaps, just as the standard English-language histories of the science of statistics neglect or omit entirely any mention of the relative frequency analysis of text in Abbasid- and Fatimid-era philology and cryptology,[1] contemporary histories of computational philology tend to reproduce that elision, notwithstanding their habit of protesting in advance any suggestion that their attention to numbers has overtaken attention to words.

The historian David Kahn has argued that "analyzing the frequency and contacts of letters is the most universal, most basic of cryptanalytic procedures."[2] While cryptanalysis, a word that entered the English language in William F. Friedman's 1923 *Elements of Cryptanalysis,* refers to the act of deciphering an enciphered cryptogram into "plaintext" form,[3] the history of Arab cryptological reflection is coeval with Arabic-language lexicography and philology, built on a Quranic scholarship whose linguistic studies documented Arabic letter and word frequencies while grappling with the question of provenance of non-Arabic words in the Quran, among other difficulties.[4] Philological debate over the provenance of non-Arabic words in the Quran has been traced from Abu Ubaida (c. 110–208 AH / 728–825 CE), who resisted the idea that the Quran contained words in any other language, to Al-Shafi'i (150–204 AH / 767–820 CE), who argued that what seemed to be non-Arabic words in the Quran were words in Arabic dialects, to Abu Ubaid (c. 154–224 AH / 770–838 CE), who imagined them as naturalized loan words and therefore as authentic Arabic, to Taj al-Din al-Subki (728–771 AH / 1327–1370 CE) and Al-Suyuti (849–911 AH / 1445–1505 CE), who were finally able to recognize and affirm Abyssinian, Persian, Indian, Turkish, Zinji, Nabataean, Coptic, Syriac, Hebrew, Greek, and Berber-derived words in the Quran as what they were.[5] Arab philologists also studied and wrote extensively about other languages and writing systems: Ibrahim A. Al-Kadi describes a work by Ahmad ibn Wahshi-yyah (d. c. 919 CE), *Shawq al-mustaham fi ma'rifat rumuz al-aqlam* (Seeker's joy in learning about other languages' written symbols), which described ninety-three alphabets and was published in 1806 in an English translation by Joseph von Hammer that was known to both Sylvestre de Sacy and Jean-François Champollion.[6]

Cryptological reflection as such begins, as far as we know, with an unrecovered treatise by Al-Khalil (c. 110–178 AH / c. 718–786 CE), whose achievements also included the production of an Arabic dictionary and studies of prosody in Arabic poetry. More a linguist than a mathematician, Al-Khalil, who nevertheless had an affinity for combinatoric exercises, assembled lists of combinations and permutations of voweled and unvoweled Arabic words. Of the lost *Kitab al-Muamma* (Book of cryptographic messages), Kahn concluded that al-Khalil's reflections, ostensibly prompted by his solution of a cryptogram in Greek, reveal that "the Arabs had not yet formulated the more analytical techniques of cryptanalysis based upon letter-frequency."[7] Those techniques emerged, and have survived, in a 841 treatise titled *Risalah fi istikhraj al-muamma* (Manuscript on deciphering cryptographic messages) by Al-Kindi (c. 184–259 AH / c. 801–873 CE), which recorded a technique for relative frequency analysis.[8] Al-Kindi presented a typology of Arabic phonetics and syntax, discussed varieties of ciphers, and described various cryptanalytic techniques, including the comparative statistical analysis of letter frequencies in a cryptogram using a sample text in the same language. Provided with ciphertext of a length sufficient for meaningful statistical evaluation, Al-Kindi demonstrated, a cryptanalyst could decipher a message by analyzing the frequency of letters in Arabic ciphertext and matching the frequency patterns to those already determined for plaintext Arabic:

> One way to solve an encrypted message, if we know its [original] language, is to find a [different clear] text of the same language long enough to fill one sheet or so and then we count [the occurrences of] each letter of it. We call the most frequently occurring letter the "first," the next most occurring the "second," the following most occurring the "third" and so on, until we finish all [the] different letters in the cleartext [sample].
>
> Then we look at the cryptogram we want to solve and we also classify its symbols. We find the most occurring symbol and change it to the form of the "first" letter [of the cleartext sample], the next most common symbol is changed to the form of the "second" letter, and the following most common symbol is changed to the form of the "third" letter and so on, until we account for all symbols of the cryptogram we want to solve.[9]

Risalah fi istikhraj al-muamma also provided a tabulation of letter frequencies in Arabic text, and Ibrahim A. Al-Kadi and Lyle D. Broemeling have argued that this early, informal description of statistical inference anticipates that articulated in the better-known 1654 correspondence of Blaise Pascal with Pierre de Fermat.[10] Other authors of extant reflections on frequency analysis in Arabic include Ibn Adlan (582–666 AH / 1187–1268 CE), Ibn Dunaynir (582–626 AH / 1187–1229 CE), author of *Maqasid al-fusul al-mutarjamah an hall at-tarjamah* (Clear chapters' goals on solving ciphers), and Ibn ad-Duraihim (c. 711–760

AH / c. 1312–1359 CE), author of *Miftah al-kunuz fi idah al-marmuz* (Treasured key for clarifying ciphers).[11]

Arab cryptological thought was described exhaustively by Al-Qalqashandi (c. 755–820 AH / c. 1355–1418 CE) in a chapter on cryptology in the encyclopedia *Subh al-a'shafi sina'at al-insha* (The light of the blind in the profession of writing).[12] Kahn argued that Al-Qalqashandi's description of the transposition and substitution ciphers of Ibn ad-Duraihim was the first published discussion of both transposition and substitution ciphers, as well as the first published description of a poly-alphabetic cipher, in which each plaintext letter is assigned more than one substitute. It was even more important, in Kahn's view, that Al-Qalqashandi also provided the first published discussion of cryptanalysis as a practice whose beginnings, as Kahn put it, "are probably to be found in the intense and minute scrutiny of the Koran by whole schools of grammarians in Basra, Kufa, and Baghdad."[13] Paraphrasing Ibn ad-Duraihim, Al-Qalqashandi provided lexicographic frequency lists of letter combinations in Arabic, instructing the cryptanalyst to begin by counting the letters in the ciphertext, looking for the symbol that marks division into words in the plaintext and comparing ciphertext letter frequencies with known letter frequencies in Arabic plaintext, working methodically from two-letter to three-letter words and then longer words.

Much of this cryptological knowledge was lost, as Kahn put it, to the European West after the collapse of the caliphates and the end of six centuries of Arab transmission of Greek knowledge: an arc of history that saw the cultural legacies of the Abbasid translation movement, which had encountered texts in dead languages as ciphertexts, themselves fading into "encrypted" obscurity.[14] While its European rediscovery or indigenous duplication is a matter of some dispute, the Latin West had meanwhile invented a cryptophilology of its own.

Western Humanism and the Elements of Style

"Authorship attribution," Hugh Craig has written, "is as old as writing itself, and its history displays a fascinating variety of problems and solutions. Groupings of texts (Homer, the Bible, Shakespeare) may have been created at times when their coherence was not especially significant, but later generations have placed enormous importance on the difference between the canonical and the apocryphal in each case."[15] The authenticating ambition of later generations, as Craig imagines it, is marked by the custodial role of philology, situated in tension with philology's temporization and indeed with its temporal*ism*. In "Idea for a Universal History from a Cosmopolitan Point of View," Immanuel Kant reminded us that the archival record of human struggle is fragile, that after a few centuries at most, many historical documents will have disappeared, and that what our descendants will value in their own history is the solutions we have devised by using ideas and by measuring ourselves against ideals. For the technician of authorship attribution, this is the predicament of a premodern philological universe bereft of corpora scaled to entice automation in the analysis of internal rather than external textual evidence. As a research field, authorship attribution thus dates itself to the Renaissance in southern Europe, albeit for the most part west of the Adriatic Sea: a time and place when the legacy of Arab Muslim philology was recognized in the forgetfulness of an awakened Europe inventing its humanism out of the selective reading of its own, suddenly apparently more substantial archives. Where the modern practice of authorship attribution in Western scholarship and administrative culture is concerned, Craig's origin story is a characteristic one: "the demonstration by Lorenzo Valla in the fifteenth century that the Donation of Constantine, which gave the Western part of the Roman empire to Pope Sylvester, was a forgery, is perhaps the most famous example."[16]

Valla's deservedly famed exposition of a scholastic hoax invites us to define modern scholarship as a displacement of the ancient and medieval historiography that either trusted or doubted its sources, with not much range in between. At the center of a new secular humanist worldview, history as a mode of thought, an active reconstruction performed by the historian, stood against premodern scholastic and systematic knowledge in the latter's rejection of historical time. The target of polemical humanists like Valla was therefore not perhaps truth as such, but a scholastic attachment to Aristotelian logic, and just as importantly, the medieval Latin in which that attachment was embodied. History as a mode of thought adopted its new, fluid form in a comparative linguistic project reimagining Latin as a medium of secular scholarly, rather than ecclesiastical communication, even as the humanists devoted themselves to a new and newly disciplined multilingualism. Valla was both typical and archetypal, some might say, in his attempt to do "something no agent contemplated—that is, to explain the different patterns of thought, Greek and Latin, by the different patterns of the languages" understood as historical artifacts in themselves.[17]

Of the expansive spirit of this humanist multilingualism, one can say two things. The first is that it embodies, in practical and procedural form, an attempt to mediate an increasingly violent conflict between two forms of sovereign authority. To adapt Djelal Kadir's words on Valla's contemporary and interlocutor Nicholas of Cusa, historical humanism's "programmatic mission . . . was to get pope and patriarch and their respective godmen to recognize the possibility of something other than their own maximal absolutes."[18] The second is that it also represents a competitive attempt to establish what we would now call a rival discipline: to authenticate and reproduce itself as *studia humanitatis,* a "philology" that displaced logic and added history to the trivium in its place. In this pursuit, humanism programmatically launched and maintained a campaign of its own, as its competition with scholasticism developed through the seventeenth century into a "war between two cultures," those of naturalism and historicism.[19]

Valla's work and thought thus sits in no little tension with a medieval European tradition of textual studies comparatively more secure in the authenticity of its materials and having little need for, or need to tolerate, such a temporalism. At the same time, as Christopher S. Celenza suggests, it is at odds with the Urtext-seeking formation of a later, nineteenth-century modern philology, conceived as a discipline of cultural authentication with an authority comparable to that of the natural sciences. In no way content merely to "correct" texts corrupted in transmission, Valla, the *"enfant terrible* of philology" in the Latin West, organized his activities around the dialogic practice of *disputatio,* and he said and wrote many things that got him into trouble, beginning with the open letter attacking the Latin style of Bartolo da Sassoferrato in 1433, by which Valla hastened his departure from his first academic post.[20] Valla's conception of language, his understanding of style, and his professional conduct itself were all thoroughly disputational, attentive to the history of usage among groups as a history of conflict. In his active investment in conflict as both object and mode of study, Valla could not have less resembled the computational philologists of today, who have embraced the political quietism of a hegemonic scholarly culture of state- and corporate-funded applied technical science and the formalist modes of attention that safely accompany it.

And yet in other ways, Valla is recognizable as a career operator, attentive to opportunities to compete for institutional space with the established scholarly culture that he imagined his persecutor. When he argued for the superiority of Latin to Greek in his *Repastinatio dialectice et philosophie* (Re-ploughing of dialectic and philosophy), it was a comparative argument characteristically justified by the notion of language as a historical determinant of culture.[21] It was also, however, a mark of Valla's leadership in a humanist campaign to establish historical scholarship as a discipline. What Donald R. Kelley called Valla's "rhetorical nominalism" not only drove him into extended, sometimes dangerous public intellectual disputes with rivals like Poggio Bracciolini, but also embodied "a considered justification for the menial tasks of humanists, not only for the special pleading of the orator but also for the apparently unfocused and purposeless pedantry of the philologist."[22] Valla may not have been the first scholar to question the authenticity of the Donation of Constantine, a close reading of which occupied a third of his 1440 *De falso credita et ementita Constantini donatione* (Oration on the falsely believed and forged donation of Constantine),[23] but he was the first to apply philological precision to it, with respect to the identification and historical periodization of words. Indeed, in the vehemence of his polemic against the document's forger, in this work, Valla can be regarded as the inaugurator of a modern humanist philological tradition that put historical textual criticism to political ends, making formal analysis a starting point for the elaboration of historical knowledge and even of polemically speculative interpretation, rather than an end in itself.[24] All of this makes him a both complex and compromising origin figure for a cryptophilology in search of its history today.

Humanism and Renaissance Cryptology

Modern Western diplomacy emerged from conflicts among thirteenth-century Italian city-states. "To the *condottieri* of the sword," as Harold J. Grimm has put it, "were added the *condottieri* of the pen," forming the administrative capacity needed to manage free mercenary armies.[25] The secularization of public life in the breakdown of a medieval social order found expression not only in the historical scholarship of the humanists, but also in the European rebirth of cryptology, understood as an administrative secularization of literary devotion to textual magic and the occult (or what Kahn loved calling "supernatural claptrap"). Perhaps unaware of the vast "lost" body of knowledge preserved in Arabic, the northern city-states had begun using simple forms of cryptography as early as 1226. The oldest extant European text describing methods of cryptanalysis is the work titled *De componendis cyfris* by Valla's contemporary Leon Battista Alberti (1404–1472), who designed a polyalphabetic cipher disk possibly inspired by a description by Ramon Llull and resembling devices that were used well into the twentieth century. Kahn credited Alberti with the publication of the first European treatise on cryptanalysis (*De componendis cifris,* 1466) and the invention of polyalphabetic substitution ciphers. For Kahn, the Renaissance, a real and permanent renascence that finally ended an entire millennium of "patchwork," "crazy-quilt" chaos in the custodianship of all forms of knowledge, is embodied in Alberti as the personification of all that made "the story of cryptology during these years . . . exactly the story of mankind." It is to Giambattista della Porta (1535–1615), author of *De furtivis literarum notis* (1563), meanwhile, that Kahn credited "the second major form of cryptanalytical technique," in probabilistic word (rather than letter) frequency analysis, as well as the earliest descriptions of cryptanalytic techniques for use against both monalphabetic and polyalphabetic ciphers.[26]

With diplomacy came postal espionage and the encoding of diplomatic correspondence, as the so-called black chambers, which were fully integrated into the postal systems, emerged to intercept and duplicate it.[27] Kahn's description of the Geheime Kabinetskanzlei of Vienna describes the qualifications for its clerks: "All European languages could be read, and when a new one was needed, an official learned it. Armenian, for example, took one cabinet polyglot only a few months to learn. . . . Young men about 20, of high moral caliber, who spoke French and Italian fluently and knew some algebra and elementary mathematics, were assigned to cryptanalysts as trainees. . . . If they proved competent, they were introduced to the secrets of the black chamber and sent to other countries for linguistic training."[28]

Where Kahn insisted that modern cryptology, emerging between the two world wars of the first half of the twentieth century, had broken completely with kabbalistic and other forms of medieval linguistic and textual mysticism, Gerhard F. Strasser was inclined to see the persistence of links between modern diplomatic cryptology and what preceded it, including European philological Orientalism and the rise of artificial languages.[29] Neither (though only Kahn is explicit about it) considered it likely that European techniques of frequency analysis developed from direct contact with Arabic sources, rather emerging "indigenously" (Kahn's word) from the cryptanalytic mandates of the black chambers and attacks on the polyalphabetic ciphers invented to defeat them. Kahn did not deny that the "cultural explosion of the Renaissance" infused European intellectual culture with the Muslim philosophy, science, and mathematics cultivated in Andalusia, but he suggested that where it was known by Europeans, Arab cryptological thought was likely to have been discarded as philological, rather than mathematical in character, too closely tied to Quranic scholarship.[30]

That may well have been true of the black chamber code clerk laboring over intercepted diplomatic correspondence, but it has the suspect advantage of obscuring the relations between state security and literary humanism that developed afterward and that persist to this day. That obscurity, we can say, redounds to the credit of the practical mathematical cryptanalyst, at least in Kahn's view, and to the relief of the literary humanist whose latter-day rediscovery of this intellectual genealogy can be reproduced through Kahn's segregation of cryptology in, and as, a domain of purely practical activity.

Egyptology

Like Lorenzo Valla, the German Jesuit Athanasius Kircher sought the rehabilitation of Christianity through the recovery of its prehistory, but his interest in cryptology was directed toward Egypt and hieroglyphic writing. Kahn regarded Kircher as having wandered too happily in mystical literary and philosophical terrain, but both Umberto Eco and John Hutchins (both less invested than Kahn in segregating intellectual from military history) saw things differently, grouping Kircher with Cave Beck and Joachim Becher as thinkers whose investments in pseudo-ideography anticipated techniques later devised for computerized "dictionary" (that is, word-by-word) translation.[31] The seventeenth-century explosion of interest in universal communication that produced the "universal character" systems imagined by both Kircher and Becher, Gerhard F. Strasser observed, also happened to "lend themselves to cryptographic use. From a mere cryptologic point of view, these systems appear to be unwieldy at first—though highly secure—but the numerical 'interfaces' they imply actually are harbingers of a new technology, the commercial codebooks introduced in the 1850s in the exploding world of telegraph communication, in particular multilingual registers. The ingenious—and 'value-neutral'—graphic rendering of such numerical interfaces as invented by Becher and refined by Schott, however, takes an even greater leap forward into the 20th century and its invention of the electronic computer."[32]

Despite ostensibly yielding to the "intellectual disease" of a "sense of universal mystery," seventeenth-century hermetic thinkers like Kircher had lived through the Thirty Years' War and worked in its aftermath, and they were attentive to the machinations of state security, dedicating their ciphers, as Eco put it, "to grand-dukes deep in military campaigns and political machinations, presenting them as arcane suggestions."[33] The mystic of the period, Eco continued, "winks his eye at the politician who will use this language as his secret code; on the other hand the cryptographer sells to the politician a cipher (that is, an instrument of power and domination) that for him, the Hermetic initiate, is also a key to supernatural truths."[34]

Napoleon's seizure of Egypt and French capitulation in Alexandria brought the Rosetta Stone to Europe (more precisely, to the British Museum) and spurred the emergence of a new, newly precise historical science devoted to processing the booty of imperial expeditionism. Jean-François Champollion's decipherment of the hieroglyphics is perhaps closest to

Kahn's historical ideal of so-called black chamber cryptanalysis, insofar as the distance of museum artifacts removed by imperial armies from their origins in both space and time offered the philologist a challenge of crystalline purity: to unlock a secret writing system "without the help of any human informant."[35] Within twenty years of the invasion of Egypt, Champollion had eliminated the "four hundred years of mistakes and illusions" encapsulated in Kircher's comparatively scattered and confused approach, to which the age of imperialism and its new philological Orientalism now brought new, determinedly practical rather than speculative solutions. In his modernity, Champollion discarded the "conventional symbolist view of the hieroglyphs" and derived their values using what Kahn approvingly named "the cryptanalytic method—substituting known values, guessing at the names, and testing the presumed values elsewhere."[36]

The Industrialization of Cryptology

A younger United States had no black chamber, though it had innovators like Thomas Jefferson, whom Kahn named "father of American cryptography" to honor Jefferson's sophisticated wheel cipher and device (used well into the twentieth century) and James Lovell, whom Kahn named "father of American cryptanalysis."[37] In Europe, cryptanalysis was industrialized in the eighteenth century, with the well-organized continental black chambers differentiating their labor functions and devising sophisticated mechanical supplements and affordances for their work, only to vanish in the revolutions of the 1840s: Vienna's Geheime Kabinetskanzlei had been shuttered by 1848, along with the Cabinet Noir in France and the Decyphering Branch in England, among others. (This might serve to remind us today that the surveillance state is a historical institution and not a historic inevitability—one that *can* be unraveled by determined, even if nonspectacular and incompletely successful resistance to absolutism.) Alongside the institutional industrialization of cryptanalysis, and contemporaneous with the liberalization that followed 1848, the mid-nineteenth century saw two key technological, one further institutional, and one broadly social development in cryptological history, which are worth noting individually here.

The first is the spread of telegraphy. Kahn imagined the telegraph as a singular medium of cryptological modernization, enabling military commanders, "for the first time in history, to exert instantaneous and continuous control over great masses of men spread over large areas."[38] The semaphore or optical telegraph systems of Claude Chappe in France, Agustín de Betancourt and Abraham-Louis Breguet in Spain, Abraham Niclas Edelcrantz in Sweden, and Lord George Murray in England were state security technologies operated from the last decade of the eighteenth century through the middle of the nineteenth. The Napoleonic wars of 1803–1815, which introduced modern signals intelligence, also set in motion the forces that swept away the monarchical black chambers and made the telegraph available for private use.

The purpose of a code, in the historical sense of the word, is communication at a distance, and thus "the very opposite of secrecy."[39] Optical telegraph systems were supplanted by the public electric telegraph during the mid-1840s, and in the new commercial use of telegraphy in business, the primary concern was speed, accuracy, and efficiency in transmission, rather than concealment. Many companies devised so-called commercial codes of their own, which assigned common standard administrative and transactional phrases to very short dictionary words. (The majority of these codes used an English lexicon, though there were some multilingual codes, such as that devised by Marconi's Wireless Telegraph & Signal Company, that used English as a pivot language, anticipating the use of similar techniques in multilingual machine translation decades later.)

The second noteworthy development is encapsulated in Charles Babbage's approach to solving ciphers. Simon Singh described Babbage's solution of the autokey cipher of Vigenère, a polyalphabetic substitution cipher whose design dated to the sixteenth century, as "the greatest breakthrough in cryptanalysis since the Arab scholars of the ninth century broke the monoalphabetic cipher by inventing frequency analysis."[40] Babbage's work on ciphers went mostly unpublished, but Kahn claimed he was the first to use mathematical notation in his solutions and to devise cryptanalytic formulas, building directly on his interests in relative frequency analysis and the mechanization of tabulation. If this is so, then Babbage's work can be understood as having anticipated not only electromechanical and electronic computing as such, but its application to the new science of cryptanalysis as it emerged in the 1920s.

A third development is the emergence of modern diplomatic historiography. The new historiographic methods and practices developed by figures like Leopold von Ranke were notable in two ways. First, for their emphasis on amassing great quantities of primary sources, and on pitting the factual authority of masses of such sources against the interpretive historiography that carried on arguments with other historiographers' interpretations, in a reconceptualization of historiography as a new science. Second, for the role that cryptanalysis had in such work, insofar as the diplomatic correspondence found in vast, newly available collections like the Venetian state archives was often enciphered. As Kahn put it, "All cryptanalysts have not borne arms for Mars. Some of the most prolific have served Clio, the muse of history. Many of these unsung heroes—the only cryptologists whose contributions enlightened all mankind—worked in the 19th century."[41]

Finally, there is a new popular interest in cryptology. Both Kahn and Singh argued that the spread of telegraphy for business communication generated widespread popular interest in cryptology. Both noted Babbage's interest in the publication of encrypted messages (ostensibly amorous in nature) in Victorian newspapers. Singh dwelled on the reflections of this fascination in the works of Jules Verne, Arthur Conan Doyle, Edgar Allan Poe, and Kahn on the U.S. presidential election of 1876, Congressional investigation into the contested outcome of which turned on the content of enciphered telegrams.[42]

From Nineteenth-Century Philology to the Structuralist "Code Wave"

In an as yet unpublished study, the literary scholar Henry Veggian set out a critique turning on the technological determinism through which the histories of the human sciences and literary criticism had been overwritten by the history of technology, in both Kahn's and Singh's work.

Veggian argued that Kahn's imagination of the telegraph as the singular medium of a general cryptological modernization, and of radio as an equally singular medium of cryptanalytic modernization, both erased "the role of literary humanism, and philology in particular, in cryptanalysis." "The means of transmission and the methods of analysis," Veggian suggested, "had developed from the entirely different fields of nineteenth century thought. Wireless telegraphy emerged from thermodynamics, where cryptanalysis had emerged from the hermeneutic techniques of literary humanism that were refined to attack technological advances during the war."[43]

Against both Kahn and Singh, Veggian argued that the origins of modern cryptanalysis lay not in telecommunications, but in the modern human sciences and specifically in literary humanism. Mid-nineteenth-century philological Orientalism and diplomatic historiography, Veggian suggested, may have played a more important role than commercial telegraphy in encouraging a popular interest in cryptology, and cryptology may have found its reflection in the works of Verne, Doyle, and Poe through the cultural authority of philology more than anything else. When in the aftermath of the Franco-Prussian War, France, the defeated power, committed itself to cryptological modernization, this, Veggian suggested, provided the historical conditions for a convergence of hermetic literary discourse and activities with military intelligence, particularly in the United States, which modeled its efforts on those of France, but where literary scholars furnished both expertise and staffing for the first U.S. military cryptanalytic intelligence units.[44]

As we have seen, Kahn acknowledged the contributions of philology to the history of cryptology up to the nineteenth century—that is, to its premodern history, as he saw it. Kahn did not entirely ignore the contributions of nineteenth-century scholars either. He dwelled at length, for example, on the career of Jean Guillaume Auguste Victor François Hubert Kerckhoffs (1835–1903), a teacher of modern languages and author of English, German, and Flemish grammars as well as a literary scholar who in 1883 published a study titled *La Cryptographie militaire* and went on to become what Kahn calls "the most active propagandist of Volapük," a widely used international auxiliary language that was displaced by the better-known Esperanto. Of *La Cryptographie mili-*

taire, Kahn reflected that "it is perhaps significant that at least three of the great books of cryptology—Kerckhoffs', Alberti's, and Porta's—were written not by narrow specialists but by well-rounded men who had one foot in each of what C. P. Snow would later call 'the two cultures' of science and humanities."[45]

And yet Veggian was correct that Kahn, like Singh, understood technology as the real motor of history. The First World War produced an enormous volume of radio traffic—a development, Kahn argued, that gave technical advantage to the cryptanalysts, who now had vast pools of data at their disposal when seeking patterns in encrypted signals. At the same time, this vast increase in data, and in the time and effort required to process it, would encourage experimentation with the automation of cryptanalysis by electromechanical means.[46] Against this emplacement of radio, data, and computation as the autonomous actor-agents of twentieth-century history, Veggian argued that the wartime staffing of both British and U.S. military cryptanalytic units by literary humanists represented a genealogical development in the history of literary humanism itself.[47]

Singh described the staff of the famous Room 40 of the British Admiralty as "a strange mixture of linguists, classical scholars and puzzle addicts, capable of the most ingenious feats of cryptanalysis,"[48] while Kahn provided the following catalog:

> Ronald Knox, who later became a Catholic priest and made a highly praised translation of the Bible; Dr. Frank Adcock, dean of Kings College, Cambridge, who was later knighted for his work as one of the three joint editors of the 11–volume Cambridge Ancient History, and who also served as a cryptanalyst in World War II; Desmond McCarthy, a widely known author and critic, later knighted, who, like Knox, joined only late in the war; the second Baron Monkbretton, who served as chairman of the London County Council from 1920 to 1930; and W. Lionel Fraser, later chairman of three substantial financial firms—Banque de Paris et des Pays-Bas, Cornhill Insurance Company, and Scandinvest Trust, Ltd.—and president of Babcock and Wilcox, Ltd.; Gerald Lawrence, the actor; and Professor E. Bullough, chiefly known as the son-in-law of the famous

actress Eleanora Duse. Less well known—sometimes unknown—
to the public, but outstanding as cryptanalysts, were Ronald
Knox's older brother, Dilwyn, who is credited with having solved
the three-letter German naval flag code in his bath, and who
found cryptanalysis so to his taste that he made a career out of it
in the War Office; Dr. John D. Beazley, then a tutor at Oxford and
later professor of classical archaeology there, later knighted;
Dr. Gilbert Waterhouse, professor of German at the University of
Dublin, regarded as a "first-class performer"; Dr. Leonard A. Wil-
loughby, lecturer in German at Oxford and later a Freeman of the
City of London; Professor E. C. Quiggin, who enjoyed considerable success with the Austrian messages; and Dr. Douglas Savory,
professor of the French language and Romance philology at
the University of Belfast, later knighted, who, after Quiggin died,
took over the Austrian traffic and produced some important
solutions.[49]

Also working in Room 40, Kahn noted, were "German university
scholars, many of whom were commissioned in the Royal Navy Volunteer Reserve so that they could wear uniforms to forestall icy looks from
the public," and women who "were enlisted to free cryptanalysts from
clerical tasks."[50] When the British M. I. 1(b) section was set up in 1915,
meanwhile, Malcolm Vivian Hay

began at once to scour the universities for bright young men,
preferably language scholars, to supplement the three original ci-
vilians on the staff: J. St. Vincent Pletts, a radio engineer from
Marconi's Wireless Telegraph Company; J. D. Crocker, a young
Cambridge scholar, and Oliver Strachey of the Indian Civil Service, who liked cryptanalysis so much that he switched after the
war from administering the East Indian Railway to codebreaking
for the Foreign Office. Hay recruited a remarkable concentration
of men who were later to achieve eminence, if listing in *Who's Who*
may be taken as an index. Among them were his chief assistant,
John Fraser, 32, later professor of Celtic as a fellow of Jesus College,
Oxford; Arthur Surridge Hunt, 45, then and later professor of

papyrology at Oxford and one of the world's most eminent authorities on ancient writing; David Samuel Margoliouth, 58, professor of Arabic at Oxford, later president of the Royal Asiatic Society and author of many works on Arabic literature and history; Zachary Nugent Brooke, 33, then lecturer in history at Cambridge, later professor of medieval history there and an editor of the Cambridge Medieval History; Edward Thurloe Leeds, 39, then assistant keeper of the department of antiquities of the Ashmolean Museum and, after the war, keeper of that first public museum in England; Ellis H. Minns, 42, then and later lecturer in paleography at Cambridge, later knighted; Norman Brooke Jopson of Cambridge, 26, later professor of comparative philology there; George Bailey Sansom of the consular service, 33, later knighted and commercial counselor of the British embassy in Tokyo and author of a Historical Grammar of Japanese and of a standard history of Japan; and Henry E. G. Tyndale, 28, later housemaster of Winchester College, one of England's great public schools, an avid mountaineer, and editor of the Alpine Journal and of the classic Whymper's Scrambles Amongst the Alps. The chief himself, Hay, became well known as a historian, writing half a dozen major historical works (most presenting the Catholic viewpoint on controversial questions) and almost as many on other subjects. His first study, A Chain of Errors in Scottish History, concerning early church history, was violently denounced and extravagantly praised. But subsequent works, such as The Enigma of James II, were received with more moderate but more extended applause, and his later The Foot of Pride, an erudite examination of European anti-Semitism, was universally lauded.[51]

The U.S. counterparts of the Room 40 humanists were to be found in MI-8, directed by Herbert O. Yardley, a onetime English major at the University of Chicago whose wartime staff included literary scholars from Chicago's English department as well as from English and Romance language departments at Yale and the University of Pennsylvania. They were also sent to the U.S. Army Signal Corps headquarters in France.[52] Literary humanists, Veggian suggested, "were ideal laborers during the early years of modern U.S. cryptology because they maintained two distinct versions of the term 'code' in their professional terminology." One of these major connotations, the modern one, was primarily business-oriented and technical, derived from the nonsecret commercial codes, which did not encrypt messages but merely compressed them by the substitution of other words and phrases of programmatically or arbitrarily shorter word length. The other connotation of "code" was broadly social and historical, equivalent to the concept of custom "in that it refers also to social mores and suggests a social or ideological understanding of a 'code' . . . which persists," Veggian noted pointedly, "in U.S. literary criticism to the present."[53]

Philology, Veggian argued, was "predisposed to cryptology during the pre-WWI era because it had sustained this functional, if vague, understanding of 'coding.' Terms such as 'code,' 'decode,' and 'decipher' loosely carried the multivalent significance of language as a dynamic and flexible historical entity." Such a predisposition marks the echoes of nineteenth-century philological scholarship in what Veggian called the "structuralist 'code wave' of the 1950s." When cryptology "escaped, together with other sciences, from philology's nineteenth century borders," it was decoupled from its existing vector or vehicle, historical humanism, floating unbound during the institutional transformations wrought by the two world wars.[54]

Mid- to Late Nineteenth-Century Stylistic Analysis

Modern biblical scholarship emerged in the mid-nineteenth century with the attribution of portions of the Hebrew Bible to different and possibly even miscellaneous sources.[55] The first proposals for the application of statistical analysis to the problem of authorship attribution in Jewish and Christian sacred texts appear to have been made by the British logician Augustus de Morgan in an 1851 proposal for the analysis of word and sentence length in the Letter to the Hebrews. After 1867, work on the comparative analysis of philosophical vocabulary in Plato's dialogues and *Laws* emerged independently in Scotland, in the work of Lewis Campbell, and in Germany, in the work of Wilhelm Dittenberger.

The former was ignored outside Scotland until close to the turn of the century, while the latter inaugurated a series of word frequency studies of the dialogues undertaken by German scholars between 1881 and 1914. In the United States, the physicist Thomas Mendenhall published studies of word length in the works of Bacon, Marlowe, and Shakespeare resting on the assumption, as Mendenhall put it, "that every writer makes use of a vocabulary which is peculiar to himself, and the character of which does not materially change from year to year during his productive period; that, in the use of that vocabulary in composition, personal peculiarities in the construction of sentences will, in the long-run, recur with such regularity that short words, long words, and words of medium length, will occur with definite relative frequencies."[56]

Where De Morgan had focused on word and sentence length as cardinal measures of text, Mendenhall was interested in measures of relative word frequency. The methodological analogy that Mendenhall proposed is worth reproducing here in its entirety:

> The nature of the process is extremely simple, but it may be useful to point out its similarity to a well-known method of material analysis, the consideration of which actually first suggested to the writer its literary analogue. By the use of the spectroscope, a beam of nonhomogeneous light is analyzed, and its components assorted according to their wave-length. As is well known, each element, when intensely heated under proper conditions, sends forth light which, upon prismatic analysis, is found to consist of groups of waves of definite length, and appearing in certain definite proportions. So certain and uniform are the results of this analysis, that the appearance of a particular spectrum is indisputable evidence of the presence of the element to which it belongs. In a manner very similar, it is proposed to analyze a composition by forming what may be called a "word-spectrum," or "characteristic curve," which shall be a graphic representation of an arrangement of words according to their length and to the relative frequency of their occurrence. . . . It has been proved that the spectrum of hydrogen is the same, whether that element is obtained from the water of the ocean or from the vapor of the atmosphere. Wherever

and whenever it appears, it means hydrogen. If it can be proved that the word-spectrum or characteristic curve exhibited by an analysis of "David Copperfield" is identical with that of "Oliver Twist," of "Barnaby Rudge," of "Great Expectations," of the "Child's History of England," etc., and that it differs sensibly from that of "Vanity Fair," or "Eugene Aram," "Robinson Crusoe," or "Don Quixote," or any thing else in fact, then the conclusion will be tolerably certain that when it appears it means Dickens.[57]

The developments that would eventually provide the tools and methods, if not the occasion, for the institutionalization of U.S. military cryptanalysis had their roots in a publicly entertaining controversy into which Mendenhall was only drawn by others. Reminding us of the enduring commotion generated by the mid-nineteenth-century "Baconian theory" of Shakespearean authorship, Marjorie Garber noted that "some sense of its magnitude can be gleaned from the fact that when, in 1947, Professor Joseph Galland compiled his bibliography of the controversy, titled *Digesta Anti-Shakespeareana,* no one could afford to publish the 1500-page manuscript."[58]

While the first recorded attributions of Shakespeare's works to Francis Bacon date to the end of the eighteenth century, they were the vehicle of enormous industry by the mid-nineteenth century, producing dedicated study societies, special periodicals, and a book market devoted to the debates, some of which endured into the twentieth century.[59] At the center of public controversy through the 1850s was Delia Bacon (1811–1859), whom Shakespeare scholars treated as a hysteric and intellectual anarchist, the detonator of an "anti-Shakespearean bomb," well into the 1960s.[60] More recently, Bacon's life and work have been reread within the history of the institutionalization of English literature as an object of study in the United States—a process in which Richard Grant White made himself a professional critical authority in Shakespeare studies by denigrating Bacon's views and actively suppressing the publication of her work (a situation into which a sympathetic Nathaniel Hawthorne decided to intervene, despite his own discomfort with challenges to the image of Shakespeare as authorial hero).[61] Although White was a public critic and not a university scholar, "he seems to have worked in concert with the increasingly academic Shakespeare establishment that emphasized textual criticism" and with it a methodological focus on the role of the literary author, the authentication of literary authorship, and the recovery of authorial intention.[62]

The "ruckus" created in "both scholarly and popular circles" by Bacon's 1856 article in *Putnam's Monthly* titled "William Shakespeare and his Plays: An Inquiry Concerning Them" may have been generated as much by Bacon's suggestion that Shakespeare's works were composed by an unnamed group of collaborators as by the associated, if competing suggestion that they were composed by Francis Bacon. Uncongenial to the spirit of the public professionalization of magazine authorship in the mid-nineteenth century on the one hand, and that of the scholarly materialization of the author in academic textual criticism on the other, Bacon's arguments proved explosive.[63]

Shawn Rosenheim has called the Baconian theory (a term naming both Francis Bacon as author of Shakespeare's works and Delia Bacon as someone closely identified with the controversy) "the cryptographic appropriation of Shakespeare," arguing that it was mediated by the cultural presence and image of Poe, of whose centrality Rosenheim observes: "it would only just overstate things to say that the cryptographic fascination with Shakespeare is a function of Poe's own writing."[64] Poe had long been regarded as someone who had added "to cryptography the glamour of illusion," even if—or precisely because—his cryptanalytic interests were casual and his skills amateurish.[65] Describing a conflict between the Egyptological legacies of Kircher and Champollion during the Egyptian revival of the first half of the nineteenth century in the United States, John T. Irwin argued that far from displacing Kircher's metaphysical exegetical approach to hieroglyphic writing, Champollion's "logical science of interpretation" remained locked in tension with it.[66] Hawthorne's (and Emerson's) sympathy for Delia Bacon might be understood in the context of this codependence of mystical and logical interpretation, whose effects were always mixed even if in the end, as Irwin argued, Champollion's secularization of the hieroglyphs inaugurated a linguistic turn in U.S. American literature: a "point in intellectual history when questions that had once been considered to be the metaphysical . . . are in the process of becoming, in the works of a writer like Melville, linguistic questions."[67]

Delia Bacon's more recent defenders have not ignored the "elitist prejudice" of her investment in supplanting the commoner "William Shakespeare" with the aristocrat Francis Bacon as a possible author of the plays.[68] Of Ignatius Donnelly's *The Great Cryptogram: Francis Bacon's Cipher in the So-called Shakespeare Plays* (1888), which presented a bibliographic and stylistic analysis of the plays followed by an intricate analysis of a cipher that Donnelly presented as authenticating Bacon's authorship, Henry Veggian wrote that Donnelly's efforts were "embroiled in the U.S. politics of social reformism and Social Darwinist elitism" and carried with them the "late nineteenth century Social Darwinist reaction against progressive social reform movements."[69] Donnelly's political career, it has been argued, was characterized by a similarly "intense conviction that there existed a simple answer, despite its seeming complexity, for a problem he confronted."[70] Donnelly's posture, a blend of agrarian nationalism with populist nativism, won him few admirers on the promotional tour for *The Great Cryptogram*, during which he was famously humiliated in a debate at Oxford University, or later in the 1900 presidential campaign for which Donnelly was the Populist Party's nominee for vice president.[71] Of Donnelly's analysis of the cipher of Bacon's authorship, Kahn observed:

> Of Donnelly's "system" it may be remarked that nothing like it has appeared in cryptology before or since. And with good reason, for the system is no system at all; there is neither rhyme nor reason to the choice of numbers that lead to the result. It may also be remarked that, in an open-code system, the hidden message controls the cover-text, which is merely a function of the hidden plaintext. Donnelly, though he worked only on a few pages of the two parts of *Henry IV,* therefore presupposed that the magnificent language of the plays all resulted merely from the inner workings of a cipher. Did Falstaff, marvelous Falstaff, exist so exuberantly only to make sure that Bacon would have the right words for an open code? The thought is hard to bear. Donnelly's murder of logic, like the slaying of Banquo, started a line of phantoms that

threatens to stretch out to the crack of doom. Among the Baconians, these apparitions are "ciphers" that are not really ciphers. Likewise, the technique of descrying them is not really cryptanalysis, and the results are not solutions or decipherments. They are the deliriums, the hallucinations of a sick cryptology.[72]

But one might say Kahn protested too much. Donnelly's ridiculous "system" had its place in a nineteenth-century cultural polysystem organized by the imaginaries of so-called Oriental knowledge, whose reflection in the hermeticism of the American Renaissance and whose maturity in modernist U.S. poetry carry implications that have yet to be sorted out even today. Against Kahn's sequestration of the "enigmatology" of a "sick cryptology," Veggian argued that "the connections between U.S. cryptology and the hermetic style were sustained" through the Second World War and into the 1950s, when they reappeared in the prose fiction of writers like Thomas Pynchon.[73] Zachary Lesser's assessment of Shakespearean scholarship as "less opposed to than implicated in the anti-Shakespeare industry" reminds us that the professionalization of analytic techniques and the construction of institutions to support and reproduce them occurs not in a vacuum, but in resistance to rival undertakings that such endeavors must banish and disavow. If the debate over Shakespearean authorship is "for academic Shakespeareans what creationism or intelligent design is for evolutionary scientists,"[74] that is because secularization itself gains neither traction, in historical terms, nor meaning as a historical phenomenon in abstraction from its relationship to an "outside" that never completely disappears.

The Baconian theory and its reactionary cultural politics found a home at one of the first privately funded, university-independent, politically conservative research foundations in the United States, the Riverbank Laboratories (today Riverbank Acoustical Laboratories) founded by "Colonel" George Fabyan, who had plowed his inherited wealth into an estate in Geneva, Illinois. Fabyan invited researchers to work on projects in acoustics and chemistry as well as genetics, the latter with an orientation toward eugenics and shaped by Fabyan's antipathy to the Midwestern progressive and reform movements rooted in Chicago.[75]

Fabyan also promoted the Baconian theory, and after Elizabeth Wells Gallup's *The Bi-literal Cypher of Sir Francis Bacon Discovered in his Works and Deciphered by Mrs. Elizabeth Wells Gallup* (1899) appeared, Fabyan invited her to continue her work at Riverbank, where she would be assisted by William F. Friedman, hired as a Cornell graduate in 1915 initially to work on genetics, and Elizebeth Smith, later known as Elizebeth Friedman. The Baconian lab at Riverbank buzzed with activity. With Fabyan's financial support, it adapted or developed special-purpose assistive devices such as the "cipher wheel" machines invented by Orville Ward Owen (a Baconian whose transatlantic manuscript-hunting expeditions Fabyan also financed) used to collate pages and align common words or passages in segments of text.

Contrasting Riverbank scholarship with that of the University of Chicago Shakespeareans, with which it had antagonistic relations, Veggian observed that the former "developed a non-historical model of interpretation; unlike the philologists, who pursued the historically inscribed significance of language, the Riverbank cryptologists culled the exegesis of the text from the settings of letters and words rather than from historical evidence."[76] Their intellectual opponents responded in kind, elaborating their own statistically grounded arguments and demonstrations purporting to expose the flawed logic and sham science of the pretenders.[77] Perhaps unsurprisingly, given the homologous methodological ambitions of the antagonists, the conflict would be resolved during the approaching war, as John Matthews Manly, chair of the University of Chicago English Department and a future (1920) president of the Modern Language Association of America, forged an "unpredictable" affiliation with the Riverbank Baconians, drawn by the "literary-formalist allure of cryptology, rather than its Baconian, Social Darwinist distortion."[78] Fabyan, aware of the impoverishment of U.S. diplomatic and military intelligence where cryptanalytic skills and resources were concerned, had offered the help of Riverbank's Baconian laboratory to the State Department, which responded by forwarding interceptions of enciphered transmissions by the government of Mexico for Fabyan's team to crack.[79] Once the war was underway, the transformation of Riverbank scholarship "from a literary-philological register to a branch of the United States' primitive security apparatus"[80] followed immediately, with Gallup readying the lab for service in decrypting German communications.

According to David Kahn, Riverbank's most important early wartime achievement was the deciphering of communications between the Indian revolutionaries of the Ghadar Party in North America and their German sponsors, with both Elizebeth and William Friedman testifying in support of the prosecution at the Hindu-German Conspiracy trials of 1917.[81] By 1917, in addition to assisting British counterinsurgency efforts in India, Riverbank was not only decrypting communications for the Department of Justice and the War Department, as well as the State Department, but training officers in six-week courses they completed before deployment to France—courses for which Friedman wrote a series of seminal technical monographs in cryptology. It was "in this manner," as Rosenheim put it, that "the cipher department at Riverbank—an organization designed for literary research—became the site for all cryptanalytic training of American officers in World War I; became, indeed, godparent to the NSA."[82]

Postwar Transformations

Both Kahn and Singh suggested that French defeat in 1871 spurred the reorganization that by 1914 had made France's cryptanalytic intelligence service one of the most advanced in Europe, rivaled only by Austria-Hungary. The Bureau du Chiffre, Kahn argued, was "the first echeloned organization in the history of cryptology,"[83] and while the United States made France its model in attempting to organize its own resources, circumstances forced it to improvise. When MI-8, the new cryptology section of the U.S. Military Intelligence Division, was established in June 1917 with Herbert O. Yardley as its head, Yardley recruited John Matthews Manly to supervise instruction in cryptanalysis. Manly, Kahn related,

> brought with him a bevy of Ph.D.'s [sic] clanking with Phi Beta Kappa keys, mostly from the University of Chicago: David H. Stevens, 32, an instructor in English, later director of the division for

the humanities of the Rockefeller Foundation; Thomas A. Knott, 37, associate professor of English and later general editor of Webster's Dictionaries . . . Charles H. Beeson, 47, associate professor of Latin, later president of the Mediaeval Academy of America, who had gotten his doctorate at Munich and knew German well enough to write scholarly works in it; and Frederick Bliss Luquiens, 41, professor of Spanish at Yale University, general editor of the Macmillan Spanish Series, and author of *An Introduction to Old French Phonology and Morphology*.[84]

Other literary scholars or writers recruited into MI-8 included Chauncey Tinker and Stephen Vincent Benét, both from the Department of English at Yale (where Tinker was a professor of English Literature and Benét was the undergraduate editor of the *Yale Literary Magazine*), James Thurber, and Manly's colleague at Chicago, Edith Rickert. To the eccentric and improvised, yet genuine cryptanalytic expertise of what Veggian called the "Riverbank anti-philologists," on which the United States had relied since 1914, was now added the legitimating disposition of the university scholar, and the harmonizing imperatives of mobilization for war provided them with a common objective. In the year before William F. Friedman was sent to France in 1918 to work with the Radio Intelligence Section, "the Riverbank Baconists and the Black Chamber Elizabethans of MI-8" thoroughly modernized U.S. cryptology, applying to problems of cryptanalysis William and Elizabeth Friedman's "antiphilological interpretive technique," which "permanently abandoned the philologist's commitment to study language as a dynamic, historical entity, thus separating cryptology from late nineteenth century methods of literary interpretation."[85]

Severing its links to the hermeneutic enterprise, a new science of cryptology defined itself by its disposition of "a new aggregation of statistical models, the production of specialists engaged in supervised, collective work, and, when necessary, the practical applications of the mechanical arts within the confines of emergent state institutions."[86] Kahn noted that increasing volumes of enciphered message traffic had spurred the refinement of statistical cryptanalytic techniques and that the complexity of the ciphers used by the new electromechanical cipher machines required both mathematical attacks and electrome-chanical assistance or automation. Advances in the statistical analysis of text flung "wide the door to an armamentarium to which cryptology had never before had access. Its weapons—measures of central tendency and dispersion, of fit and skewness, of probability and sampling and significance—were ideally fashioned to deal with the statistical behavior of letters and words. Cryptanalysts, seizing them with alacrity, have wielded them with notable success ever since. . . . The cryptology of today is saturated with mathematical operations, mathematical methods, mathematical thinking. In practice, it has become virtually a branch of applied mathematics."[87] To this, Veggian added that "unlike literary study, which was not bound to temporal exigency, William Friedman's treatment of encoded texts as closed systems with recurring behavioral patterns solved the problem of time that plagued the cryptologists: the accelerated selection and interpretation of messages permitted the new U.S. cryptologists to decode a text before its military or intelligence value had expired."[88]

Returning briefly to Riverbank in 1920, William and Elizebeth Friedman departed again when William was offered a position in the U.S. Army Signal Corps, then hired by the War Department to teach at the Signal Corps School at Camp Alfred Vail. Friedman rose to become the Signal Corps' chief of cryptanalysis in 1922, then, following the closure of Yardley's postwar Cipher Bureau (MI-8) by Secretary of State Henry L. Stimson in 1929, director of the new Signal Intelligence Service (SIS). Unsurprisingly, given Friedman's commitment to cryptology as a new science, the second-generation cryptologists Friedman hired to work in the SIS were mathematicians with doctoral degrees in the subject and no professional interest in literature. If this marked the irreversibility of the "massive institutional reforms that shifted cryptology from a marginal, post-philological science to a mechanized institutional apparatus,"[89] it was, interestingly, hardly the end of John Matthews Manly's personal involvement in those reforms. Veggian showed that Manly, appointed a reserve intelligence officer upon returning to Chicago's English department, continued to correspond with Yardley and to support U.S. military intelligence by promoting the work of the Friedmans.[90]

The mathematization of cryptanalysis and its operational divestment from philology proceeded in Europe as well. The Polish intelligence reforms established during the Polish-Soviet War of 1919–1921, which led to the establishment of the Biuro Szyfrów in 1931, responded to the codebreaking prowess of mathematicians like Stefan Mazurkiewicz, Wacław Sierpiński, and Stanisław Leśniewski. As Kahn put it, the reforms "recognized that the increased volume of communications, foreshadowed by World War I, was mechanizing cryptology, that these cipher machines operated not on linguistic entities, such as words, as did the codes that were then popular, but on individual letters that would, for example, separate the *t* from an *h* in *the,* and that consequently, what was needed to solve them were not classical scholars and philologists but mathematicians. They might reconstruct a cryptosystem without ever reading a word of plaintext, not unlike the way William Friedman worked when he devised the index of coincidence."[91]

Pers Z, the cryptology service of the German Foreign Office, divided its cryptanalytic section into a cipher team that "was heavily mathematical in personnel and approach" and a code team that took a predominantly linguistic approach. Werner Kunze, who directed the cipher team, had begun working on British ciphers in 1918 and "may well have been the first mathematician employed in a modern cryptanalytic office."[92] A similar shift occurred in British cryptanalysis, with a "concerted effort to balance the staff" of Room 40, hitherto "dominated by linguists and classicists," by the addition of mathematicians.[93] Rudolf Schauffler, who with Adolf Paschke had directed Pers Z's linguistic code team, would go on after the war to obtain a doctoral degree in mathematics, a shift reflected more broadly in the philological sciences that furnished the wartime intelligence agencies with their founding personnel: in 1930, the decipherment of Ugaritic cuneiform by Hans Bauer, an Orientalist at the University of Halle, was accomplished with primarily statistical techniques, drawing on Bauer's wartime work as a cryptanalyst for German intelligence.[94]

"Not only scientists," Carol S. Gruber observed of American college and university faculty upon U.S. entry into the war, but "humanists and social scientists as well sensed in the war situation an opportunity to win confidence in their disciplines, to stimulate interest in them, and to accomplish necessary reorganization and reform."[95] That a cryptanalysis both mathematized and mechanized under emergency conditions and for the purpose of advantage in total war would be reapplied to the antecedent pursuits of demobilized scholars, whose work was conceived under different conditions and with different goals, was probably inevitable—though its continuance or renewal need not be, and the opportunistically active or passive forgetting of its genealogy ought to be opposed. Following his return to the Department of English at the University of Chicago in 1919, Manly devoted himself to a methodological reform of literary scholarship modeled explicitly on the antiphilological modernization of cryptology. For all intents and purposes, what Manly proposed in the address he delivered to the membership of the Modern Language Association of America as its 1920 president was a "Bureau du Chiffre for the U.S. humanities":[96] a reimagination of literary humanist scholarly practice conforming to the scientific model of specialized supervised or collaborative research, addressed to problems whose scale threatened to paralyze an individual scholar. A new mathematically oriented and mechanized cryptanalytic military intelligence had organized the solitary philological "chamber analysts," Manly reminded his audience, and new collective modes of technical labor in literary scholarship were bound to follow.[97] (Of cryptography's modernization, Kahn observed that "the science at last outgrew the mode of operation that had dominated it for 400 years. This was chamber analysis, in which a single man wrestles with a single cryptogram alone in his room."[98])

Edith Rickert, Manly's University of Chicago colleague who had worked alongside him in MI-8 and who would labor alongside him on the eight-volume variorum *The Text of the Canterbury Tales,* applied herself to the cryptanalytic reform of literary scholarship with such dedication that Manly would proclaim her 1927 handbook *New Methods for the Study of Literature* "the sign and the cause of a new era in the study of literature."[99] Rickert was explicit about the origins of her work, writing in her preface titled "To Skeptics" that "its root lies, strangely enough, in the methods of code analysis used in the Code and Cipher Section of the Military Intelligence in Washington, during the war. . . . The defense for its appearance now," she offered, "is the crying need for some book to turn the study of literature in a new direction."[100] Rickert's articulation of a practice of close reading modeled on cryptanalysis is entertaining to regard amid the excitement of latter-day digital humanists who would have us believe that their cryptanalytic derivation of a "distant reading" is unprecedented in literary studies.

The Road to Computing

Fewer philologists served U.S. intelligence agencies as cryptanalysts during the Second World War than had served in that role during the war preceding it. This is not to underestimate their contributions, which were concentrated elsewhere, mainly in research and translation. Remarking on the historical amnesia on campus during the 1970s at the very institution, Yale University, whose literary scholars and historians helped to establish the Central Intelligence Agency in 1947, Robin Winks noted that "history was . . . the best discipline for the gathering and evaluation of intelligence information, in part because it enabled individuals to assimilate and reorder into meaningful patterns an enormous variety of data." Academics, Winks argued, were temperamentally ideal for intelligence work:

> Academics do not often suffer from identity crises, because their identities are within their work: they are, in that sense, at work all of the time (some literally so, in part from fear of inquiring too closely into the actual value of the work being done, which would challenge the elite status and the basis for individualization, and in part because work—doing that which one does well—is a buffer against one's incompetence in other areas of human endeavor). These are precisely the kinds of individuals valuable to the OSS or the CIA, and especially to the work of researching and analyzing intelligence data.[101]

Established in 1942, the Office of Strategic Services (OSS) began contracting research projects to new institutes established at Stanford, the University of California at Berkeley, the University of Denver, Columbia,

Princeton, and Yale. "No one at the universities," Winks remarked, "appears to have protested these ties, and university presidents and professors awarded contracts and consultantships, at times going well beyond supplying or analysis of information, as when Cal Tech manufactured rockets for the Army."[102] Those sent abroad by the OSS used their university affiliations as cover, as in the case of Joseph Toy Curtiss, assistant professor of English at Yale, who traveled to Istanbul in 1942 as a scholar collecting materials for Yale's library. In Istanbul, Curtiss resided at Robert College, ostensibly translating German documents for the U.S. military attaché and occasionally teaching an English course alongside the U.S. Army reserve officers that had replaced the departed U.S. civilian teaching staff. Fraternizing with other Yale faculty and administrators serving in various positions in Ankara and Istanbul, Curtiss gradually worked his way into direct service to OSS's Istanbul branch, in time becoming acting head of the X-2 Counter-Espionage Branch and then chief of OSS Istanbul.[103] (Living up to its reputation, wartime Istanbul hummed with intrigue, including some of a purely philological nature: Winks noted that "the OSS had to withdraw the entire first edition of the Turkish grammar prepared by a member of staff who had been trained in linguistics at Yale" because the staff member's Turkish informant had maliciously misled her regarding the conjugation of "I am"—supposedly printed "I fuck."[104])

Curtiss was already on his way to Turkey when Norman Holmes Pearson, a Hawthorne scholar who completed his PhD at Yale in 1941 and joined the Yale faculty as instructor in English,

> plunged into helping Charles S. Walker in his role as Yale's "Secretary of War," writing a series of letters to thirteen universities . . . to find out what English departments were doing to assist in the war effort. He received notably useful replies from [George F.] Reynolds [Shakespeare scholar at the University of Colorado], and also from the three other state institutions to which he wrote (Indiana, Iowa, Rutgers), while some universities—Harvard, notably—gave him a waffly response. (Later Pearson was to observe that state universities, having to account to non-scholarly—and sometimes scholarly—taxpayers, knew a lot more about making

quick decisions than private institutions would ever know.) . . .
English departments weren't doing much, Pearson found, for the
history, political science, and economics departments had moved
out first; Yale was the exception, thanks to Dean DeVane.[105]

Trained by OSS in 1943 and sent to London to work in X-2, Pearson
served as a liaison between X-2 and U.S. staff at Bletchley Park. Work in
the estate's Hut 3, which translated, analyzed, and routed the intercepts
deciphered in Hut 6, was directed by Frederick W. Hilles, another faculty member in Yale's English department, who supervised a multilingual staff of 183 holders of advanced degrees from the Ivy League, major
private and public research universities, and elite liberal arts colleges.[106]
By itself, Shawn Rosenheim joked, "the X-2 network could, in fact, have
been considered one of the better university English departments in
America. Among others, Pearson handled Yale English professors Louis
Martz and Eugene Waith; Edward Weissmiller, winner of the 1936 Yale
Younger Poets award; and Richard Ellman, whose subsequent work on
Joyce might be thought of as a form of biographical decryption."[107]

After returning to Yale as an assistant professor of English in 1945,
Pearson became a promoter of the work of the poet H. D. (Hilda Doo-
little) and eventually her literary executor, while providing the new
Central Intelligence Agency with memorandums on such topics as
"controlled enemy agents" and suggesting the recruitment of advisors
from the ranks of faculty in English, foreign languages, and history.[108]
Pearson's most substantive accomplishment was the promotion and institutionalization of American studies, Yale's program in which he directed from 1963 until his death in 1975, and which is just one item of
evidence in what Winks called the "major impact" of OSS's R&A section on scholarship in U.S. universities from the 1940s to the 1960s.[109]

Both Winks and Rosenheim noted that the submergence of literature
and literary scholarship in military research and administration, in
these cases, did not end with the war. Just as John Matthews Manly, appointed a reserve intelligence officer upon return to the University of
Chicago English department, remained in contact with Yardley and
Friedman while pursuing his cryptanalytic reform of philology as president of the Modern Language Association of America, the Yale scholars

of the OSS were never fully demobilized—though unlike Manly, many of them appear to have abandoned scholarship. Winks observed that they "seemed to take too long to get back into stride. For whatever reason . . . there was a flourishing of brilliant teaching . . . and a long silence of the pen," while Rosenheim remarked of Pearsons's return to Yale that his "career as a critic never regained its momentum, and he ended up running the Yale American Studies program 'as if it were the CIA.' "[110]

Cryptography, the enciphering of a message, had been automated by the Enigma cipher machines marketed commercially since the 1920s and adapted for military use. After the Biuro Szyfrów cracked a German military Enigma cipher in 1932, subsequently sharing their techniques with British and French analysts, both the U.S. Navy Combat Intelligence Unit commanded by Thomas H. Dyer, the "father of machine cryptanalysis,"[111] and William Friedman's SIS began using IBM tabulating machines, "convert[ing] as many [cryptanalytic] tasks as possible to mechanical operation."[112] As they had been since the early 1920s, the cryptanalytic service personnel who supervised these operations were mathematicians. "Foremost in the battle against Enigma," Kahn wrote, "was a new breed of cryptanalyst. For centuries, it had been assumed that the best cryptanalysts were experts in the structure of language, but the arrival of Enigma prompted the Poles to alter their recruiting policy. Enigma was a mechanical cipher, and the Biuro Szyfrów reasoned that a more scientific mind might stand a better chance of breaking it."[113]

At Bell Laboratories, Claude Shannon's concurrent work on cryptology and the mathematical theory of communication, from 1941 onward, were in his own words "so close together you couldn't separate them,"[114] drawing their insights into natural-language redundancy from the cryptanalyst's principal technique, comparative frequency analysis. "The astonishing stability and universality of the phenomenon of letter frequency," Kahn warned his readers, "is not often realized." Admitting that "the more the cryptanalyst knows about a language, the more easily he can solve cryptograms in it" and that "if he has never seen a sentence in the language, then the solution is virtually impossible," Kahn was unable to refrain from adding: " 'virtually' because the alternations of vowels and consonants common to all languages may yet afford some clues."[115]

The first electromechanical and electronic computers would be constructed after 1941 for two quite different applications. One of these applications was purely computational (the calculation of ballistics trajectories), while the other was primarily textual, if no longer either philological or linguistic. That story, the story of computing as such, is not one I will dwell on here, as others have done a more than adequate job of it. But it is here, in Kahn's portentous insistence that "other activities besides cryptanalysis depend upon the fixity of letter frequency,"[116] and that new meaning is to be found in the latter's nonmeaning—that is, that it is possible to solve a cryptogram "in a language that one 'does not know,' provided that 'not knowing' means only that one does not understand the sense of the words"[117]—that we are presented with the cryptophilology of our era: that is, of the era of computing, which enjoins us to encounter any and all text as enciphered and responsive to automated computation.

3

Machine Translation

A Tale of Two Cultures

Machine translation (hereafter "MT") was the first imagined broadly cultural, rather than narrowly and strictly practical, military application of the electromechanical and electronic computers developed by the United States, the United Kingdom, and Germany for aerodynamics and ballistics calculations and cryptanalysis during the Second World War. Although the mathematicians and engineers who dominated work on MT often insisted that they were working exclusively on practical problems, it is unlikely that they were entirely unfamiliar with the intellectual genealogy of their project, which stretched back at least to the final decline of Latin and the rise of philosophical rationalism in seventeenth-century Europe. During the second half of the seventeenth century, constructed universal taxonomic, arithmetic, or logical languages capable of replacing Latin and refining the communication of thought were imagined in different ways (and with different levels of both sincerity and sophistication) by Francis Lodwick, Thomas Urquhart, Cave Beck, George Dalgarno, Johann Joachim Becher, Athanasius Kircher, John Wilkins, and Gottfried Leibniz, among others. The profusion of international auxiliary languages that accompanied the late nineteenth-century period of European imperialism built on these earlier, more speculative efforts, in some cases developing active international communities of fluent speakers (notable examples include Volapük, Esperanto, and Ido). Many such projects emphasized both the potential universality of a rationally planned language, in itself, and its role in translation, mediating the difference of existing natural languages and ameliorating the conflict that difference creates. In this respect, at least, the postwar internationalism of early MT research can be situated squarely within the Euro-American or Euro-Atlantic intellectual tradition we call modernity, shaped by the historical concurrence of secularization, nationalism, and empire.[1]

Mechanical or mechanizable translation methods were implied by both philosophical and practical auxiliary languages, the ideal of which was to restrict each single word to a single unambiguous meaning (thus John Hutchins, for example, refers to the works of Beck, Kircher, and Becher as "mechanical dictionaries"[2]). By contrast, the "machine" in "machine translation" designates a nonhuman translating agent, designed to take the place of the human translator sooner or later, and ideally altogether, at least for some of the earliest researchers in the field. As in the field of artificial intelligence (AI), which like computational linguistics has its origin in early work on MT, the goal of fully automated natural language processing, sufficiently accurate to pass the so-called Turing test by persuasively simulating the discourse of a human being, represents the cultural power of the speculative imagination, in this work: from 1949 to 1966, both enthusiasts and skeptics described fully automated high-quality translation (FAHQT) in mythic terms, as a "holy grail." It structured debate across the entire field, pitting theoretical against pragmatic approaches (and optimistic and pessimistic assessments of work of each type), strongly influencing public perception of the research, and leading in time to collapse and retrenchment.

Hutchins and Evgenii Lovtskii remind us that the first recorded proposal for the construction of a translating machine appeared in a patent granted to Petr Petrovich Troyanskii, a "forgotten pioneer" of MT, in the Soviet Union in 1933. (Troyanskii's writings of the 1930s and 1940s were neglected until after 1954, when Soviet MT programs were launched in response to growing publicity for work in the United States.)[3] Troyanskii imagined a labor-saving device used by monolingual human operators who were ignorant of the source language to be translated—though he did insist that at least one human operator, whom he designated "the editor," would have to be fluent enough in both source and target languages to check and refine the machine's output. In addition to human "post-editing," this machine, which Troyanskii proposed would be useful in "translating from and into languages of minor nations of the Soviet Union," also relied on human "pre-editing" of the text, replacing word stems and endings with what he called "logical symbols" borrowed from the grammar of Esperanto.[4] But the rational idealism so typical of early MT work can be found here, too, in the emphasis Troyanskii placed on the relocation or displacement to the machine of the cultural labor of language learning and translation, and on the benefits it offered to a world culture in which genuinely bilingual or multilingual professional translators were extremely scarce (and whose time and labor capacities were finite). In a 1947 paper titled "On a Translation Machine Built on the Basis of Monolingual Language-Translation Methodology," Troyanskii imagined a "universal logical make-up in all languages" accessible using "about 25 universal international symbols of logical parsing for all languages . . . capable of rendering without exception all relations and the slightest shades of human thought" and ensuring "absolutely exact translation into other languages without distortion of meaning."[5] Troyanskii stressed the advantages, to the 99 percent of the world's population that he regarded as functionally monolingual, of thus being able to translate "foreign journal articles and books into one's own language without knowing the language of the original."[6]

The imagination of a logical interlingua manipulable by a machine resurfaced in the postwar writings of Warren Weaver, the mathematician and engineer who served as a director at the Rockefeller Foundation and the U.S. Office of Scientific Research and Development (OSRD) during and after the war, and who authored an extended interpretive introduction to Claude Shannon's "The Mathematical Theory of Communication," the founding paper in information theory that emerged from Shannon's wartime work at Bell Laboratories. (Weaver seems not to have been aware of Troyanskii's projects.) In discussions during 1946 with Andrew Donald Booth, who was then beginning work on the construction of computers at Birkbeck College at the University of London, Weaver speculated about new applications for the Colossus code breakers constructed during the war at Bletchley Park, suggesting that cryptanalytic techniques might be applied to the translation of natural languages. Weaver would pursue this approach for some time, writing in a 1947 letter to the cybernetics researcher Norbert Wiener: "When I look at an article in Russian, I say: this is really written in English, but it has been coded in some strange symbols. I will now proceed to decode."[7] The discouraging response that Weaver received from Wiener and from figures like the British literary critic I. A. Richards (a proponent of Basic English) was offset by the enthusiasm expressed by others (such as Vannevar Bush, former director of the OSRD and president of the Carnegie Institution for Science) and by Alan Turing's endorsement of MT in a 1948 report to the United Kingdom's National Physical Laboratory.[8] The memorandum titled "Translation" that Weaver distributed to his circle of acquaintances in July 1949 revisited this earlier discussion and correspondence, referring to Shannon's information theory as well as the sinologist Erwin Reifler's work on comparative semantics in English and Chinese, and foregrounding a "war anecdote" related to Weaver by William Prager, a mathematician at Brown University. The German-born Prager, who had emigrated to Turkey during the war before arriving in the United States, had encoded a sentence in Turkish for one of his colleagues to practice a deciphering technique. "The most important point" about the fact that his experiment succeeded, Weaver asserted in his memo, was "that the decoding was done by someone who did not know Turkish, and did not know that the message was in Turkish."[9]

The conclusion Weaver drew from this, that a logical basis for all existing languages might be manipulated using cryptanalytic techniques, was quickly discredited. Still, its basic impulse, which one might call the neutralization of culture through the segregation of soluble engineering problems from potentially insoluble philosophical problems, pervaded subsequent work in MT as a constant temptation. In many ways, the story of MT is the story of an attempt to assert the independence of computation from culture and at the same time to assert the dominion of computation over culture: a story in which applied science arguably played a much more aggressive, even hostile role in the postwar university than C. P. Snow cared to recognize in his polemic against the division of "two cultures."[10] Often enough, as Norbert Wiener admitted in describing the origin of his work in cybernetics, the institutional culture of applied science was driven by the opportunism of engineers seeking access to social power and cultural prestige, looking for "something to do" (Wiener's words) with the resources being placed at their disposal in an arms race with the Soviet Union. In thus seeking a "niche" (Wiener's word) in the power complex of the postwar era, prosperity came with making one's work appear useful above all else.[11]

While the prominent role in MT research of German and Austrian Jewish refugees like Reifler, Yehoshua Bar-Hillel, and Hans Reichenbach no doubt reflects their firsthand experience of the Nazis' irrationalist "neue Kulturkampf" as much as a refugee's simple need to survive, it also reflects their intellectual roots in the positivist attack on philosophy in 1920s Berlin and Vienna, and the triumphalist culture of Anglo-American empiricism that had sheltered them was now launching its own culture war. In their introduction to *Machine Translation of Languages: Fourteen Essays* (1955), an edited volume that included the full text of Weaver's 1949 memorandum, Booth and W. N. Locke defined MT as "the completely automatic substitution of a different language for the language of a given text, the ideas being kept unchanged," stating that they intended to "leave aside, for the present, such philosophical points as the possibility of expressing any idea in written or spoken words, and the difficulties arising from the known fact that certain languages contain words descriptive of situations which have no parallel in other tongues." Admitting that one-to-one correspondence between word meanings in the source and target languages assumed an "ideal process" that was "by no means necessary, or even possible in general," they declared nonetheless preferable the practical advantages conferred by its "tacit" assumption as a basis for experiment, dismissing "philosophical" objections as finally irrelevant: "So much for purely philosophical views of translation, which are hardly likely to find any general measure of agreement either among linguists or among students of ideas. We proceed to a more special consideration which is bounded on the one side by what is useful and on the other by what is practicable."[12]

Weaver placed the neutralization of culture in the service of an internationalist ideal, describing the multiplicity of human languages as a "world-wide translation problem" that "impedes cultural interchange between the peoples of the earth, and is a serious deterrent to international understanding." Contrasting the Second World War anecdote related to him by William Prager with the U.S. military cryptanalytic efforts of the war that preceded it, Weaver lamented the time that had been spent identifying languages in which encoded messages had been composed. In Weaver's view this was time squandered, since cryptanalysis itself had provided measures of letter frequency, combination, and interval that were "to some significant degree independent of the language used." That languages had certain "invariant properties" statistically "common to all languages," Weaver opined, "may be, for all I know, a famous theorem of philology." Believing it supported such speculation, Weaver invoked the work of the nineteenth-century Orientalist Max Müller, who had been Oxford University's first Professor of Comparative Philology, and (apparently unaware of Müller's contempt for them) onomatopoetic-echoic "bow-wow" theories of the origin of human language, suggesting that all human beings had identical vocal organs producing similar ranges of sounds, "with minor exceptions, such as the glottal click of the African native." Phonological and graphic correlations between words in English and Chinese had been demonstrated by Reifler, Weaver noted, while Reichenbach, a founder of the Berlin Circle who had "also spent some time in Istanbul, and, like many of the German scholars who went there . . . was perplexed and irritated by the Turkish language," had discovered common features of the basic logical structures of otherwise very different languages.[13]

· · · ·

THE SECTION OF WEAVER'S MEMO TITLED "Translation and Computers" recapitulated the history of his ideas about MT and his correspondence with Wiener in 1947, which Weaver excerpted liberally. Weaver reflected on his first letter to Wiener, in which he had suggested that "a most serious problem, for UNESCO and for the constructive and peaceful future of the planet, is the problem of translation, as it un-avoidably affects the communication between peoples." Acknowledging the likelihood of "semantic difficulties because of multiple meanings, etc.," Weaver had briskly moved on to what really interested him, which was to speculate about whether "it were unthinkable to design a computer which would translate. Even if it would translate only scientific material (where the semantic difficulties are very notably less), and even if it did produce an inelegant (but intelligible) result, it would seem to me worth while." Asked if he thought this "worth thinking about," Wiener had replied with a dismissal of "any quasimechanical translation scheme" as implausible, given the vague "boundaries of words in different languages" and their extensive "emotional and international connotations."[14]

Weaver took up the question of literary translation, conceding that mechanical word-for-word transposition of literary prose or verse would fail owing to "problems of idiom, multiple meanings, etc." Happily, he noted by way of contrast, the technical discourse of mathematics was haunted by no such polysemy, so that "one can very nearly say that each word, within the general context of a mathematical article, has one and only one meaning." Unwilling to rest here, however, Weaver complained that skepticism about generalized application of MT was not "appropriately hopeful," and went on to suggest four distinct possible methodological approaches to fully automated mechanical translation of language in general. One, Weaver explained, would focus on the relationship of meaning to context, bringing brute force computation to bear in resolving multiple meanings by inferring as much context as necessary (less for technical and scientific writing, more for literary prose and verse) from the "statistical semantic character of language" in general. Another would focus on semantic logic, on the assumption that despite its "alogical elements," "written language is an expression of logical character." A third approach, extending the first and based on Shannon's work on the statistical character of communication, would simply treat translation as cryptanalysis. "Perfect" translation, Weaver admitted, was "almost surely unattainable"; but the advantage of statistical semantic study was that it addressed the "statistical character of the problem" rather than the perfectibility of a solution. A chief purpose of his memorandum, Weaver declared, was to stimulate such work. Finally, describing the "deep use of language invariants" as "the most promising approach of all," Weaver imagined languages as towers erected on a common foundation with an open basement, and translation as a traversal of that basement, rather than "shouting from tower to tower":

> Think, by analogy, of individuals living in a series of tall closed towers, all erected over a common foundation. When they try to communicate with one another, they shout back and forth, each from his own closed tower. . . . But, when an individual goes down his tower, he finds himself in a great open basement, common to all the towers. Here he establishes easy and useful communication with the persons who have also descended from their towers. Thus may it be true that the way to translate from Chinese to Arabic, or from Russian to Portuguese, is not to attempt the direct route, shouting from tower to tower. Perhaps the way is to descend, from each language, down to the common base of human communication—the real but as yet undiscovered universal language—and then re-emerge by whatever particular route is convenient.[15]

Emphasizing the generality of his interest, Weaver noted that such a project, "whether or not it leads to a useful mechanization of the translation problem . . . could not fail to shed much useful light on the general problem of communication."

· · · ·

WEAVER'S MEMORANDUM PROVED GALVANIZING. By the end of 1949 research groups had been formed at MIT, UCLA, and the University of Washington, where a team was led by Reifler, the most prominent of a very few MT researchers whose training was in a discipline other than mathematics or engineering. (Hutchins notes that post-Bloomfieldian linguists were generally skeptical about this enthusiasm, especially the inordinate interest taken in statistical analysis and classification of logical and semantic universals across languages.)[16] Very early work focused on word-by-word dictionary translation, the results of which some pronounced "tantalizingly good,"[17] but which led others, such as Reifler, to conclude that human pre- and/or post-editing would be indispensable. Papers and reports published in the early 1950s dwelled on limited hardware storage capacity and access time as inhibiting progress, while divisions emerged between the theoretical and "perfectionist" approach of the MIT group, aimed at the long-term goal of high-quality translation, and the empirical and operational approach of Reifler's group at Washington, funded by grants from the Rockefeller Foundation and the U.S. Air Force from 1952 onward.[18] Beginning in 1950, Reifler, who appears to have been the first to respond in writing to Weaver's memo,[19] circulated a series of papers titled "Studies in Mechanical Translation," using his credentials as a scholar of comparative semantics, a translator, and a teacher of Chinese and German as foreign languages to promote MT research from a humanist perspective.

In "The Mechanical Determination of Meaning," included in *Machine Translation of Languages: Fourteen Essays*, Reifler set aside his earlier reservations about MT as a "new expansion of the empire of the machine" and declared fully automated translation both worthy of pursuit and an achievable goal. Reifler argued that work on mechanical solutions was justified by the labor-intensiveness of translation, the scarcity of translators, and "the ever-increasing volume of important publications in many languages." Stating that as a scholar of comparative semantics, a translator, and a foreign-language instructor, he had initially regarded MT as altogether impossible, but later came to see "certain limited possibilities" for MT in concert with a human pre-editor, Reifler then discarded the latter position as well, declaring that human pre-editing itself "could be completely mechanized." Reifler distinguished the "MT linguist," who would focus on the explicit, partly context-independent, "less formidable" graphical forms of language, from the traditional linguist, who focused on spoken language as a primary symbolization. The MT linguist working on a mechanical translation problem, Reifler suggested, could restrict his attention to specific problems formulated using single language pairs, rather than being distracted by problems of language in general—and he need not be distracted, Reifler added, by questions of meaning beyond accuracy in translation. Asserting that "all languages actually do have a number of features in common," especially logical features of grammar, Reifler argued that completely mechanized translation "based entirely on the conventional form of the original text," rather than pre-edited or post-edited by a human operator (or composed using a special monosemantic lexicon), ought to be both possible and accepted as possible. Only a mechanical process that could handle multiple meanings without human assistance, Reifler opined, could "really deserve the name of MT." Insofar as it would have to handle polysemy and "intended nongrammatical meaning," fully automated MT, he concluded, could lead to "general-purpose translation machines, capable of translating even poems, as long as unconventional or even 'bad' prose is satisfactory."[20]

．．．．

IN "HISTORICAL INTRODUCTION," their preface to *Machine Translation of Languages,* Locke and Booth provided an overview of MT research completed to date and speculated about future directions, noting that fully automatic text readers would be needed to read printed and hand-written input material and that MT had thus far been conceived only for written language: "The conversion of the time-varying sound patterns of a spoken language into the space-varying ink-on-paper pattern of the written language is a translation problem in its own right." They noted that storage media providing a ten-million-word capacity appeared to be the most capacious available; that most researchers were focusing on bilingual Russian to English and German to English translation, but that there were many more languages to which one might want to apply MT; and that a "multilingual machine in which the input would be translated into any of a number of output languages or vice versa" would require input to be first translated into an "interlanguage" of a character "completely logical with simple, regular word formation and grammar." Erwin Reifler, they noted, had proposed Chinese for this role; but "the logicians . . . and others believe that an artificial language would be more appropriate." In a digression on conjugations and the divergence of different languages in grammar, more than in lexis, they observed that "on the grammatical side, much remains to be done before a machine can be built that will 'translate' in any true sense of the word." Acknowledging that the processing of syntax would require complex programming, they noted that "this work is particularly difficult because linguists have to adopt a wholly new point of view if their analyses of language are to be no longer simply understandable to other human beings but entirely translatable into a series of machine operations."[21]

In a section titled "Dictionary," Locke and Booth observed that current MT did not try to achieve output of "literary quality," but merely output useful "to a reader who wishes to glean the ideas contained in the original text." Later, turning to literary language again, they admitted that "turning a masterpiece of literature written in a foreign language into a respectable translation is one of great difficulty." Arguing that it was, however, an "extreme position" to hold that such a task could not be accomplished, they opined that "this view seems to us overpessimistic." Discarding their earlier caution regarding the modest prospects of MT of literary quality, Locke and Booth closed "Historical Introduction" by declaring the translation of literary language to be a goal worthy of pursuit: "It seems not unreasonable," they wrote, "to anticipate thoroughly literate translations of literary works as good as published run-of-the-mill translations." Given sufficient storage capacity, they argued, a computer could certainly handle the reproduction of rhyme and meter; indeed, given sufficient storage capacity, they were confident that a computer might be entirely successful in "identifying the ideas contained in the original text and expressing these in terms of stored phrases." This, they declared, "would thus be no translation of the words at all, but merely a transposition of semantic content from one language to another." "Poetic phraseology" was not only not resistant to MT, in this sense—it was "particularly susceptible" to MT. The translation of poetry, Locke and Booth concluded, thus "seems hardly more extravagant now than an automatic dictionary did ten years ago."[22]

* * * *

AS THE FINAL FRONTIER FOR COMPUTATION and its ultimate test, the translation of literary language would become a middle note of MT research, pervading both the speculations of researchers themselves and the popular press coverage that increased dramatically after a public demonstration of Russian-to-English MT on January 7, 1954, at IBM's Technical Computing Bureau in New York. Showcasing the work of a team at Georgetown University led by Léon Dostert, a professor of French who had served as Eisenhower's interpreter and organized language services for the Nuremberg trials, the so-called Georgetown demonstration was the first working implementation to advance beyond word-by-word translation and incorporate elements of grammar.

The goal of the Georgetown project, Dostert stated in his contribution to *Machine Translation of Languages,* was to eliminate the need for human pre- or post-editing: "We set out to feed in the normal language at the input, without prior human processing, and we aimed at obtaining clear, complete statements in intelligible language at the output."[23] Dostert described an initial experiment using a lexicon of 250 terms in Russian and English, beginning with a "card test" in which Russian sentences written in romanized script were successfully translated by human translators unfamiliar with the Russian language, who followed a mechanical lexical and syntactic "lookup" procedure that could also be performed by a computer.

Dostert defined translation as the transference of meaning from a patterned set of symbols found in one culture to another patterned set of symbols found in another culture. Linguistically, he suggested, the problem of translation was a syntactic problem, not a problem of usage: even when translation was performed by a human being, the transference of meaning was achieved through the two "basic operations" of lexical selection (selecting a correspondence in the target language) and the syntactic manipulation or arrangement of output. Dostert acknowledged that "language items are fluid entities which carry meaning determined by a number of factors" including context, which is where "mechanical translation encounters most of its difficulties." Such difficulties were in no way intractable, he suggested, but would require the development of a systematic code for the contextual determination of meaning and a "core syntax, common to several languages" to serve as a pivot or medium of transfer. Dostert was confident that with each additional language integrated into such a core syntax, less additional programming would be needed, "since we are likely to find that many of the comparative or contrastive mechanical syntax operations in any two languages occur in other languages as well." In general, Dostert argued, such extralinguistic determinants of meaning as cultural norms or reference, usage history, and the specific historical context of an utterance or act of writing "need not, in my opinion, become a subject of major preoccupation in the immediate research in mechanical translation."[24]

* * * *

LIMITED AS IT WAS, Dostert's "Georgetown demo" made an impression and received a great deal of publicity, and reactions to it ranged from euphoria to dismay, though not always in predictable ways or from predictable quarters. In memoirs of the period, Dostert's assistant Muriel Vasconcellos recalls the attacks of "language experts, particularly translators" on the authenticity of the Georgetown demonstration,[25] while Anthony Oettinger, who after producing the first doctoral dissertation on MT would lead a research group at Harvard starting in 1954, recalls finding Dostert "a bit of a fraud" and the Georgetown demo "contrived."[26] It would appear, indeed, that the acquired technocratic optimism of a humanist like Reifler was paralleled all along by the gradual disenchantment of some of the mathematicians and engineers working on MT. As early as 1951, Yehoshua Bar-Hillel, appointed that year to the first funded research position in MT, in MIT's Research Laboratory of Electronics, wrote that FAHQT was an unachievable short-term goal, noting in a paper presented at a four-day MT conference the following year that it would be possible for MT output to be grammatical and make sense, and therefore be accepted as a correct translation, "but still be dead wrong." Observing that multiple possible translations imposed constraints of labor or processing time and cost, as well as storage capacity on the feasibility of MT, Bar-Hillel declared himself concerned "not so much with how to select from the huge number of tentative translations the one (or the few) appropriate one (or ones), as with what to do if none of the translations offered is appropriate."[27]

William E. Bull, Charles Africa, and Daniel Teichroew cautioned still more skeptically that in such cases "no translation at all would be less dangerous than a wrong or misleading one." Distinguishing failure in MT from apparently successful but incorrect results, they noted that while the former was marked by untranslated source words or phrases left in the product, the latter might be impossible to detect if the product was intelligible. Scorning "the spurious marvels of Basic English," they argued that while relative frequency analysis might contribute something to MT efficiency, it should never be used to justify restrictions on word storage. By contrast with the small set of words that constrain grammar and syntax and therefore are used by any speaker who makes sense, the number of additional "dictionary words" that may be freely selected by any speaker was, they wrote, "theoretically infinite"—and most choices occur so infrequently as to be inferentially meaningless.[28] "There does not exist," Bull et al. concluded, "nor is there any probability of devising a method of sampling all human behavior which will provide data that can predict either all the necessary machine routines or the total vocabulary needed when a random segment of discourse is presented for translation." This, they concluded, "is discouraging but inescapable." In their view, the MT researcher facing this fact had two choices: "Either we must attempt to close the open system of human behavior by establishing arbitrary restrictions (new givens), or we must restrict investigations to that portion of human behavior which is determined by the existence of special closed systems. In either case, there is a large residue of questions to which statistical data will provide no answers. The recognition of this fact, at the outset, will save time and energy."[29]

. . . .

ALONG WITH DOSTERT'S "GEORGETOWN DEMO," the year preceding the 1955 publication of *Machine Translation of Languages* saw the launch of Margaret Masterman's Cambridge Language Research Unit at Cambridge University and of Oettinger's group at Harvard, along with the first issue of the journal *Mechanical Translation,* published at MIT, and the formation of the first Soviet research groups. It was the beginning of a golden age for MT, defined by major international conferences, a critical mass of important publications, and in the United States, easy access to generous government, military, and private funding even before the Sputnik crises of 1957. John Hutchins suggests that while this influx of funding after 1954 was driven mainly by Cold War geopolitical objectives, the cultural imagination of artificial intelligence, both among the public and among scientists and engineers themselves, may have helped boost support for MT research as well.[30] Between 1954 and 1960, Reifler's group at Washington worked on a Russian-to-English system for the U.S. Air Force's information retrieval systems at Rome Air Development Center in New York; Noam Chomsky joined the MT lab at MIT, developing work on syntax that would influence the direction of subsequent work on MT, though Chomsky himself would come to feel that MT was "pointless" and "hopeless";[31] and research groups formed in the Soviet Union, Italy, France, Belgium, West and East Germany, Czechoslovakia, Hungary, Romania, Japan, China, and Mexico, while expanding in the United States and the United Kingdom.

Some MT researchers cautioned the public, and their own scientific and technical colleagues, that successful MT would likely be limited to technical and scientific prose and that MT of literary prose was unlikely. Others explicitly proposed a goal of low-cost but acceptable "poor translation,"[32] and still others, like Oettinger, made a point of rejecting outright the fantasy of translating literary prose or verse. Observing in his contribution to *Machine Translation of Languages* that "it is in the translation of the vast volumes of technical literature now inaccessible to the vast majority of American scientists that automatic devices are likely to be most useful," Oettinger argued that "one-to-one correspondences are the exception, not the rule" in natural languages and that the definition of a manageable problem required modesty of ambition. Oettinger deliberately restricted his own speculation to the manageable problem of technical Russian and technical English, rejecting the application of MT to "all possible discourse." Russian-language technical literature, he suggested, was "likely to have a sufficient degree of statistical homogeneity to make possible" the design of a working MT system for such documents. But of MT of literary language, Oettinger argued that "there would be no point in designing machinery to perform a certain task if the whole task had to be done first in order to design the machinery. It is this consideration which, coupled with respect for esthetic sensibilities, rules out the application of machines to literary works of art, since these often shine by virtue of their deviation from the statistical norm."[33]

• • • •

PUBLIC SKEPTICISM ABOUT MT FOUND JOURNALISTIC expression in joking and mockery, such as the story retailed by Hutchins about the translation of two idioms, "Out of sight, out of mind" and "The spirit is willing but the flesh is weak," from English to Russian and back again. "According to some accounts," Hutchins notes, "the first came back as *invisible insanity* and the second was *The whiskey is all right but the meat has gone bad;* according to others, however, the versions were *Invisible and insane* and *The vodka is good but the meat is rotten;* and yet others have given *invisible lunatics* and *the ghost is willing but the meat is feeble.*"[34] Occasionally, this was matched by a certain levity in the professional publications of MT researchers themselves. "A mechanical translator, like the sorcerer's apprentice," noted Booth and R. H. Richens in "Some Methods of Mechanized Translation," "is unable to desist. It will continue to translate even when not required, as for example, when it encounters proper names. The context will almost certainly prevent misunderstanding, but the reader must be prepared for Tours to come out as *turn / tower (plural)* and for Mr. Kondo to appear as *Mr. near wistaria.*"[35]

For the most part, speculation about MT of literary language was a motif in framing discussions, a way to probe public opinion—and perhaps bait campus humanists—with provocative conjecture. Some researchers suggested that MT might be applied in extending long-since mechanized modes of literary study itself. *Mechanical Resolution of Linguistic Problems,* a volume published in 1958 by Booth with two of his doctoral students at Birkbeck, Leonard Brandwood and J. P. Cleave, described their use of "digital calculators" in the stylistic analysis of Plato's dialogues as venturing "like Daniel, into the den of [our] colleagues in the Faculty of Arts."[36] Others followed with less trepidation, triumphantly announcing a "change in the climate of opinion among literary scholars" presaging a "revolution in literary studies."[37]

Better than by anyone else, what Hutchins described as a peak of optimism around 1959[38] was registered by Émile Delavenay, a scholar of D. H. Lawrence and head of UNESCO's Department of Documents and Publications, in a slim volume self-translated from the French original titled *An Introduction to Machine Translation*.[39] MT, Delavenay argued, promised a "new analysis of linguistic phenomena . . . with a technology of language, made possible by the application of electronics to the signs in which thought materializes in the form of language." Although computers could not use human language, in their performance of logical operations, Delavenay argued, they could mimic a subset of human mental processes with greater-than-human speed and efficiency. As the difference between scientific and literary prose was a difference of degree, not a difference of kind, there was no reason to see literary prose as a barrier to the machine-assisted general logical classification of knowledge, which Delavenay thought might someday provide a universal "atlas of meanings" as useful to literary researchers as to scientists.[40]

Like John Matthews Manly before him, and like others since, Delavenay imagined literary scholarship broadly transformed by collectivization, with new forms of collaboration in scientific "real time" replacing the "laborious scholarship undertaken by one man at the beginning of a lifetime of patient work." On the question of MT of literary prose, Delavenay made lemons into lemonade, observing that incomplete or partial output including untranslated words might be read as preserving the "local color" of the source—in a French translation of a novel composed in Hindi, for example, for which "a mixed vocabulary peculiar to such a translation" could even be established in advance. And when it came to that "question which has long lain in wait for us," the question "Will the machine translate poetry?," there was, Delavenay intimated portentously, "only one possible reply—why not? . . . From the Cartesian absolute of metalanguage to the mystic absolute of pure poetry," he opined, "there are differences not of kind but only of degree." Comparing the translating computer to the pantograph, noting that that latter was now regarded as a simple, no longer sacrilegious mechanical tool, Delavenay closed *An Introduction to Machine Translation* by placing MT alongside phonograph recording and the mechanical reproduction of images "in the first rank of modern techniques for the spread of culture and of science."[41] It is worth examining Delavenay's brief yet highly demonstrative and anticipatory text more closely.

• • • •

DELAVENAY WENT OUT OF HIS WAY to imagine anxious readers of *An Introduction to Machine Translation,* beginning with the reassurance that in applying electronic computation "to the signs in which thought materializes in the form of language," MT researchers were not creating a substitute "robot brain," rather merely "a tool at the service of the human intellect." His own focus, Delavenay declared, was not on the word "machine," but on the word "translation" in the phrase "machine translation." At the same time, in what would become a characteristic gesture, Delavenay insisted on MT as a domain of its own, separated from traditional philology by its currency and modernity. The atomic age was an age of science, he argued, and "automatic translation corresponds to a real need of our time": scientific knowledge was increasingly fragmented by specialization, with scientists needing translation of work by other scientists to be "available in real time." MT research focused on existing language behavior, rather than on the history of languages: "without wishing to offend the classicists, the problems requiring solution today are those of quantity and speed."[42] The atomic age was also a postimperial age of nationalism, Delavenay suggested, with newly decolonized nations eager to ground their national cultures in vernacular languages and at the same time to assert their contributions to a "universal culture." Such nations demanded translation not only of science textbooks and literacy readers, but also of "the great works of world literature." Yet even here, he predicted, scientists needed to lead the way, because linguists were "held in the leading strings of a historical and literary training which continues to direct the study of language towards the traces of the past rather than towards the possibilities of the future."[43]

Delavenay closed the first chapter of *An Introduction to Machine Translation* by explicitly disavowing Warren Weaver's imagination of translation as cryptanalysis. Cryptanalysis, Delavenay argued, operates on and within a natural language that cryptanalysis makes legible to both sender and receiver of an enciphered message, but "translation from one language to another requires something else altogether." Although information theory would indeed prove useful to MT, as Weaver had predicted, "the originality and individual nature of discourse" would always place limits on the utility of statistical laws. In the book's second chapter, "Computers and Language," Delavenay emphasized on the one hand that the human mental operations that a computer could mimic could already be understood as mechanical tabulating operations, and on the other hand that the so-called intelligence of a computer could do no more than reproduce the intelligence of the programmers who had programmed it. The activity of computer programming, he suggested, was both bounded and limited by "a world of strict conventions from which ambiguity or possibility of interpretation are excluded.... Everything in this system is predetermined and inhuman." The numeric encoding of the human-readable signs of a writing system had to be retranslated into human-readable signs in order to be useful. "It is important to remind ourselves," Delavenay wrote, "of this fundamental difference between human language and what has been called, by extension and by analogy, machine language."[44]

·   ·   ·   ·

REASONABLE ON THEIR OWN TERMS, such caveats seem nonetheless crafted to license increasingly aggressive assertions of the extraordinary, indeed world-historically novel impact and utility of computing. At times, Delavenay's reassurance of his reader seems little more than a vehicle for that reader's imagined anxiety, even its intentional provocation—suggesting that Delavenay was in no way finally persuaded of MT's value and that he had concluded, consciously or otherwise, that the case could not be made independently of what amounts to a politics of fear and a wager on futuristic bluster and intimidation. Presenting a review of MT research to 1960, the third chapter of *An Introduction to Machine Translation* praised the "bolder" recent work that had discarded the modesty and the modest ambitions of dictionary translation for pursuit of the ideal of "completely automatic, grammatically correct translation." Enthusiastically endorsing Reifler's reconsideration of the necessity of human preediting, Delavenay insisted that the work presented at the landmark MT conference of 1956 at MIT had demonstrated that advances in computing would "shortly make it possible to extract from conventional writing, without complementary signalization, all essential grammatical information."[45]

In the book's fourth chapter, meanwhile, Delavenay speculated affirmatively, even eagerly, about what he called the "philosopher's stone of machine translation": an interlingua determined either a posteriori, from the analysis of existing languages, or a priori and programmatically, as part of a "universal translation programme applicable to all languages." In a fifth chapter focused on problems of syntax, Delavenay remarked of the phrase "the King of England's Empire" that it would always be "enigmatic to the machine," providing insufficient context for resolving polysemy (the empire of the King of England, or the King of the empire of England?). "In such cases," Delavenay noted, "a reviser must remain the only final resort." At the same time, he insisted that as the syntax of a language was slower to change than its lexis, such polysemy presented a problem "relatively limited in scope" and already quite manageable with current hardware.[46]

Idioms, Delavenay suggested in a chapter titled "Lexical Problems of Automatic Translation," were "fossil" or "vestigial" units of meaning whose use "introduces an extra-linguistic element into language" in the form of specially specific, often outright exclusive context that is wholly determinative of meaning. If as such, he opined with breezy confidence, idiom was a serious obstacle both to MT of everyday language and to MT of literary prose and verse, it presented no particular problem to MT of scientific discourse. To be sure, he admitted, some intractably "genuine polysemy" inhered in all human uses of language, with which even human translators might struggle without success: MT could not be expected to do better in that respect. And yet, Delavenay insisted immediately, the probabilistic analysis of polysemy was feasible, and could help MT programs to learn to choose between likely and unlikely meanings—for example, of the French *temps,* by comparing its frequency of use to mean "time" with its frequency of use to mean "weather." A "national terminological centre and translation laboratory," Delavenay speculated, might maintain a centralized dictionary for scholarly discourse in a given language; by proceeding from the lexicons of the most precise of the sciences (mathematics and astronomy) to those of the least precise (the human sciences), one might in time expand it to encompass all those images and figures of speech representing "traps set by non-Cartesian thought on the path of all translation which seeks to be exact and faithful." Thus, he expected, might be overcome the weakness of the human sciences, who tended "to confuse language the tool of their analysis, with language the object of their study, because the subject of their work has no material being other than in words." Indeed, Delavenay insisted, from this point we might move on to still "bolder enterprises," integrating even literary prose into a "general logical classification of knowledge."[47]

*   *   *   *

BUT STORM CLOUDS WERE GATHERING. By 1959, Bar-Hillel's drift from enthusiasm to "profound gloom"[48] had produced a report for the U.S. Office of Naval Research concluding that FAHQT was not only un-achievable in the short term, but impossible regardless of the level of resources devoted to it. The report was republished in expanded form in 1960 in the journal *Advances in Computers,* which brought it to public attention. Reviewing a half-million-dollars' worth of MT research supported by federal funding during 1958, Bar-Hillel's discouraging assessment was a foreshadowing of things to come: John Hutchins has noted that "there can be few other areas of research activity in which one publication has had such an impact."[49] Léon Dostert of Georgetown was forced to defend MT research at congressional hearings in 1960, but he did so successfully, and the U.S. House of Representatives Committee on Science and Aeronautics endorsed MT's promise not only for science and military intelligence, but for "the exchange of cultural, economic, agricultural, technical, and scientific documents that will present the American way of life to people throughout the world." Still, at the NATO Advanced Summer Institute on Automatic Translation of Languages held in 1962, Bar-Hillel was publicly pessimistic, and it is possible that Mortimer Taube's attack on MT in *Computers and Common Sense* (1961) influenced public perception as well. For his part, Anthony Oettinger recalls a culture at MIT that was "intolerant of deviationism," forcing him to grant Hubert Dreyfus and Joseph Weizenbaum "'political asylum' in my offices" to write their critiques of the intellectual premises of AI. By 1963, both Oettinger and Victor Yngve, Bar-Hillel's successor at MIT, were giving up on MT altogether, and the program at Georgetown shut down when the funding Dostert had successfully defended before Congress in 1960 was not renewed.[50]

Oettinger's work at Harvard had begun in 1949, while he was still an undergraduate, and involved contacts with I. A. Richards, Roman Jakobson (then head of Harvard's Slavic department), Carol Chomsky, and Warren Plath, brother of the poet Sylvia. Oettinger recalls that when he joined the Automatic Language Processing Advisory Committee (ALPAC) of the National Academy of Sciences, convened in 1964 to assess progress on MT, "I knew that I was probably going to end up by taking my own research field 'down the drain' but I already had the firm conviction that MT was not going anywhere and that it made no sense to perpetuate a fraudulent belief that something might be achieved."[51] Oettinger describes a culture of casinoized grantsmanship, with both U.S. and Russian researchers engaged in "a kind of amiable conspiracy to extract money from their respective governments, playing each other off with various 'experiments' and 'demonstrations' that sometimes bordered on fraud."[52] ALPAC's report, issued in 1966, was deeply skeptical of researchers' claims that MT was needed to help process Russian-language technical literature, observing that the present supply of human translators "greatly exceeds the demand" and that "There is no emergency in the field of translation. The problem [of translation] is not to meet some nonexistent need through nonexistent machine translation."[53] It stated flatly that to date, "without recourse to human translation or editing . . . there has been no machine translation of general scientific text, and none is in immediate prospect" and observed that after eight years of work, the Georgetown group still could not produce output that was usable without post-editing. It described the Mark II system at Wright-Patterson Air Force Base in Dayton, Ohio, derived from Reifler's work for the Rome Air Development Center, as dependent on human post-editing, and noted that J. C. R. Licklider, then head of the U.S. Advanced Research Project Agency's Information Processing Techniques Office, had counseled IBM not to invest in MT product services. "Unedited machine output from scientific text," it concluded, "is decipherable for the most part, but it is sometimes misleading and sometimes wrong (as is post-edited output to a lesser extent), and it makes slow and painful reading."[54] Finally, ALPAC's report noted that "in some cases it might be simpler and more economical for heavy users of Russian translations to learn to read the documents in the original language," adding that many U.S. scientists already did just that, that instructional resources were available for those inclined to make use of them, and that acquiring basic reading facility in Russian was not likely to divert critical quantities of a researcher's time.[55] Regarding the labor cost of using human translators to post-edit MT output, it quoted Robert T. Beyer, a physicist at Brown University, who observed that

> I found that I spent at least as much time in editing as if I had car-ried out the entire translation from the start. Even at that, I doubt if the edited translation reads as smoothly as one which I would have started from scratch. I drew the conclusion that the machine today translates from a foreign language to a form of broken En-glish somewhat comparable to pidgin English. But it then remains for the reader to learn this patois in order to understand what the Russian actually wrote. Learning Russian would not be much more difficult.[56]

• • • •

THE ALPAC REPORT'S IMPACT WAS DEVASTATING: by 1968, The Association for Machine Translation and Computational Linguistics had dropped the phrase "machine translation" from its name, as the ten U.S. research groups active in 1963 dwindled to three, with research vir-tually shut down in the United Kingdom and significantly reduced in Japan and the USSR.[57] Hutchins has argued that ALPAC's assessments were selective and narrow in scope, and in some ways quite unfair;[58] but subsequent developments suggest that the goals of much MT work to 1965 had never been as practical and philosophically circumspect as its proponents had claimed. In a strikingly self-reflexive and self-consciously literary essay published in a 1967 volume of essays edited by Booth and titled simply *Machine Translation*, Ida Rhodes offered an elaborately stylized disavowal of the perfectibility of translation in gen-eral, suggesting that the most intractable problem was the "lack of cor-respondence in basic concepts" between some languages and implying that "mechanical translation" was quite simply a contradiction in terms. Rhodes mocked what he called "the ridiculous claims disseminated with regard to the prowess of the electronic computer," which he wrote was superior to the human in only one, comparatively unimportant aspect: speed.[59] Rhodes concluded that the nondissociability of mental processes from meaning ("semantic implication") would come to be recognized as "the Waterloo of MT."[60]

By that point Victor Yngve was ready to face what he called the "semantic barrier," admitting in his contribution to the same volume that "we have come face to face with the realization that we will only have adequate mechanical translations when the machine can 'understand' what it is translating and this will be a very difficult task indeed."[61] But in their contribution to Booth's *Machine Translation,* O. S. Kulagina and I. A. Mel'cuk were still speculating about conquest of the "gnostic-encyclopedic problem" by a new science capable of describing human knowledge of "extralinguistic . . . external world situations" in formal notation.[62] It took ALPAC's destruction of the legitimacy of the grand narrative that MT researchers had invented, along with the funding stream that sustained it, for work in the field to move finally and completely beyond the metaphysical objective of FAHQT, resigning itself to a durable human-computer symbiosis. Hutchins notes that it was only after the ALPAC report, in subsequent work on interactive human-computer translation workstations, that professional translators were invited to join MT research efforts *as* translators, rather than as models for their computer surrogates or post-editors of their output.[63]

Also shaping MT's fortunes after ALPAC were the genuine social, economic, and internal political needs of Canada and the European Communities, multilingual polities that recognized language plurality at the level of the state and embodied it in public policy. The Canadian and European situations stand in stark contrast to that in the United States, also a multilingual polity but one historically intolerant of public multilingualism. While the European Commission (EC) adopted an English-to-French Systran system in the mid-1970s and launched the development of its ambitious Eurotra multilingual system, the Traduction Automatique de l'Université de Montréal (TAUM) group produced METEO, a service for translating weather bulletins between English and French that operated until 2001. In the United States, MT development after 1965 was sustained by the Mormon Church's investments in bible translation, which kept work going at Brigham Young University,[64] and was otherwise left to the commercial sector.

* * * *

WRITING IN THE MID-1980S, Hutchins described a decade of "realistic optimism"[65] in the new work on MT that emerged around 1975. Released from the dream of FAHQT, MT would find lasting if limited practical application, as well as recognition for its contributions to subsequent work in computational linguistics, natural language processing in AI, and indexing and abstracting. Peter Toma's Russian-English Systran system, based on work at Georgetown, replaced the Mark II at Wright-Patterson Air Force Base in 1968 and was used by NASA during the Apollo-Soyuz project, while the English-to-French implementation developed for the EC was joined by French-English and English-Italian implementations between 1978 and 1981. Today, Systran, whose portfolio of product suites for home, business, and enterprise users offers translation in fifty-two language pairs, still provides services to the European Union. More projects would fail along the way: AVIATION, a TAUM project for translating aircraft maintenance manuals, was cut by the Canadian government in 1981 when it exceeded its budget, and development of the Eurotra system by a research consortium at the universities of Grenoble, Saarbrücken, Manchester, and Pisa was discontinued in 1994 after fifteen years of labor failed to produce a working prototype. Still, there is no doubting the vitality of what Makoto Nagao, leader of the Japanese government's Mu project during the early 1980s, called a "language industry" supported by the "language engineering" of postwar information societies[66]—even if, like many of those who inherited the metaphysical legacy of MT's golden age, Nagao was perhaps too eager to rewrite its history. ("No one," he has objected, "would say that automobiles are no good simply because they cannot be driven through swamps!"[67])

More recent defenses have revived the liberal internationalism of the postwar years, suggesting that MT provides speakers of minor languages with relief from domination by a lingua franca, allowing them to preserve their own languages and linguistic cultures.[68] Observing that MT research achieved intellectual maturity only when it relinquished the goal of FAHQT and resigned itself to the mediations of a human translator, the same authors noted in 1994 that Carnegie Mellon University researchers working on "knowledge-based" MT have had to scale back goals originally formulated in the late 1980s, given very modest achievements to date.[69] Such anecdotes suggest that the "gnostic-encyclopedic problem" has retained its temptations. Along with the amusingly (to some) mistranslated English-language signage now coloring public space in cities like Beijing, Tokyo, Moscow, and Istanbul, no-cost public access to crude but functional web-based MT is reflected in the literary production of pseudo avant gardes like the "Flarf poets" who emerged in the United States in the mid-2000s. These culturalizations of the cryptophilology known as "MT" certainly support Hutchins's 1986 observation that "there is now a growing realization that for many recipients stylistic refinements are not necessary; it appears that on the whole users are more content with low-quality texts than translators and post-editors"[70]—but they also give it something of a twist.

Cryptophilology, II

"When a complete history of literary data processing is written," Dolores M. Burton has suggested, "its links to machine translation will have to be explored."[1] More than thirty-five years later, the history Burton anticipated in 1981 has still not been written. Early work on the automated generation of concordances and word indexes, Joan Smith reflects, accompanied "some attempts at machine (assisted) translation which were not very good; likewise some attempts at machine understanding and original composition; and a diversity of other studies on verse and prose; also use of a computer as an aid in lexicography, the making of dictionaries."[2] The term "concordance," associated to that point almost exclusively with biblical philology dating to the thirteenth century, in which a concordance often included quotations of passages for each word, came to be used as an equivalent for a word index, which typically only contains references to tokens for each word in a text. "Perhaps the clearest link between machine translation and automated concordance / word-index generation," Burton remarked of this shift, "is the work of Andrew D. Booth."[3]

Along with Booth's edited volumes published in 1955 and 1967,[4] I have already mentioned *Mechanical Resolution of Linguistic Problems* (authored with Leonard Brandwood and J. P. Cleave), an account of experiments at the Birkbeck College Computational Laboratory on "the application of digital calculators to linguistic problems"; and I have already mentioned that its authors imagined themselves as venturing, "like Daniel, into the den of [our] colleagues in the Faculty of Arts."[5] The self-serving portentousness of this comparison, made in a book published during a year of responses to Sputnik I including the setting aside of U.S.-British estrangement over Suez, passage of the U.S. National Defense Education Act and National Aeronautics and Space Act, the formation of the Advanced Research Projects Agency, and vast increases in appropriations for the National Science Foundation, suggests that the imagined hazards of such a venture were straw men and scarecrows devised for a particular rhetorical purpose. Booth, Brandwood, and Cleave made it clear that the roots of their interest in the statistical properties of language lay not in the scholarly arts but in telecommunications engineering and its preoccupation with efficient transmission, and they recognized that the surge of interest in machine translation following the circulation of Warren Weaver's 1949 memo had been driven primarily by engineers, rather than by specialists in the study of language. Postwar stylistic analysis, as Booth, Brandwood, and Cleave saw it, had now freed itself from the classic philological preoccupation with problems of authorship attribution in relation to scriptural and literary canons—turning instead, by the mediation of MT research, to problems in the computational processing of technical prose. At Birkbeck, Booth saw his Department of Numerical Automation, which sponsored work on text parsing, dictionaries, Braille output, and natural language translation, as engaged in work building on Brandwood's research on style in Plato, which picked up where the British and German work on that topic had left off in the mid-1930s, but at the same time breaking with such research's origins and stated purpose or justification. Since "the frequency analyses required in machine translation are of the same generic type" as those traditionally employed in the philological construction of a concordance, Booth, Brandwood, and Cleave wrote, it was natural to imagine such work as having a new, common, yet at the same time schismatic or internally displaced origin.[6]

The Concordance Era

Reflecting on the Automatic Language Processing Advisory Committee report of 1966, Roberto Busa insisted that ALPAC had exposed nothing more than minor, arbitrary shortcomings in "linguistic knowledge"[7]— as if Erwin Reifler had not been indispensable to the legitimation of MT from a linguistically expert perspective, and as if ALPAC's report had not made a point of both emphasizing existing reading fluency in Russian among U.S. scientists and engineers and highlighting the superfluity of proposed technical solutions to what the committee regarded as a manufactured problem and a "nonexistent need."

Both Busa and John W. Ellison, who had also begun integrating theological textual studies with electromechanical computing in the mid-1940s, justified their work through a combination of appeals to efficiency and contempt for what they regarded as outmoded methods. Ellison ostentatiously reported being "astounded to discover" in 1945 that scholars like William H. P. Hatch, "the dean of manuscript scholars at that time," were "essentially counting on their fingers as they studied manuscripts," and that things had not changed much by the 1960s: "the scholars who are most involved in textual studies at the present feel that the subjective intuition of the scholar is going to make the greatest discoveries. They are still at work with the older methods, essentially counting on their fingers!"[8] Boasting of having been "the first humanist to walk into Harvard Computation Laboratory with a specific problem wanting to use the computer," when he requested time on the Harvard Mark IV whose construction was still in the planning stage in 1950, Ellison noted an encounter with the man who would later take such an unsparingly critical view of work on MT:

> In 1951, I went back to Harvard to learn how to program Mark IV. I was shown through the computer by one of the assistants, and as I came out of Mark IV (you could walk around inside computers in those days), Dr. Aiken was waiting for me. "You've seen the computer?" I said that I had. He turned to the assistant and said, "Find him a desk. Show him where he can get supplies." Then turning to me, he said, "When you want to know anything,

ask someone. When you want to think, go to your desk and sit down and think. I hope you have a very pleasant summer." That ended my formal instruction on how to program a computer!

After sitting at my desk and thinking for an hour, I was asked by someone, "How are you doing?" I said, "I wish I knew." He suggested that the librarian could supply me with descriptive material, and that after reading it, I might be ready to ask some questions. The temporary librarian was Anthony Oettinger, who was there also learning how to use the computer, because he had the idea that he might possibly be able to translate Russian into English on a computer.[9]

But it was the work of Busa, above all, which in its massive scale, if extremely narrow focus, challenged a "'theological' diffidence towards computer-aided studies."[10] Busa's 1946 dissertation drew on the ten thousand handwritten cards of a concordance to the works of Aquinas, a project whose computationalization over the next thirty-some years would become his life's work. Typifying the "heady mixture of idealism and hustle that fostered so many early computer projects," Busa's pursuit of the support of IBM's Thomas J. Watson along with Cardinal Francis Joseph Spellman, R.C.A. Laboratories, and the Library of Congress may not have been quite as successful as humanities computing enthusiasts would have us believe, but there is no denying Busa's resourcefulness and industry.[11]

IBM owned the Hollerith patents and had focused on tabulating equipment since the First World War, and Busa decided that electro-mechanical card machines would be necessary to advance his work. As Thomas N. Winter points out, Busa's first new project, a word index and concordance to four hymns of Aquinas assembled using a card machine, involved "no computers, no programming" in the senses those terms acquired later, and "not exactly" or "not yet" a vision of computing applied to humanities research.[12] Busa used card machines until 1956, when the Centro per l'Automazione dell'Analisi Letteraria (CAAL) was established in Gallarate and Busa began collaborating with Paul Tasman at IBM New York. In 1957 Tasman programmed an IBM 705 computer to process cards for the CAAL's projected index of the Dead Sea Scrolls, and Busa began reproducing the card entries of his Corpus Thomisticus on magnetic tape. By 1964, Busa had a staff of sixty including four programmers and a much larger group of machine operators working on texts in nine languages and four alphabets on a range of texts "dating from Aristotle to nuclear physics abstracts."[13]

In the meantime, Harry Josselson and Howard Hyatt had published *The Russian Word Count and Frequency Analysis of Grammatical Categories of Standard Literary Russian,* providing tabulation of a million words of Russian prose processed with an IBM machine in 1953; Ellison had published the first computer-generated concordance (of the Revised Standard Version), which had been assembled in 1957 using a UNIVAC; and the first of the so-called Cornell concordances supervised by Stephen Parrish, a concordance to the poems of Matthew Arnold, followed two years later.[14] The year 1957 was a "highpoint in the history of automated concordance construction," which saw the publication of Guy Montgomery's word index of the poems of Dryden, completed on tabulating equipment by Montgomery's colleagues after his death.[15] Burton has described the labor economy of Ellison's project in detail:

> Ellison, who deplored the idea that scholars with two or three doctoral degrees apiece should sit around sorting words, believed that the necessary concordance could and should be produced by a computer. Because Mark IV could code only numerical data, Ellison turned to Remington Rand's Univac, which would accept alphabetic input. He outlined the logic of the program in a day and a half. . . . To prepare the text for processing, five women working at "Unitypers" hammered away for five months on metal tape, transcribing the approximately 800,000-word text of the Bible. The resulting 400 reels of metal tape were then transferred to four reels of magnetic tape. As an accuracy check, ten other women punched the Bible text onto cards, ran them through a card-to-tape-converter, and produced four additional rolls of magnetic tape. Univac then went to work for five hours comparing the two sets of tapes for discrepancies, after which mistakes were corrected, and a single accurate set of four tapes was prepared. This entire process of preparing the input text required nine months. . . .

The total time of 1200 to 1300 hours still put Univac ahead of James Strong, whose concordance to the Authorized Version of the Bible was published in 1894 after 30 years of manual indexing.[16]

In 1958, Thomas A. Sebeok and Valdis J. Zeps began work at Indiana University on their word index to the text of folk songs in Cheremis with Hans Peter Luhn's KWIC (Key Word in Context) project and the foundation of Bernard Quemada's Laboratoire d'analyse lexicologique at Besançon following in 1959 and, in 1960, the launch of a wide variety of projects: Brandwood's aforementioned word index to Plato, P. J. Wexler's word index to Racine, Antonio Zampolli's index to Italian phonology, and Roy Wisbey's medieval German concordances.[17] A major conference in 1960 on mechanical methods of literary analysis and lexicography, convened in Tübingen, drew the participation of members of Thesaurus Linguae Latinae, the Mittellateinische Wörterbuch, and the Historical Dictionary of the Hebrew Language, along with the Vetus Latinus Institute at Beuron and the Deutsche Akademie der Wissenschaften.

Through the mid-1960s, European work focused on word indexes, with new centers like Mario Alinei's Mechanolinguistic Center of the Italian Institute, University of Utrecht (CMLIU) continuing to draw on their roots in MT research of the 1950s. In the United States, the Cornell concordances to Yeats and Emily Dickinson followed the Arnold concordance. In the 1960s and 1970s, concordance programs like UNICON, DISCON, and TRICON, which had emerged from early MT work on word-by-word or "dictionary" translation, were used for the production of Miguel Civil's dictionary for Sumerian literary texts, Lawrence V. Berman's concordance to Maimonedes's *Guide for the Perplexed,* and Paul Pillsbury's concordance to the West Saxon Gospels. MT research also produced a concordancer written by Kenneth F. Scharfenberg with Philip H. Smith Jr. at the IBM research center in Yorktown Heights and used by Alice M. Pollin to produce the Cornell concordance to plays and poems of García Lorca and by Smith and Jess B. Bessinger to produce the Cornell concordance to *Beowulf.* Richard L. Venezky's BIBCON was used to produce a concordance of the Rushworth Gospels gloss of Matthew, a working Pope concordance, and a concordance to Céline's *Voyage au bout de la nuit,* among other projects, while concordance programs like WATCON, LEXICO, UNICORN, and COCOA began incorporating other features designed for text analysis.[18]

With the concordancers came the first known attempts to provide instruction for humanist scholars who had research computing needs but insufficient knowledge of programming. The later 1960s have been deemed a period of "settling in," consolidating the pioneering work accomplished to date.[19] The establishment of the Literary and Linguistic Computing Centre at the University of Cambridge, the LLCC's sponsorship of a major conference on literary data processing in 1969, and the publication of the Association for Literary and Linguistic Computing Bulletin in 1973 all marked this consolidation, though during the same period, Busa's center at Gallarate was closed (in 1966) and work on the Index Thomisticus moved to Pisa, briefly to Boulder, Colorado, and then back to Italy, this time in Venice.

Major concordance projects struggled with the logistics of making their results available for use. Ellison regarded the problem of publication to be "formidable":[20] while the publisher Thomas Nelson was willing to meet the expense of setting Ellison's concordance in type,[21] the Cornell concordance to Arnold was produced on a line printer without any lowercased characters or punctuation. Later, photocomposition from magnetic tape enabled Emmett G. Bedford and Robert J. Dilligan to preserve the typography of the Twickenham edition of Pope in their 1974 concordance,[22] appearing the same year that Busa began publication of the first volumes of his Index Thomisticus after twenty-five years of philological labor.

One might say that having undertaken such a project and having devoted most of his life to it, it was impossible for Busa to avoid the conclusion that, as Burton put it, the apparently purely mental operation of analytically transforming written language from one intelligible form (poetry or prose) into another (word lists) might be mechanized, as a "mechanical, or as he termed it, 'material' component"[23]—a sentiment (it is a sentiment) resonant with those used by early researchers in MT to justify their endeavors and the comparatively massive quantities of time and funding devoted to them. "In the 1950s," Busa wrote retrospectively, echoing MT researchers who had moderated their more grandiose claims in the face of skepticism and outright mockery, "newspapers were contrasting the rude and crude technology to the gentle and frail humanity: as if machine [*sic*] could endanger human thinking. Today specialization lead [*sic*] to a subtler and deeper problem, that of the incommunicability between disciplines, a kind of entropy and decadence of the culture."[24]

One finds such subterfuge in Ellison's retrospective statements as well: to illustrate his imaginative insinuations regarding an "ingrained opposition" to computational philology rooted ostensibly in the "fear that the scholar will be displaced somehow," Ellison offered an anecdote about the resistance of leading scholars of contemporary Iranian languages to the data processing projects that Ellison and his colleagues had wanted to "push" (his word), and another about scholars' refusal to support the data processing work of a doctoral student in Turkish. Reproducing the Orientalism of a common linguistic fantasy about the mathematical regularity of the Turkish language, Ellison opined indignantly that the latter "has a very peculiar kind of grammar, but one that would lend itself very readily to computer analysis."[25]

Ellison found it undignified for scholars with advanced degrees to sit around counting "on their fingers"—which meant that someone else, usually a woman who was not a distinguished scholar (but who might well be married to one), performed the labor of data entry while the eminent scholar supervised. While the philological products may be valuable, the labor compacts of early literary data processing are unflattering, and the eagerness of pioneers in postwar literary and linguistic computing to scale and accelerate their work using computers have yet to be measured in any systemic context, such as that marked by the toxic underground vapor plume left by IBM's Plant No. 1 campus in Endicott, New York, which happens to be where some of the Cornell concordances were first processed—and where the company's skeleton crew today monitors the extensive fume pumping and groundwater monitoring equipment and the ventilation systems installed in homes and other buildings occupied by 2,500 people.

Busa appears to have entertained none of the misgivings of Norbert Wiener, a genuine technocrat at the genuine center of the new postwar world order, when it came to the costs of modernity. Busa suggested that "being a priest, people often consider my presence in computer science as exotic, like if you met a camel in your Marktplatz. But it is precisely as a priest that I am doing what I do. In fact analyzing texts leads to realizing the presence of the mystery of God at the roots of human understanding and talking." Regarding the divergence of his and Wiener's views late in their careers, Busa recalled that "when, July 18, 1956, Norbert Wiener visited me at Gallarate, we agreed about it. Later he published a booklet [titled] 'God and Golem—Cybernetics impinges on religion.'"[26] Anticipating a "language industry" that would "explode" once fully automated indexing and abstracting had matured, Busa assigned philology to the task of adapting linguistic data to the "computer [sic] potentials and ways of operating. . . . Computer science as far as artificial intelligence on texts, cannot go further without an enhancement and deepening of our philology;—no present grammars, no present vocabularies provide enough information for programming practical services in automatic processing of texts;—even less adequate to it is the knowledge which each educated programmer has, or is able to derive from the grammars and dictionaries, of his own language, today."[27]

Busa's reasoning on these and related topics contains much that deserves praise: he saw the Anglophone linguistic foundations of computing as a liability to the extent that it embedded "structures . . . simpler than those of many other languages," and he had harsh words for programmers who failed to grasp "how big a mistake it is to process words as they process digits: when their semantics is processed too, words are deeply heterogeneous even within the same sentence, while within the same file digits and numbers are homogeneous."[28] Too, Busa was careful to imagine a "new philology" that might retain some of its traditionally retrospective character while working in concert with informatics, provided that "a quality-leap and new dimensions" were achieved first. Often enough, however, such cautious wisdom seems less intended than deployed in clearing the air for excitable speculation, a combination that makes Busa another of the great characters in the linguistic history of computing, someone who both intelligently and impatiently looked forward to a grand integration of human effort in the transformation of both material and intellectual life, the likes of which has never been accomplished and likely never will be:

> Too often computer is used to reach the same targets as before, using the same methods as before. . . . Philologists must create new

strategies for new goals, when using computers. The skills of a taxi driver are of no use for piloting a jet plane and traffic regulations in the skies are tremendously different from those on ground. . . . The new philology will explode into a "language industry" when our mind has analyzed micrologically the elements and the steps of the macrological intuitions by which we grasp the global meaning of sets of words composing a text. New interactive methods and strategies of linguistic research are expected. They will be the spring, the engine, the soul of such new philology. Young people find in it enormous quantities of work to which to apply their creative ingenuity.[29]

Busa seemed to delight in sentencing "young people" to a life like his own, comprising potentially lifelong labor on potentially interminable accumulative projects of both massive scale and minute scope— deliberately divorced from "all terminologies specifically adopted by philosophers of language"[30] and other things that set young people's minds on fire. "If so much was done without the computer," Busa wondered ecstatically, "how much more should the young people of today be able to achieve with the computer?"[31] Busa not only had no pity for those to be put to labor in such industry, on the more or less familiar terms that young people seldom get to set or control; he was even proud of the fact that computing, far from relieving the scholar of her labor, actually added to it. In most other domains, Busa noted, the automation of repetitively performed tasks diminished the total expenditure of human effort; not so in computing's application to philology, where the automation of the duplication, classification, sorting and searching of records all produced output that must be verified by a human being if it is to be reliable and useful: "computer [sic] allows the researcher to perform much less secretarial work, but imposing on him higher quality decisional intelligent activities in closer time. In the end, using computer, a researcher has to work much more than before. . . . For the Index Thomisticus, we used no more than 10,000 machine hours (including punched cards machines), but 1,800,000 man hours."[32] Such prideful recitations of large numbers are a characteristic component of Busa's reflections on his own work: "I have punched and processed 6 million cards. I started to use IBM computers as soon as they existed. I have put in I/O more than half a billion records, containing either one line or a word with its 'internal' hypertext: of texts of 18 languages and 8 alphabets. I have photocomposed by computer 80,000 pages. I have entered into computer by optical scanner 12 million characters. Finally I have compressed, without any loss of information, into 120 million bytes on a CD-ROM the 1,630 million bytes of the Thomistic Latin corpus with its hypertext."[33]

Authorship Studies

In time, automated concordance generation techniques would be incorporated into the authorship-focused computational philology that had preoccupied the so-called Baconians of the late nineteenth century. Today, historians of contemporary "stylometry," describing an evolution from early unitary invariate approaches focused on a single statistical characteristic of a text (for example, word length), to multivariate analytic techniques in the postwar era and on to machine learning research today, regularly cite the casual but well-publicized essays of Thomas Mendenhall in the 1880s, as well as the statistical studies of George Zipf and G. Udny Yule in the 1930s and 1940s, as precedents for their work.[34] The unitary invariant approaches of Mendenhall and William Benjamin Smith, a mathematician at Tulane University who published his work on the Pauline Epistles under the name Conrad Mascol, imagined style as represented by a "characteristic curve" describing a relationship between word length and relative word frequency unique to the prose of a particular writer.[35] With wider availability of academic computing, more sophisticated multivariate analytic techniques began to appear in the 1960s, and what Michael Brennan and Rachel Greenstadt call the "classic example case,"[36] Frederick Mosteller and David L. Wallace's authorship study of the Federalist Papers, *Inference and Disputed Authorship: The Federalist,* was published in 1964.[37]

   "Stylometry's best known success," a "landmark in the field" and "arguably the most famous and widely cited statistical analysis of authorship,"[38] Mosteller and Wallace's study is widely credited with having launched "nontraditional" or automated authorship studies, a mode of stylistic analysis that broke with prewar scholarly traditions resting on "human expert-based methods." (Efstathios Stamatatos suggests that work in this field through the 1990s is best regarded as "computer-assisted rather than computer-based," rarely taking as a goal something closer to complete automation, as one might say of the machine learning projects developed subsequently.[39]) Applying a Bayesian classification procedure using thirty function words (that is, common, topic-independent words: prepositions, conjunctions, articles), Mosteller and Wallace were able to reproduce existing scholarly consensus by assigning authorship of the twelve disputed essays to Madison "purely on the basis of statistically inferred probabilities and Bayesian analysis."[40] Indeed, Mosteller and Wallace "viewed their work as an application of statistical discrimination methods rather than as a means of settling the Federalist dispute,"[41] about which Mosteller appeared to have been entirely ignorant. Looking back, Mosteller had this to say about the origin of his work:

> When I worked at the Office of Public Opinion Research with the social psychologist Hadley Cantril, beginning in 1940, I got to know Frederick Williams, a political scientist. He and I collaborated on some articles in the study of public opinion that appeared in a book edited by Hadley Cantril. One day in 1941, Fred said, "Have you thought about the problem of the authorship of the disputed Federalist papers?" I didn't know there were Federalist papers, much less that both Hamilton and Madison had claimed authorship of some of them. I had attended an engineering school where very little classical literature was taught at the time. I had, however, been reading in the statistical journal *Biometrika* articles by G. Udny Yule and by C. B. Williams (a different Williams) on the resolution of some disputes about authorship.[42]

Mosteller's and Wallace's study sparked "a tremendous resurgence" of stylometric research[43] that included projects in the 1960s and 1970s focused on the vocabulary of seventeenth-century poetry and the influence of Petrarch, on the influence of Philo Alexandrus on the Epistle to the Hebrews, on high- and low-formulaic stanzas of the Nibelungenlied, and on works by Mikhail Aleksandrovich Sholokhov and Fyodor Dostoyevsky.[44] The newly sophisticated multivariate approaches developed with access to computing, it is claimed, "not only made statisticians feel more comfortable with their analyses," but advanced the field in a manner that facilitated claims on, and to, humanities scholarship.[45] A breakthrough was achieved in the work of John Burrows, who in the late 1980s and early 1990s published a series of papers whose impact rivaled that of Mosteller and Wallace's study.[46] Using a variety of methods applied to the relative frequency and distinctiveness of use of function words in the works of Austen, the Brontës, and Byron, among others, Burrows is said to have "tapped into that subconscious usage of words for which, at the lexical level, stylometrists had been searching for effective quantifiable descriptive measures."[47]

Methodological Questions and Issues

Why should humanist scholars, especially literary humanists, care about stylometric authorship attribution? Patrick Juola's response to that question is "because 'style,' and the identity underlying style, has been a major focus of humanistic inquiry since time immemorial." And yet because that in itself is perhaps neither sufficient nor persuasive alone, Juola also dwells on stylometry's range of applications outside of literary study, in not only historiography and journalism, but computer security, civil and criminal law, and signals intelligence.[48] A recent second "explosion" of research in nontraditional authorship attribution, Juola suggests, is marked on the one hand by the disciplinary migration of such techniques into medicine, law, and forensics, along with computer science and cybersecurity, and on the other by technical progress toward the fully automated "objective" inference of authorship using dynamic statistical techniques and very large corpora.[49]

As far back as 1958, Booth and his collaborators in *Mechanical Resolution of Linguistic Problems* had suggested that stylistic analysis would have to leave its origins in philology behind if it was to fulfill the potential of computing to make human communication both more rapid and more efficient. "Nowadays," they wrote, "it is not so much the styles of individual authors that need to be investigated as the styles employed in different circles": the prose of scientific and technical research literature, of journalistic publication, and of the civic institutions of the state.[50] In time, the postwar liberal justification for MT, that it would help to ensure international peace through clear and eternally present communication, would yield to internally oriented legitimations. Today it is common enough to encounter tautologically structured expositions such as the following definition of "computational stylistics" as meaning nothing more than the application of computation: "Computational Stylistics aims to find patterns in language that are linked to the processes of writing and reading, and thus to 'style' in the wider sense, but are not demonstrable without computational methods."[51]

Juola deliberately defines stylistic authorship attribution as broadly as possible: "any attempt to infer the characteristics of the creator of a piece of linguistic data."[52] Others, such as Moshe Koppel and his collaborators, have begun by identifying a specific, ostensibly fundamental subproblem, making it a pretext for generalization: "given two (possibly short) documents, determine if they were written by a single author or not. Plainly, if we can solve the fundamental problem, we can solve any of the standard authorship attribution problems, whether in the idealized form often considered or in the more difficult form typically encountered in real life."[53] In authorship *attribution,* the researcher begins with samples of writing by multiple authors and attempts to attribute authorship of an anonymous text to one of those authors. In what Koppel and Efstathios Stamatatos call authorship *verification,* on the other hand, the researcher works with the known and possible writings of a single author.[54]

Juola divides authorship attribution problems into three categories: "closed class" problems, beginning with definitively attributed sample texts by a set of authors; "open class" problems, in which the attribution of sample texts is tentative; and "profiling" problems, the object of which is to determine specific properties of authorship (single or multiple authorship, native or acquired linguistic proficiency, national standard variation, gendered usage, and so on).[55] One thing that all of these classifications and subdomains seem to share are assumptions about the concept and the history of authorship itself—assumptions that are fairly described as fundamental, meaning that they either assume the concretion and the scrutability of the object of study, or they assert such concretion and scrutability tautologically, as the justification for the research program focused on it. Often enough, what may at first seem to be unselfconscious assumptions turn out to be polemics in something not quite disguise, broadcasting aggrieved antipathy to those currents of twentieth-century European and North American literary and cultural theory that ostensibly did so much to undermine given, unchallenged, or unexamined concepts of authorship. "Since the 1970s," as Hugh Craig has put it, "the traditional scholarly activity of determining authorship has been conducted with a certain unease, resulting from the work of the French post-structuralists Roland Barthes, Michel Foucault, and Jacques Derrida, who, in undermining what they saw as the bourgeois individual subject, displaced the author as the primary source of meaning for texts." Interpreting more recent cognitively oriented research approaches as blessing a rollback of that unease, Craig notes happily (or hopefully) the "signs . . . that models of authorship are evolving from the post-structuralist 'author function,' an intersection of discourses, toward a concept more influenced by the workings of cognitive faculties."[56]

Others present themselves not as rejecting the challenges of radical theory to authorship, but as complementing those challenges or even accompanying them, "providing an alternative means of investigating works of doubtful provenance."[57] Still, more often than not, such complementarity finds its limit in the concept and practice of interpretation associated with ostensibly traditional work in literary studies, insofar as the stylometrician must insist tacitly on the unconscious character of stylistic decisions in order to justify a subdivision of the scholarly field to accommodate her own, specifically computational (and thus "nontraditional") enterprise. Craig makes the point clearly when he writes that "the search for stylistic markers which are outside the conscious control of the writer has led to a divergence between literary interpretation and stylometry."[58]

Necessarily assumed as well (either straightforwardly or strategically) is the "richness" or "diversity" of an author's vocabulary necessary to give the products of relative frequency analysis plausible meaning.[59] Such assumptions themselves rest fatally on constraints imposed on the domain of study, excluding nonfluent uses of language of all kinds. Too, there is the assumption that an author is "honest in his writing style": that is, not deliberately attempting to deceive the stylometrician or to otherwise protect herself from analysis.[60]

That stylometricians have been generally both meticulous and conscientious in documenting their challenges and setbacks along with their hopes suggests that the form of these assumptions is more often strategic, indeed self-consciously so, than unmindful or inconscient. It seems fair to give the range of that documentation some closer attention.

Methodological Challenges

1. Relations with ostensibly traditional literary scholarship, on the one hand, and with radical literary theory, on the other. Confident as early as 1967 that "it has become unnecessary to apologize for the quantitative approach," Louis Milic nonetheless took care to warn his fellow stylometricians of the need to face "the implication that the artist's work can be compassed in measurable quantities." "It is not my belief," he continued, "that everything of importance about a writer's performance can be identified, much less measured. I am even willing to admit that the measurable may turn out to be peripheral or secondary, though I would hope that this were not so. But I would say in my defense that the process of measuring is not autotelic: it ends are literary, bound to a fundamental interest in the writer and his work. And the mechanical process is always preceded by a knowledge of the text and accompanied by a devotion to its literary qualities."[61]

Better than by anything else in more recent literature, the article-length disciplinary histories and analyses of stylometry published by David I. Holmes, a statistician holding a faculty position in a department of mathematics and statistics, articulate the double voice of the stylometrician, anxious to reassure the "traditional" literary scholar on the one hand, while launching broadsides on the radicalism of literary theory on the other. "Throughout this story of stylometry's evolution," as Holmes puts it, "it is important to emphasize to the humanist that stylometry presents no threat to traditional scholarship. In the context of authorship attribution, stylometric evidence must be weighed in the balance along with that provided by more conventional studies made by literary scholars."[62] Such reasoned care is paired with a closing citation of Burrows's "timely reminder" that "Literary theorists ... are not entitled to deny that literary works are marked by the particular stylistic habits and, by a not unreasonable inference, the intellectual propensities of their authors."[63]

Thus while "stylometry presents no threat to traditional scholarship," it is clearly not also true that "literary theorists" pose no threat to stylometry. In forging an alliance with the first group against the second, Holmes appears to believe that "hesitation by literary scholars and mistrust of such a blatantly quantitative approach may be alleviated by choosing the least contestable mode of analysis, namely that of counting"[64]—a deeply eccentric hope, to be sure, since far from being placated by mere counting, the imagined old-fashioned literary humanist with whose anxiety level Holmes is so concerned might well be more hostile to mechanistic counting than to anything else. Craig, by contrast, meets the real issue here directly, noting correctly that for such traditional scholarly "individualists," "a full explanation returns to the irreducibly unique self-expression of the human agent," and that the emphasis on freedom is incompatible with the "systematic comparison which has been the basic method of stylometrics and the more recent computational Stylistics."[65]

Only slightly less plausible than his proposed solution, given the fractious state of affairs in U.S.-based literary studies for the last half century, is Holmes's conjecture that "the major problem inhibiting stylometry's acceptance within humanities scholarship is that, as yet, there is no consensus as to correct methodology or technique."[66] Stylometricians seem to imagine that it is the production and presentation to "traditional" literary humanists of a coherent body of computationally generated knowledge about literature that will ensure their welcome into the fold: a sentiment suggesting remarkable obtuseness where the disciplinary history of literary study in the latter half of the twentieth century is concerned.[67] Stylometry's struggle "to gain acceptance within the halls of traditional humanities scholarship" during the two decades after Mosteller and Wallace published their study was followed by an acrimonious public debate between Andrew Morton and M. W. A. Smith that only "confirmed distrust of the intrusion of statistical methods into humanities scholarship": "if stylometry had its 'dark age,'" as Holmes put it, "then surely this must be it."[68] Another, somewhat less acrimonious, but no less damaging episode of the 1970s and 1980s was Robert Valenza's discrediting of the results of the technique applied by the statisticians Bradley Efron and Ronald Thisted to questions of Shakespearean authorship: of this occasion, publicity for which "brought stylometry out of academia and into the newspapers," Holmes observed that "stylometry, it seemed, had once again been its own executioner."[69] Indeed, though it should not surprise anyone familiar with the fates of the publicity-seeking academic movements of the past, what Holmes calls the "age of 'pop' stylometry" has not, on balance, been kind to its practitioners.

One need not condone Stanley Fish's attacks on Milic's work to recognize the cohabitation in Milic's perspective of a likable caution and reason on matters of technical dispute and an attitude to intradisciplinary relations that can only be called comically reactionary. The challenge posed to what Milic called the "basic theory of style" by "postmodern critics who assert the death of the author" was, he opined, "derived from a mixture of Marxism and victimization theory" and "based on the belief that language is a tool of society's system of oppression of the weak and that it controls what can be thought and said, that when the writer writes, it is actually the language that speaks the writer, who has no control over the product; hence no individuality and presumably no individual style is possible." Conceding the point on "specious" grounds—"this notion is speciously attractive because it has a grain of truth—that the language governs to a great extent what we can say and think though it does not compel us one way or another"—Milic went on to dismiss it as "otherwise pointless and false to all experience."[70]

But it was not only alien (principally French) "postmodern theorists" whom Milic saw obstructing the due progress of a temperamentally nativist, empirically oriented Anglo-American stylometry or computational stylistics. The German philologists were equally at fault in their refusal to disambiguate style from interpretation:

> In discussing the basic theory of style, I have limited myself to what I think of as the scientific approach to style, identifying the peculiarities of the prose style of individuals. But there is another purpose, which surfaces now and then to give substance to the "humanistic" intention of investigators and whose absence has often given rise to complaints that humanistic computing was failing of its real purpose. This is the expectation that stylistics should be of help in the interpretation of literature, found both in pre-computational as well as non-computational work in stylistics. It is most classically expressed in the work of such different scholars as Spitzer and Riffaterre, in which for example a particular device of style (the presence of series or lists) is associated with a particular trait of character or world view (Spitzer on Claudel) or used to explain a certain effect (Riffaterre on Hugo's vocabulary). Because such work is not replicable, it is not scientific in tendency and therefore technically lies outside the limits of this survey, however interesting, plausible, or illuminating its conclusions may be. But this literary-critical expectation continues to inform many computational studies, whose authors do not clearly realize the problems they create by bringing it in.[71]

Reflecting on the "anti-humanist motivation" that he understood as the target of Fish's critiques in the two chapters on stylistics in *Is There a Text in This Class? The Authority of Interpretive Communities*,[72] Craig warned his colleagues to take Fish seriously as having "provided the most root-and-branch challenge to stylistics," a challenge that "should be compulsory reading for any beginning stylistician." "Fish is speaking as a humanist," he explained: "he sees stylistics as an attempt to make interpretation mechanical and thus to exclude the human." Fish, Craig continued, rejected "the claims of stylistics to a special 'scientific' validity," adding, in what is nothing if not a non sequitur, that "it is possible . . . to propose an alternative motivation for stylistics, that is, the uncovering of patterns of language use which because of their 'background' quality, or their emergence on a superhumanly wide scale, would otherwise not be noticed; and the testing of hypotheses about language use where some empirical validation seems possible and appropriate."[73]

It is true enough that Fish was explicit in describing stylometry as "an attempt to put criticism on a scientific basis," "a reaction to the subjectivity and imprecision of literary studies" attempting "to substitute precise and rigorous linguistic descriptions" for "the appreciative raptures of the impressionistic critic." Fish was unsparing in his characterization of stylometry as aiming for the "elimination or control of interpretation by identifying a set of context-free elements or primes," in a hypostatization of that impressionistic subjectivity "given free reign by an elaborate machinery that hid from them and from their readers what they were in fact doing." And the declared basis for Fish's opposition, in the speech-act theory of J. L. Austin as interpreted by John Searle, and more specifically in its rejection of the inert autonomy of the text on which stylometry, as Fish saw it, had come to depend, is well known and well understood.[74]

Both Craig and Burrows have noted Fish's accusations of arbitrariness, in this context, and of "circularity," in stylometricians' methods, and done their best to defend stylometry from it.[75] Still, one might say that going well beyond methodological skepticism, it is the essayistic irreverence of someone like Fish, when it comes to the platitudes of any scholarship that takes itself so seriously, that was more deeply in play, here: and that when Fish wrote of a stylometric procedure that has "been executed, but . . . hasn't gotten you anywhere," we might say that he was remarking first of all something like the mere busyness of the stylometricians—their dedication to continuity and constant activity at any cost. As Fish put it: "Milic provides a clear example of one of the basic maneuvers in the stylistic game: he acknowledges the dependence of his procedures on an unwarranted assumption, but then salvages both the assumption and the procedures by declaring that time and more data will give substance to the one and authority to the other. It is a remarkable non sequitur in which the suspect nature of his enterprise becomes a reason for continuing in it."[76]

More recent critiques, such as that of Brian Vickers, have chosen to dispute assumptions about the English language common to work in stylometry: that it is acceptable to elide syntax with grammar, to fragment syntactic units into subsyntactic grammatical elements measured by their relative frequency in a text or corpus, and to take or process such measurements using computational techniques derived from work on non-linguistic data (for example, genetics).[77] Such attacks are more susceptible to rebuttal on methodological grounds, by invoking the arms race in which the promise of some new, as yet unrefined technique can always be imputed against criticism.[78] In the absence of any other ambitiously sweeping critique following that of Fish, enclosed turf warfare has encouraged gaslighting:

> It is reasonable to say that the extreme skeptics about "stylometry" or "non-traditional authorship attribution studies," those who suggested that it had similar claims to useful information about authorship to those of phrenology about personality . . . have been proved wrong.[79]
>
> There are enough successes to suggest that computational stylistics and non-traditional attribution have become essential tools, the first places one looks to for answers on very large questions of text patterning, and on difficult authorship problems. It is worth noting, too, that the lively debate provoked by computational work in stylistics and authorship is an indication that these activities are playing a significant part in a much wider contemporary discussion about the relations of the human and the mechanical.[80]

2. *Eclecticism and amateurism.* We can thank the stylometricians for the honesty with which they sometimes reveal the poverty of the middle ground in their own advocacy. Writing of what is really "at stake in computational linguistics," Craig imagines, in the best case, "a powerful new line of evidence in long-contested questions of style," and in the worst, "an elaborate display of meaningless patterning." Such polarization is perhaps inevitable in context of two very consistent demands that stylometricians make of themselves: one, that they be understood as unjustly marginalized, even where their methods are carefully consonant

with the best of ostensibly "traditional" scholarship on the same questions; and another, that everything in their contributions to work on those problems stands or falls on the necessary resort to computing, in addressing those problems' putatively novel scale: "For the moment we can note that this sort of work remains under challenge, and is still largely ignored by mainstream humanities disciplines. It is worth reflecting also that though all its procedures individually predate the digital age, the combination in this sort of analysis is inconceivable without the computer."[81]

Looking back at the three decades that followed the advances of the 1960s, Milic noted "progress in the accumulation of data, in the creation of databases and archives, in the ingenious construction of software and the energetic processing of texts, as well as an appreciation among literary scholars that the use of computers was not the sign of a deranged mind." "But," he continued, "and this is a major-league BUT, measured against the expectations that we had twenty-five years ago and more, I must say the net is disappointing." Faulting what he saw as a nearly complete absence of effort to replicate or improve the results of previous studies, and the "superficial, political, idiosyncratic, contentious rather than constructive" character of attempts to describe methods in theoretical terms, Milic at once deplored the state of the art in stylometry and expressed hope that "maturity" would bring real progress.[82]

Not much has changed, if respected and reliable chroniclers and assessors of work in the field are to be taken at their word. Joseph Rudman is determined to maintain the image of aggrieved marginalization, even against what appears to be resistance from the more affirmative among his colleagues at large: "contrary to what many practitioners of the non-traditional proclaim," he writes, "there is not widespread acceptance of non-traditional authorship attribution. For example, in my area, eighteenth-century English Literature, most scholars feel that there is a long way to go before they accept the results."[83] But Rudman is by far the most aggressive (indeed controversially so) of contemporary stylometricians when it comes to facing squarely and narrating methodological struggles and failure, alongside struggle for legitimacy and recognition in the humanities. The relentlessness of Rudman's disappointment, chronicled in his numerous periodic reviews of progress in the field, is matched only by his stubbornness in resisting the conclusion that stylometry is not usefully scientific, but rather deeply quixotic and thus entirely at home with the literary scholarship that rejects it for its technical pretensions, especially in the claims on literary scholarship that it makes in the name of automation. Juola has joined Rudman in this pessoptimism, noting that the increased attention garnered by research in authorship attribution in the early to mid-2000s "has not created a consensus on the best way to approach it. Quite the opposite; there are probably more ways proposed today than there have ever been before." "More annoyingly," he continues,

> most of the proposed methods "work" if one sets the bar low enough. But, as the old joke has it, a hundred fools are not equal to one wise man—and similarly, a hundred unreliable analyses are not likely to yield a gold standard. . . . With the exponential growth of digital-only texts and the increasing need to validate or test the legitimacy of questioned digital documents, there is an obvious need for proven techniques and best practices with good track records. Unfortunately, the current state of affairs does not present this. Instead, as several recent surveys have shown, we have a collection of thousands or millions of different techniques, most of which work (in the sense of better than chance) but there are no clear front-runners.[84]

Of Mosteller and Wallace's classic study, among others, Juola observes that "these studies, while excellent in themselves, also illustrate the issue at hand; the results cannot be directly compared, as they use not only different corpora, but also different pre-processing, different feature sets, different numbers of features, and different classification technologies. It is not clear that we can expect the same accuracy from other analyses using these techniques in other settings."[85] Brian Vickers may have seized upon such admissions in constructing an image of "turmoil" exacerbated by the additional "acute critiques of quantitative, machine-driven" approaches that followed, but the fact is that Vickers's harshest words have been those quoted from either Rudman's or Juola's writings themselves.[86] Here we must ask ourselves if any movement that has internalized the objections of its critics to the point of rearticulating them, in what they believe is their own defense, can truly believe in the value of its pursuit.

3. *Disorganization in the object.* Here, too, Juola assesses the issue soberly: "Human language can be a very difficult system to study, because it combines a maddening degree of variability with surprisingly subtle regularities. In order to analyze language with computers, it is usually necessary to make simplified models of language for analysis." Of such "simplified models" of the "high-order regularities" in language, on which such models focus instead of on language's "maddening degree of variability," Juola describes three grades: at the low end of the scale of complexity, "bag of words" models that work with lists of unordered word tokens; at the intermediate level, probabilistic models that preserve the "short-range" dependencies of several words in context; and at the high end, the context-free grammars "often used for describing computer languages," which can account for a limited set of "long-range" structural dependencies, and context-sensitive grammars that "are available but are still more computationally intensive yet, to the point that they are not often used."[87]

The dangers of reduction are noted everywhere in stylometric research literature, though hope for relief through advances in computing power alone seems every bit as typical today as it was in the early days of MT. As if to acknowledge the likelihood that computing's material finitude will never be overcome, others are eager to transvalue reduction as enabling: "There is a strong instinct in human beings to reduce complexity and to simplify: this is a survival mechanism. Rules of thumb can save a great deal of time and effort. Stylistics is born of this instinct."[88] Where the inevitability of the corruption of data, or the impossibility of achieving "clean" compilation to begin with must be acknowledged, it is acknowledged—though mainly, it would seem, on the way to expedient solution: "For the cleanest possible samples, all extraneous material that did not come from the author's pen (or keyboard) should be eliminated, a task requiring extreme care and knowledge on the part of the researcher."[89]

Stylometry's receptivity to the culturalization of information theory performed by Warren Weaver marks it as what I have been calling a cryptophilology. Burrows is direct: "The 'redundancy' defined by communication-theorists," he has written, is the stylometrician's "ultimate support: if English bears its meanings with a high enough degree of 'redundancy,' even a crude instrument will receive its more important 'messages' and enable a skilled interpreter to draw valuable conclusions."[90] (Other stylometricians have embraced the different model of information implicit in measures of so-called Kolmogorov or Chaitin complexity. Despite being unfortunately "formally uncomputable," Juola suggests, "Kolmogorov complexity is of interest as an unattainable ideal."[91])

4. *Limits of the object, as an object representative of culture at a scale that is widely or intrinsically important or interesting, or otherwise generalizable or justifiable as an object of interest.* The statistical properties of "language," as imagined by stylometricians, are only the statistical properties of *a* particular language. Tractable or not, the challenges posed by semantic context to statistical measures of text in one language are dwarfed by the intractable challenge posed by multilingualism understood properly as interlinguistic context—that is, as a context of difference, not positive relation. Writing in 2005 of the "special urgency to analyzing Arabic in online communications" provided by the "ramifications of terrorist organizations such as Al-Qaeda," Ahmed Abbasi and Hsinchun Chen noted that at the time, "little multilingual research exists," with the overwhelming mass of research in authorship identification tightly coupled to, even dependent on, characteristic features of English, from documented letter and word frequencies to patterns of word segmentation that cannot be generalized to other languages, especially those unrelated to English.[92] Though such troubles are redressed by the vast supplementary resources supplied in the name of national security applications, there remain fundamental, possibly incommensurable differences in the techno-scientistic methodological ambitions of stylometry and those of the broader historical philology it leaves behind. David Mimno notes that "in contrast with scientific research, one of the key challenges in working with humanities scholarship is the presence of multiple languages. Contemporary scientific research is published predominantly in English, and attention tends to be focused on recent work."[93] To date, the extension with multilingual corpora of the

outputs of recently popularized techniques such as topic modeling appears to be limited to work with corpora *designed* for multilingualism (Wikipedia pages, for example). Such ambitions share the restrictively narrow provenance of the corpora used to launch Google's statistical MT service, which were originally produced for SYSTRAN's European Union language service in the 1970s.

Cognitive impairment, or something representing it, represents another challenge: triggered by mental illness, aging, or other, nondeclinist factors including exceptional creativity or creative range, changes in a single individual's otherwise ostensibly characteristic writing style might invalidate the indispensable assumption that any author can be identified by a "stylistic signature."[94] A still greater challenge is represented by the text corpus itself taken *as* a corpus—that is, as a domain whose circumscription, or bounding, is also a circumspection, an extrusion of what it cannot include if it is to proceed unimpeded. I will not belabor this point here, since it is something that stylometricians, and computational philologists more generally, appear simply incapable of facing in their work, perhaps because their work is simply impossible without the segmentation—indeed, the gerrymandering—furnished by the concept of data. As Alberto Melloni has put it, "Pope Pius XII's silence on the subject of the *shoa* during World War II is well known—but we do not have a list of the words used in that silence."[95]

5. *Failure and bad publicity.* Rudman's most recent assessment reminds stylometricians that they are still wandering in the desert, unable to come up with a "proven theory after more than forty-five years and fifteen hundred publications," and no closer than they have ever been to acceptance "in the main, by either the literary or the scientific community." Confident as he claims to be that "a 'comprehensive' theory will evolve" eventually, Rudman nevertheless adds to his prior assessments a list of thirteen new "high-profile" problems faced or created by work in nontraditional authorship studies in the fifteen years from 1997 to 2012. Among the thirteen are Donald W. Foster's discredited attribution of the apocryphal poem "A Funeral Elegy" to William Shakespeare, Foster's embarrassment as a stylometric expert consultant and witness in the murder case of six-year-old JonBenét Ramsey, and John

Burrows's retraction of his attribution of "A Vision" to Henry Fielding. Of the latter, Rudman observes that "Burrows's shift is something that every good scientist should do—search for errors or improvements in their experimental methodology and self-correct. But this 'up and down' reporting of results has added to the 'let's wait until they get it right attitude.'"[96]

It is hard not to conclude that stylometricians, who so often appear to believe that the reconciliation of the "two cultures" of applied science and the literary humanities is not only imminent, but embodied in their own affinities and activities, are in truth trapped in a twilight zone between a culture of science that values novelty but only rewards it upon replication, and a culture of the humanities that values neither scientific truth nor novelty, though it sanctions the ideal of *Wissenschaft*. At times, the vibration represented by eagerly publicized, then retracted results, in a research endeavor seeking validation as a science while simultaneously courting the approval of its parascientific parent, seems less the routine self-correction of science than a neomania peculiar to projects with no real direction. As usual, Rudman is brutal: "the main purpose of too many studies (well into the hundreds) is to present a new, a novel method that always is better or almost as good as the old one. . . . What is disturbing about this is that most practitioners are not yet using established techniques and methodologies to solve real world problems. They are not verifying, not replicating studies. With all of the innovating and improving, will we ever reach a valid and accepted method?"[97] Among Rudman's many other indictments: a "Babelesque" professional lexicon, beginning with the nomenclature designating the field itself— "stylistics, stylostatistics, stylometry, stylometrics, authorship identification, authorship investigation, authorship categorization, authorship recognition, authorship verification, authorship attribution, and nontraditional authorship attribution"; expediency, in resorting to corrupted but available data (from Project Gutenberg and Google Books, among other sources), in leaving controls incomplete, and taking other shortcuts to obtain the results desired; failure to disambiguate the variable of authorship from other variables, such as gender or genre; failure to "deedit" "extraneous text" including "foreign language," which would "interfere with a valid non-traditional study"; cherry-picking of statistical techniques, adapting techniques "designed for fields not only outside of stylistics but also outside of Linguistics"; and the possibility of invalidation of the field's seminal study by Mosteller and Wallace, if it turns out that the disputed essays were more often collaborations of Madison with Hamilton (Rudman notes that "none of the over ninety non-traditional studies of the Federalist papers that came after" that of Mosteller and Wallace have attempted to reproduce it).[98]

Juola has added the following: failure to compare or cross-validate the accuracy of techniques that have achieved success only in experiments of small scale; "the ease of writing computer programs to implement whatever techniques are found," which "provides a seductive path to misuse and to unwarranted claims of accuracy"; and (echoing a point also made by Rudman) the analytic improvisation and indeed incompetence of many stylometricians: "most non-traditional authorship attribution researchers do not understand what constitutes a valid study."[99] Of course, the line between impatience and incompetence is not always clear: Juola describes the discrediting of Andrew Morton's stylometric adaptation of the CUSUM technique (adopted in the early 1990s by British criminal defense attorneys to raise doubt about the provenance of their clients' confessions) as one of "stylometry's best known failures," suggesting that "the negative publicity of such a failure has cast a substantial shadow over the field as a whole."[100] Of Foster's misattribution of "A Funeral Elegy" and the debate that unfolded in the journal *Computers and the Humanities* in the years that followed, Juola observes:

> From a purely scientific perspective, this cut-and-thrust debate can be regarded as a good (if somewhat bitter) result of the standard scholarly process of criticism. Unfortunately, for many non-specialists, this well-publicized failure was their only exposure to the discipline of stylometry, and the greater the hype that Foster managed to create, the greater and more notable the eventual fall. This public collapse of a well-known stylometric attribution may have unfortunately created a public perception of inaccuracy, hindering uptake of the results of attribution research by mainstream scholars. Indeed, given the overall accuracy of Foster's studies, the

perception is probably greater than the reality, and much of the hindrance is unjust.[101]

The parallels here with what Anthony Oettinger called "'experiments' and 'demonstrations' that sometimes bordered on fraud" during the golden age of MT are unmistakable—as is the anxious demand that a few rotten apples not be permitted to spoil the barrel. For all on which they otherwise agree, Rudman and Juola appear to have parted ways on stylometry as a cryptophilology. As Juola puts it: "some researchers, most notably Rudman, argue that authorship attribution simply should not be automated, that the difficulties and potential pitfalls outweigh the value of any possible product. [My review of the situation here] takes a more optimistic view, while hopefully not downplaying the difficulties."[102]

Rudman's position is the exception: most stylometricians would rather abandon the project of reconciliation with literary scholarship than abandon research automation. That would likely be for the best, though the elasticity of the reasoning offered suggests little confidence that anyone else will offer stylometry a home. Cautioning that "a well-founded computational stylistics works with tendencies rather than rules," Craig insists on its segmentation from "traditional philology," whose mode of "intensive study" is too narrow for the "superhuman reach and memory of the computer." "Stylistics," Craig suggests, "may be thought of as the epidemiology of textual study: its methods allow general conclusions about the relationship between variables. Those which have high counts together form a syndrome. Once this is identified, the researcher can seek out a mechanism to explain it, as medical researchers might isolate the cell pathology which lies behind the epidemiological link between the incidence of smoking and that of lung cancer."[103] But the advantage of the analogy with the domain of medicine, where the pressure of mortality obtains tolerance for "general conclusions" when no other alternative exists—and within which even a long-lived human stylometrician will herself be decisively outlived by most of the well-preserved, reproduced and disseminated textual artifacts with which she spends a career working—is unclear, and Craig makes little effort to defend it at length.

With some justice if also surely with some subterfuge, Juola suggests that those relying on the results of authorship attribution studies "are not necessarily either statistics professionals or literature experts, but may include teachers looking for signs of plagiarism, journalists confirming the validity of a document, investigators looking at a crime, or lawyers arguing over a disputed will." It is hard to see how a responsible teacher weighing an accusation of plagiarism, a responsible journalist confirming a detail or its provenance, or especially a responsible detective, forensics investigator, or attorney should be thought of as "casual" users of such results, and how they would necessarily be *more* satisfied than a literature expert with results requiring a "built-in confidence or reliability assessment, and to the greatest extent possible, a built-in safety net" acknowledging that their reliability cannot be guaranteed.[104] We can accept this as a reasonable statement, just as we can accept John Hutchins's claim that similarly "casual" users of MT output can be satisfied by results that are imperfect but serviceable. But nothing should prevent us from costing such statements out, as the Automatic Language Processing Advisory Committee did in its 1966 report on MT, asking how much money and other resources it is sensible to devote to something that doesn't work as advertised.

Key Concepts and Techniques

A closer look at some of the key concepts and techniques in stylometry may help to clarify both the promise it offers, according to the stylometricians, and the haplessly intractable difficulties it also appears to face.

   1. Style. Where the prime technique in stylometric research is relative frequency analysis of one form or another, the prime object is of course "style," the target of measurement. There is considerable enthusiasm in stylometric research circles for the genetic concept of a "stylome" and for the biometric security concept of a stylistic "fingerprint"; even where the pursuit of such analogies is framed hypothetically, it is with an eagerness belying the caution that also often performed or projected:

However the discipline may develop in the future it cannot be said that there is as yet such a thing as a stylometric fingerprint: a method of individual style which is as reliable as a fingerprint as a criterion of personal identification. . . . At the present time no one knows whether there are such features of style as not enough data has been collected. . . . Perhaps—some say—by 2001 stylometric profiles of all citizens will be on file in the F.B.I. if not yet in Scotland Yard.[105]

. . . it is unclear if individual language forms can be classified in terms of a "stylome," a set of measurable traits of language products. Here we will attempt to identify such a stylome, more specifically a stylome which is extensive enough to be able to distinguish between pairs of language users on the basis of their language use.[106]

Juola accepts both "authorial fingerprint" and "human stylome" as acceptable names for the object of "assumption of most researchers" in stylometry, adding of the latter that "there are good theoretical reasons for assuming that such a trait might exist."[107] In technical terms, the concepts "fingerprint" and "stylome" stand for analytic objects of a complexity far surpassing the models implied by early univariate statistical techniques measuring average word length or similar characteristics. Though Holmes acknowledges that "stylistic 'fingerprints' do not always remain stable . . . perhaps a writer becomes less stylistically innovative after an early 'peak of diversity' as certain words and patterns become increasingly preferred,"[108] this challenge is accepted as manageable for as long as the concept of authorship itself remains stable, ensuring that shifts in style can always be reconciled. Even "diachronic changes in cognition, such as those of the early stages of Alzheimer's disease"[109] are imagined as manageable challenges. Deliberate deception is another matter, and Rudman remarks disapprovingly of designed obfuscation techniques that frustrate the goals of nontraditional authorship attribution.[110] Indeed, researchers in Drexel University's Privacy, Security, and Automation Laboratory have defined their own work in "adversarial stylometry" against the fundamental and, as they see it, mostly unchallenged assumption of work in the area: "that the author of an unknown document has been honest in his or her writing style."[111]

In practical terms, a stylometric researcher's concept of style is defined by a unit of analysis. While that unit may vary, to be analyzed by computational means natural-language text must first be encoded or otherwise re-represented schematically as data, and in practice such representation relies on or is otherwise fundamentally linked to the (linguistic) concept of a word.[112] As David Mimno puts it, "the fundamental unit of text is the word, which we define here as a sequence of (unicode) letter characters."[113] As mentioned previously, from Thomas Mendenhall's proposals in the 1880s onward, word metrics were long central to stylometric research, and they were not meaningfully extended beyond the word itself as a primitive unit until advances in computing processor power and miniaturization, as well as increases in the mass and availability of machine-readable text, enticed stylometricians to attempt to measure features of syntax and semantics, as well. Juola notes the many forms of word metrics discarded along the way, from word length measured in letters or syllables to sentence length measured in words, to measures of the distribution of parts of speech, of ratios between types (the unique form of a word) and tokens (the recurrent form of a word in text),[114] and of semantic features like synonymy. Still, even contemporary stylometric techniques that look well past the word as an atomic unit are hardly discarding it: the modeling techniques (clustering, vectoring, and others) of so-called latent semantic analysis (LSA) and latent Dirichlet allocation (LDA) are still grouping words by frequency of occurrence, even if they are no longer simply listing and counting words or throwing them in an imaginary "bag" for analysis (referring to so-called bag of words approaches). In this, they do very little to meet the critiques of someone like Brian Vicker, who has pointed to the stylometric fragmentation of language, in its very preparation for analysis, as something like a fatal first step.[115]

Much the same can be said, for example, for factor analysis techniques such as principal components analysis (PCA), designed to focus on correlations between variables rather than counts. Burrows and Craig insist on the "exploratory," rather than "determinative" character of the insights made possible by PCA, but their advertisement of this benefit would be fairly described as clamantly, even fatuously determinative in itself, demanding that potentially disruptive difference be circumscribed if it is to be recognized at all: "Broad authorial differences emerge as the most important factors when two authorial sets of characters are arrayed together in PCA. Characters speak in measurably different ways, but the authorial contrasts transcend this differentiation. The diversity of styles within an author always remains within bounds. The idiolects which contribute so strongly to the variety and amplitude of drama and to the creation of a social world are evident, but only within a larger framework of persistent authorial proclivities and specialisations."[116]

2. *Automation.* With the exception of Rudman, who seems decisively isolated in his resistance, automation is a sine qua non for the stylometricians. An outsider could be forgiven for the impression that much work in stylometry is devoted to exploring the automation of the analysis of language first of all, and that the oft-declared and, it is implied, means-independent goal of producing new knowledge is in fact little more than an afterthought or strategic justification. This conflation of a research means (automated analysis) with a research end (knowledge), or to put it differently, the demand that putatively novel research means be considered research ends in themselves, has been a characteristic feature of computational philology from the start. What Andrew D. Booth and his collaborators emphasized, in taking stylometric research on Plato as a case study, was not the value of such research to knowledge of the works of Plato themselves but the benefit that such work "can be carried out with increased speed and accuracy through the aid of an electronic computer."[117] Almost a half century later, Juola still touts the putative "greater ease of use and improved accuracy" of computational means,[118] despite the abundance of evidence accumulated in that half century and reviewed by Juola himself, among others, suggesting that "ease of use" and speed of computational philology as a means have failed to help researchers produce results of acknowledged value.

Rudman prefers the phrase "non-traditional authorship attribution" to the many alternatives that place more emphasis on computation because "it gives deference to the long tradition of authorship attribution done before the use of the computer and sophisticated statistics,"[119] while Craig goes out of his way to distinguish "stylistics" as "open-ended and exploratory" from its "sibling" authorship studies, efforts in which "aim at 'yes or no' resolutions to existing problems."[120] Still, one might say that neither deference to tradition nor the "open-ended and exploratory" seems the first thing on the mind of the stylometrician eager to demonstrate how fast and efficient computational philology can be. Like Booth and his collaborators, David L. Wallace and Frederick Mosteller, the latter a statistician who "didn't know there were Federalist papers, much less that both Hamilton and Madison had claimed authorship of some of them," are unapologetic about their true interests, priorities, and goals: "We apply a 200-year-old mathematical theorem to a 175-year-old historical problem, more to advance statistics than history. Though problems of disputed authorship are common in history, literature, and politics, scholars regard their solutions as minor advances. For us the question of whether Hamilton or Madison wrote the disputed Federalist papers has served as a laboratory and demonstration problem for developing and comparing statistical methods."[121]

3. *Scale.* In stylometry the imagined *scale* of a problem, its primary materials or other pretext or precondition, or its potential or actual results is presented as a cipher of potential knowledge whose exposure and solution is beyond human analytic capacity in one way or another (mundane or sophisticated); whose challenge can be met only by automation; and whose revelation by an automated computational procedure confers an authority equal to that of evidence whose value is assessed by hand, or by eye. As Craig put it, "The claim for computational stylistics is that it makes available a class of evidence not otherwise accessible (i.e., not to the naked eye)."[122] Beyond "the relatively unimportant task of testing the authenticity of unknown texts," Alvar Ellegård wrote in 1962, "frequency dictionaries" were keys to "a wide range of linguistic problems [including] the spread of new words and forms of expressions, the appearance and disappearance of dialectal differences and stylistic fashions, the semantic problems of homonymy and polysemy, to name only a few topics." "What is important," Ellegård

concluded, is not the "trifling matter" of "solution of the literary mystery," but "the systematic survey of the field of enquiry that work on the problem necessarily leads to."[123]

Burrows makes a persuasive case (albeit one resting on hyperbolic speculation about "hitherto inaccessible regions of the language") for delegating to automated procedures the analysis of "more than 26,000 instances of 'the' in Jane Austen's novels"—a task that certainly does "defy the most accurate memory and the finest powers of discrimination" in human-powered scholarship.[124] Of this example chosen deliberately as an illustratively "extreme case," programmatically terrifying in its tedium, one might observe that its imagined extravagance is far from incongruent with the introspective micrologies of philology in its modern form, dependent on the institutions and institutional resources of the national language culture of an imperial nation-state and devoted to a historical period defined by the history of that national language, exemplified by the literary works of great authors. Roberto Busa enjoyed hyperventilating about "the huge change in dimensions that has occurred" as "the computer enables us to perform a complete census on texts of tens and hundreds of millions of words,"[125] but his extraordinarily long life's work was devoted almost exclusively to the many, many words of one single author, Thomas Aquinas (who as it happens had studied at some of Europe's earliest modern universities).

Though like those of both Holmes and Rudman, David Mimno's relationship to professional humanities research is abecedarian, he has a great deal to say about what humanities scholars have done in the past and what they might do in the future to respond to new hypothetical imperatives of scale:

> Humanities scholarship has traditionally focused on the careful, detailed reading of small numbers of high-value texts. Over the past decade, large-scale digitization projects have vastly increased the quantity of cultural heritage material, to scales well beyond the amount of text any single scholar could meaningfully process. This development raises a vital question: how, if at all, should the work of humanistic scholarship adapt to the presence of orders of magnitude more potential source material? From the perspective

of traditional scholarship, little has changed: the fact that most of recorded human intellectual output is now accessible does not increase the ability of a scholar to read it. Clearly, if there are to be fundamental advances in our ability to understand the past they must come from the fact that this material is now available for computational processing.[126]

Mimno ascribes three potential benefits to the computational processing of such material. First, automated analysis of collections of research literature could provide general knowledge guides not only for students and the curious public, but for cross-disciplinary researchers as well. Second, it might offer "quantitative measurement of intuitions" like the stories a discipline tells itself about the rise, fall, and return of intellectual trends, measuring such stories against patterns in published research literature. Third, it might support the attentive or "close" reading of a specific text by assisting in selection criteria beforehand and generating context on demand during the process.[127]

Mimno's first suggested benefit is a reasonable one, though one might certainly object that encyclopedias have existed for at least 2,000 years and that the value of an automated production whose accuracy would still be subject to question is unclear. His third suggested benefit is a reasonable one as well. The second is quite fanciful, if we imagine that the automated computational processing of a collection of research literature is likely to produce anything less or more than *another* story about a discipline, a cryptophilology no less contestable than any other. Mimno is wise to discard the ergodicist's fixation on the concept of surprise, arguing that "such tools are useful to scholars" because "the observations made using automated analysis are often not surprising to experienced scholars and other experts in the particular field"[128]—but this argument, with the great merit of rejecting obfuscation, has the greater misfortune, in the very same gesture, to beg the question of value. Some may welcome the productively alienated confirmation of their own knowledge, but many others are likely to need little from ostensibly advanced, but indubitably expensive techniques for research duplication.

Stylometry and Security

Mimno acknowledges that in using simplified models and corrupted data like that provided by the Google Books project, one inevitably discards "substantial amounts of information contained in syntactic relationships," but he justifies that sacrifice by appeal to the simplicity, "robustness," and extensibility of those models and the promise of "major changes in research practice" that they offer. David Bamman and David Smith are more cautious, suggesting of the Internet Archive's collection of Latin texts that "while we might hope that the size and historical reach of this collection can eventually offer insight into grand questions such as the evolution of a language over both time and space, we must contend as well with the noise inherent in a corpus that has been assembled with minimal human intervention." Observing that "problems plague . . . massive collections in their use for scholarly research, not only in the quality of the image scans and the resulting OCR but also in the metadata itself that describes the texts," Bamman and Smith insist that "the first research question we must ask"—not the last, as other such researchers might prefer—"is what tasks such a huge collection is best suited for in the face of such noise."[129]

Such questions are, by and large, not being asked today, at a moment determined by promises not yet tested and bills yet to come due. One might return in this context to Robin W. Winks's history of the roles played by humanist scholars in the wartime and postwar creation of the intelligence agencies of the government of the United States. Of the decline of such scholars' relationship to the agencies, which had persisted through two world wars, Winks observed that

> in the end, what happens is what happens, and all the instructions about what ought to happen, should happen, the predilections about what will happen, are overtaken by events. University scholars do not much like that phrase, "overtaken by events," for it suggests that events have a momentum of their own and that academic analysis is not sufficient to account for what happened. One can suggest dozens of reasons why the CIA shot itself in the foot and can present dozens of arguments as to why academe and

the intelligence community had, by the late 1960s in much of the country, by the mid-1970s in nearly all, put so much distance between themselves.[130]

For Winks, the public alienation that took hold "as more and more people became convinced that the U.S. Army, the U.S. State Department, the U.S. intelligence community, and the U.S. president was lying to them about what was happening in Vietnam" was central to academic disenchantment with the opportunities the agencies offered. The area studies programs focused on southeast Asia produced by the latter war are "dead in the United States today," Winks wrote in 1987, because "the dog bit the hand that fed it: most authorities on Southeast Asia in American universities joined the antiwar movement." And while the democratizing post-Second World War expansion of U.S. academe, measured by accessibility and the near-universalization of higher education as well as by the scale of its infrastructure and operations (including its scale of remuneration) had its role to play here on its own, Winks also stresses that by the 1970s "academics had discovered that they were not quite as close in thought to the process of intelligence as they had once believed." A chasm had opened between the intelligence agencies' way of explaining their own failures—by lamenting the insufficiency of data and demanding license to collect more—and the values of a newly wary academic culture, whose personae "tended to think that it was not faulty intelligence but political judgment that was producing disaster, and many believed that simply throwing more research at the problem would not solve it."[131]

This conflict of approaches to the formulation of problems and to their solution is still with us today, reanimated by the aggressive deference of the cryptophilologists to the vast scale of text data generated by recent digitization projects (and exposed by social media platforms and services). Over and over, we are told that the abruptly established accessibility of very large quantities of computationally encoded text is a watershed disrupting and reorganizing the production of knowledge with a violence that demands our deference—as if the concurrence of an explosion of so-called digital libraries and the aggressive expansion of a security state devoted to text and data mining, after

2001, along with a public entertainment culture virtually obsessed with forensics, were unworthy of any ethically evaluative remark *or* political comment.

That is not to say that the cryptophilologists avoid remarking this concurrence, even construing it as a correlation. On the contrary, some are more than content to emphasize it. For Efstathios Stamatatos, the story of the 2000s, as a decade, is the story of how a

> plethora of available electronic texts revealed the potential of authorship analysis in various applications . . . in diverse areas including intelligence (e.g., attribution of messages or proclamations to known terrorists, linking different messages by authorship) . . . , criminal law (e.g., identifying writers of harassing messages, verifying the authenticity of suicide notes) and civil law (e.g., copyright disputes) . . . , and computer forensics (e.g., identifying the authors of source code of malicious software) . . . in addition to the traditional application to literary research (e.g., attributing anonymous or disputed literary works to known authors). . . . Hence, (roughly) the last decade can be viewed as a new era of authorship analysis technology, this time dominated by efforts to develop practical applications dealing with real-world texts (e.g., e-mail messages, blogs, online forum messages, source code, etc.) rather than solving disputed literary questions.[132]

Similarly, Abbasi and Chen remark of their work on "the Dark Web project, a research initiative to identify and evaluate individuals and groups that use the umbrella of online anonymity to support extremist and terrorist activities," that "the speed, ubiquity, and potential anonymity of Internet media—email, Web sites, and Internet forums—make them ideal communication channels for militant groups and terrorist organizations." It is natural, therefore, for the project of "analyzing Web content" to have "become increasingly important to the intelligence and security agencies that monitor these groups." "Authorship analysis can assist this activity," they conclude, "by automatically extracting linguistic features from online messages and evaluating stylistic details for patterns of terrorist communication."[133]

"However," Abbasi and Chen add in what strikes one as a double non sequitur, "authorship analysis techniques are rooted in work with literary texts, which differ significantly from online communication. Furthermore, the global nature of terrorist activity necessitates the analysis of multilingual content." The cryptophilologist's containment in her work (as distinguished from her private life) of ethical questions both simple and complex often seems a willful blindness (it takes no genius to observe that online anonymity can and does accompany both socially constructive, constitutionally protected speech and behavior *and* the socially destructive behavior of agents who require active restraint by the state).

Donald W. Foster, the Vassar College professor of English who enjoyed a privileged relationship with the U.S. Federal Bureau of Investigation and other law enforcement agencies until his disgrace as the mistaken accuser of Steven Hatfill, a suspect in the 2001 anthrax attacks,[134] has described the intoxication of the academic cryptophilologist transported into the amoral domain of the security imperative:

> The arcane world of dusty archival libraries suddenly melted into a blur of political intrigue and criminal mayhem. This was not entirely un-Shakespearean in itself, but I was unprepared for the transition from academic discussions of fictional violence and cupidity to being a principal in cases involving corporate fraud or political scandal or homicidal violence. The methodology I used to ascertain the provenance of the "Funeral Elegy" . . . was immediately understood by prosecutors and other probers as a useful tool for unmasking the identities and hidden hands behind terrorist tracts, blackmail letters, and the like. The scientific analysis of text—how mind and the hand conspired to commit acts of writing—can reveal features as sharp and telling is anything this side of fingerprints and DNA. Although we disguise our writing voice, it can never be fully masked. After the crime, the words remained. Like fingerprints and DNA. . . . Early in 1996 when I analyzed the text and concluded that reporter Joe Klein was the "Anonymous" author of *Primary Colors,* his colleagues forgave him for lying to their faces faster than he has me for telling the truth

in *New York* magazine. But on the basis of that highly visible display of what was an arcane scholarly method, I have for the past several years been called into service, by press or police, as a gumshoe. Not even after *Primary Colors* did it occur to me that my field of critical expertise might have application and usefulness outside academia—not until November 1996, when I was asked to examine the writings of a former university professor, Theodore J. Kaczynski. . . . Having entered literary studies in 1978, the same year in which Ted Kaczynski began his bombing crusade, I was now presented with a fresh challenge: to develop a science of literary forensics, to adapt for the courts and, later, for criminal investigations a methodology that was originally intended for the study of anonymous poems, plays, and novels.[135]

Foster may or may not have known how typical, rather than atypical his role was of the literary scholar in the twentieth century, notwithstanding the amnesia imposed by the turmoil of the 1960s and 1970s—an amnesia that Robin Winks tells us he wrote *Cloak and Gown* explicitly to redress.[136] After 2001, the concept of "authorship profiling" promptly appeared in stylometric research publications, marking a readaptation of authorship attribution techniques to new security applications in antiterrorism policing and counterinsurgency warfare, general forensics, and consumer market research.[137] Juola's discussion of the initially concealed authorship of Michael Scheuer's *Imperial Hubris: Why the West is Losing the War on Terror* is focused entirely on the question of whether the book was a "sophisticated forgery" and whether its arguments were more or less credible depending on who claimed authorship[138]—with not a thought for the question of why the book may have been published "anonymously" or what its political goals may have had to do with that. Juola goes on to remark on the segmentation and cultivation of "specific corpora representing the specific needs of specific communities"—sets of literary texts collected for analysis devoted to literary problems, for example—as distinct from "corpora of web log (blog) entries, email, and so forth—document styles that are used routinely in investigations," which more directly serve the interests of law enforcement.[139] But this strikes one as an activation of the political unconscious, insofar as in their more excitable moments, cryptophilologists eagerly conflate scholarly and security applications of the same analytic techniques.

During the interval immediately after 2001, widespread interest in techniques for "unmasking" concealed authorship, along with an aggressive disinterest in questions of privacy, was formalized in the multivariate analytic technique with that name developed by Moshe Koppel and his collaborators. In and of itself, "unmasking" is no more or less necessarily sophisticated or successful than any of the other techniques on offer in contemporary stylometric research focused on questions of authorship. But the deliberately excitative name chosen for the technique indexes its stance toward authors who deliberately attempt to conceal authorship through alterations of writing style, from Rabbi Yosef Chaim of Baghdad, the nineteenth-century subject of the sample "literary mystery" discussed in Koppel et al.'s 2007 paper introducing the technique,[140] to contemporary student plagiarists as well as anonymous "online writers" whose political or existential motives for assuming anonymity never seem to enter the cryptophilologist's calculations.[141] Some researchers deliberately elide privacy with inclarity, in such aggressive methodological proclamations as that of Hagen Hirschmann and his collaborators: "The explicit and available coding of annotations with the data [in historical corpora] allows other researchers to understand and follow an analysis. Results become reproducible, a huge step forward from the sometimes unclear and 'private' analysis of many historical studies."[142]

It appears to have been left entirely to a single U.S.-based research group at Drexel University, including Michael Brennan, Rachel Greenstadt, and Sadia Afroz, among others, to consider the ethical and political context of what the group calls "adversarial stylometry," and to develop a technical response informed by that context. Juola has briefly considered the "active malicious alteration of writing style," noting laconically that "this problem is not entirely confined to the forensic realm (there are many other reasons that one could want to disguise one's true authorship), but it is a specific concern for forensics and takes on a heightened importance."[143] But the Drexel group's only really articulate antecedents are Gary Kacmarcik and Michael Gamon, who were willing to specify what Juola was content to leave merely implicit:

While there are clearly many reasons for wanting to unmask an anonymous author, notably law enforcement and historical scholarship, there are also many legitimate reasons for an author to wish to remain anonymous, chief among them the desire to avoid retribution from an employer or government agency. Beyond the issue of personal privacy, the public good is often served by whistle-blowers who expose wrongdoing in corporations and governments. The loss of an expectation of privacy can result in a chilling effect where individuals are too afraid to draw attention to a problem, because they fear being discovered and punished for their actions.[144]

Actively developing obfuscation techniques and releasing free software packages for the anonymization of documents, Kacmarcik and Gamon deserve recognition for both noting *and* actively embodying, in their work, resistance to the potential for abuse of stylometric techniques. Brennan, Greenstadt, and Afroz, whose research has produced techniques for what they call "imitation" and "obfuscation" counterattacks on authorship identification and end-user implementations such as the Anonymouth utility, have concluded that "even naive users lacking in expertise in the field of stylometry, linguistics, or even literature can successfully perform imitation and obfuscation attacks."[145] Making the case for "a multidisciplinary approach to privacy and anonymity," Brennan, Greenstadt, and Afroz offer their work to "privacy-conscious individuals," to assist them in taking "steps to maintain their anonymity in the face of advanced stylometric techniques."[146]

. . . . .

"IT IS AMONG LIFE'S IRONIES," John Burrows has observed, "that, throughout the international community of humanities scholars, so many of us are uncomfortable with numbers. For, at the heart of our customary work are tenets that we share with statisticians."[147] Burrows offers a reasonable, if deliberately abstract catalog of the methodological proclivities that humanities scholars ostensibly share with statisticians and a reasonably graceful invitation to the former to set aside their ostensibly psychological discomfort and open the door to cooperation.

Though they adopt the stance of the research technician and even of the scientist, in their dealings with humanist scholars, the stylometricians might well be imagined as among the most deeply crypto-romantic of us all, insofar as their incessant longing for, and maneuvering toward, more and deeper contact between the two intellectual cultures for which they themselves feel equal affinity suggests a profoundly antimodern desire to reunite and reconcile the disciplines—as if the historical process of their differentiation had been merely spontaneous or volunteered, and thus just as likely to roll back at the exertion of will. And though the stylometricians even adopt, at times, the stance of the "traditional" philologist whose counting on fingers they are so eager to transvalue, they seem profoundly uncomfortable with the polemical, specifically anticolonial and anti-imperial intellectual energies that thinkers like Edward W. Said, Paul Bové, and Aamir Mufti, among others, have reinvested in returning to philology as a counter-Enlightenment that claims for science not only a decisively modern position within a differentiated Two Cultures the terms of relation in which cannot be set by science alone, but also a broader and usefully insoluble or antinomian problem: that of the memory of historic, even epistemic violence in its power to shape, even to constitute the historical record.

What we call the sciences represent one form of modern secularization; the humanities represent another, different form of that historical process, one that has proved inassimilable to the sciences for historical reasons, rather than as a matter of will, as the opportunists would have it. We call it secular humanism, or historical humanism. In many ways the literary humanities in particular deal with secularized versions of the ethical questions that were once the domain of religion. Such questions are never resolved, as problems in engineering are resolved, because they are rooted in the conflicts and contradictions of human life and indeed, of all life and nonlife. Research technicians of all kinds, bound as they are to a domain of constant activity, have too little time—and often little real need or desire—to address such questions. So that people turn elsewhere, if often incoherently, inarticulately, and angrily, shooting first and aiming later. But that itself is one way of explaining why the traditional literary humanities are still very much alive and are not much or at all needing salvation by self-appointed "digital" successors.

C. B. Williams, who was generous enough to leave his reader "to decide for himself whether the statistical study of language is a symptom of sanity or of insanity,"[148] was also worldly enough to know that far from being intrinsically uncomfortable with numbers, "many a scholar in the literary humanities would say with Sir Thomas Browne, 'I have often admired . . . the secret Magick of numbers,' and would be as impressed by their mystical properties as was Browne himself." Still, Williams too hedged his bets, opining that "a naïve awe of statistics is no doubt less common than a flat contempt—equally unreasoning—for anything remotely resembling Thomas Gradgrind's subordination of imagination, fancy and taste to the bloodless, soulless rigidity of facts and figures." In truth, the scholars whom Williams imagined as working in a space "between these extremes," who "have encountered the serious use of numerical analysis in humanistic research" and who "have seen sophisticated quantification making a solid, recognizable contribution, without becoming an end in itself,"[149] may well not be the eager new cryptophilologists, bearing their historical amnesia and the both anxious and ignorant self-congratulation for which such amnesia is the very condition of possibility—but rather the counter-Enlightenment philologist whose long memory of conscription into war has generated something far more nuanced than "flat contempt" for "numbers." A computational philology that would "include every lingua franca and every language that became a major instrument for the development and preservation of culture"[150] can be little more than an agent of the self-congratulatory self-study of empire where it fails to attempt to account for the profound, indeed unimaginable violence through which every such "major instrument" becomes what it is.

·· 5 ··

The Digital Humanities
and National Security

Between November 16, 2010, and March 21, 2011, Patricia Cohen, then Arts and Ideas Editor for the *New York Times* (subsequently an economics correspondent), wrote four articles for the *Times* under the rubric "Humanities 2.0," which the newspaper advertised as a new "series about how digital tools are changing scholarship in history, literature and the arts."

The first of the four, published with the print title "Digital Keys for Unlocking the Humanities' Riches" and a different title—"Humanities Scholars Embrace Digital Technology"—for the web, featured a photograph of Martin K. Foys, identified in a caption as "a medievalist at Drew University, with a detail of an 11th-century map of the world." Then an associate professor of English at Drew, Foys was presented in collar and tie under sweater vest and blazer, his head and upper torso a figure to the ground of the "map" in question—in truth a fabric projection screen displaying a blurred image of a software application window, itself displaying an image of a hand-drawn map overlaid with hand-drawn red and green annotations.

It is worth quoting Cohen's opening gambit in full: "A history of the humanities in the 20th century could be chronicled in 'isms'—formalism,

Freudianism, structuralism, postcolonialism—grand intellectual cathedrals from which assorted interpretations of literature, politics and culture spread. The next big idea in language, history and the arts? Data. Members of a new generation of digitally savvy humanists argue it is time to stop looking for inspiration in the next political or philosophical 'ism' and start exploring how technology is changing our understanding of the liberal arts."[1]

Suspended a few lines of text above this last sentence, caught less than halfway to a smile, Foys's expression was indecisive. Clearly, Cohen's readers were intended to understand that Martin K. Foys, medievalist at Drew University, was a representative member of this new, less politically and philosophically inclined generation of digitally savvy humanists who, freed of the preoccupations of the past, were ready to get down to work on the present and the future. And yet at a time when one of the world's wealthiest billionaires refused to remove his hoodie even for the most serious business of the chairperson and CEO of Facebook, Inc., one of the world's biggest collectors of big data, the incongruity seemed not only sartorial, but ekphrastic. As evidence of digital savviness goes, an "eleventh-century map of the world" marked with what looked like red crayon seemed a hard sell.

Was it Martin K. Foys, medievalist at Drew University, from his vantage point in the foreground of this tableau, who was arguing that it was time to stop seeking the next political or philosophical "ism"? One wondered about that. Was it Foys opining that the exploration of the impact of technology on the liberal arts represented an alternative to such "isms" and their grand cathedrals? Did Foys believe that a new focus on the impact of technology on the liberal arts was not or could not be, more or less precisely, just one more such "ism"? What, one wondered, might Foys say in response to the suggestion that such a rotation, not to mention Cohen's imagination and approval of it as such, was itself tendentiously political? The more one considered Foys's demeanor, the more sheepish he seemed.

One could only say with certainty that Foys had responded to Cohen's interest in his work, and that he had permitted himself to be photographed. One could be forgiven for having had words put in one's mouth, couldn't one? Regardless of which was the real focus here, professor or projection screen, map or territory, Cohen's opening lines did capture the zeitgeist in all its tensions. On November 16, 2010, the United States was two to three years into the Great Recession, with the unemployment rate rising to 9.8 percent in October, gold valued at $1,400 per ounce, and the right-wing Tea Party movement reaching its first peak of influence on U.S. electoral politics. The EU-IMF bailout of Greece in May had imposed the predatory austerity measures whose consequences had yet to be concretely imagined, while a rescue deal for the erstwhile "Celtic Tiger" of Ireland was in preparation for December. The orgy of violence tendentiously dubbed the "Arab Spring" by its spectators was just about to begin.

News and commentary published that November in the *Chronicle of Higher Education,* the leading news source for higher education in the United States, had included such headlines as:

> "U. of Central Missouri Details which Programs will Be Cut" (November 5)
> "AAUP Challenges SUNY-Albany Program Cuts" (November 5)
> "Arbitrator Orders Florida State U. to Rescind Layoffs of Tenured Faculty Members" (November 5)
> "Louisiana State U. Campuses Take a Hit in Midyear Budget Cuts" (November 7)
> "Changes at Kean U. Get Enrollment Up and Faculty Down" (November 7)
> "Provosts and Financial Officers Meet in Search of Common Ground" (November 7)
> "In a Washington Minute—Spending for Pell Grants and Research Is on the Line" (November 8)
> "U. of Minnesota's Largest College Pleads for Resources, Plans for Downsizing" (November 9)
> "Nevada's Cuts in Health Benefits Could Hurt" (November 9)
> "Many Faculty-Senate Leaders at Doctoral Institutions Lack Clout, Survey Finds" (November 9)
> "Donations by the Wealthy Dropped Sharply in the Recession" (November 9)
> "With New Increase, Cal State Tuition to Be 60% Higher Than in 2008" (November 10)

"British Students' Protest of Tuition Rise Turns Violent"
(November 10)

"Policy Group Suggests Limiting Tenure and Encouraging Use of
Community Colleges to Reduce Costs" (November 10)

"Deficit-Reduction Panel Proposes Ending In-School Interest
Subsidy" (November 10)

"Despite Violence, British Students Plan More Protests against
Austerity Measures" (November 11)

"Report Predicts English Universities will Opt for Highest
Tuition Fees Possible" (November 11)

"Under Pressure from State, College of Charleston Slashes
Tuition Increase" (November 14)

"Compensation of 30 Private-College Presidents Topped
$1-Million in 2008" (November 14)

"With Revenue Drying Up, Educators Look to Productivity as an
Answer" (November 15)

And:

"Decoding the Value of Computer Science" (November 7)

"AAUP Plans to Develop New Guidelines for Corporate-
Sponsored Research" (November 8)

"The Politics of Creating New Programs and Defending Old
Ones" (November 10)

"Carnegie Mellon Announces New Engineering Partnership in
India" (November 11)

"21st-Century Studies: Peter Wood Cites the Center for
21st Century Studies at the University of Wisconsin at Mil-
waukee as an Example of the Fashionable Nihilism that is
Eroding Public Support for the Humanities" (November 12)

And:

"A Look at the Scrivener for Windows Beta" (November 1)

"Gamifying Homework" (November 3)

"Getting Your Work Done with Social Media" (November 9)

"Why I Love My Label Maker" (November 9)
"Use RSS to Keep Up with Favorite Online Services"
   (November 11)
"Scheduling Email with Boomerang" (November 12)
"Use WordPress and GCal to Create a Dynamic Course Cal-
   endar, Part 1" (November 12)
"How Teaching Changed My Mind about the iPad"
   (November 15)
"Use WordPress and GCal to Create a Dynamic Course Cal-
   endar, Part 2" (November 15)

This last sequence was the work of ProfHacker, a group blog for the *Chronicle* written disproportionately by U.S. based college and university English professors. To be fair, "Weekend Reading: Electoral Hangover Edition" (November 5) was their work as well. What had the ProfHackers recommended we read, on that day in U.S. political history? A "scary factoid from the University of Maryland's Future of Information Forum," consisting of a Google employee's claim that "90% of users don't know that [the key combination] CTRL-F" activates a feature permitting the user of a web browser to search for text on the page. A report from the Pew Research Center's Internet & American Life Project finding that 4 percent of online adults used location-based services like Foursquare and Gowalla. Apple, Inc. product evangelist John Gruber's explanation of how to browse the web without Flash plugins. An advice column titled "Twitter for Adults."

"Weekend Reading: Electoral Hangover Edition" also included an endorsement of Soylent, "a crowd-powered interface . . . that embeds workers from [Amazon] Mechanical Turk into Microsoft Word," which Jason B. Jones described as "the most interesting experiment in interface design I've seen in a while."[2] It is with memory of such lighthearted reference to what Moshe Z. Marvit, writing in the *Nation*, has called "one of the most exploited workforces no one has ever seen"[3] that one reads Cohen's descriptions of Martin K. Foys's research projects and the projects of other "digitally savvy humanists"—whom the ProfHackers, quite likely with both more forethought and more commitment than Foys, imagined themselves representing. Foys, Cohen explained, was motivated to "collect, house and connect more than 350 years of scholarship" on the eleventh-century Bayeux Tapestry depicting events of the Norman conquest of England. ("It is almost impossible to study traditionally," Foys declared in Cohen's quotation.) Cohen, helpfully comparing the scale of this artifact to that of a football field, added that since "no one person could digest the work's enormous amount of material, and no single printing could render it accurately . . . Mr. Foys created a prize-winning digital version with commentary that scholars could scroll through. Such digital mapping has the potential to transform medieval studies, Mr. Foys said."

So large (two-thirds the length of a football field!) and so detailed as to resist the "traditional" study of a lone scholar. That seemed a challenge indeed. And yet nonetheless, overcoming what might seem to be analogous obstacles, Foys, Cohen told us, had created a digital version of this enormous artifact, including added commentary and other resources. All by himself? Perhaps. Cohen was not inclined to ask questions. Foys's "latest project," she wrote, moving on briskly, "which he directs with Shannon Bradshaw, a computer scientist at Drew, and Asa Simon Mittman, an art historian from California State University, Chico, is an online network of medieval maps and texts that scholars can work on simultaneously." This latest project, Cohen informed her readers, is "distinct from most scholarly endeavors" in that "it is communal. The traditional model of the solitary humanities professor, toiling away in an archive or spending years composing a philosophical treatise or historical opus is replaced in this project with contributions from a global community of experts."[4]

To take Cohen's fatuous words seriously, rather than as glib at best and mendacious at worst, is to wonder why such comparison is needed. No straining is needed to conclude that Cohen's construction of a new class of "digitally savvy humanists" imagines a non- or predigital scholarly solitude that can never have existed, if only because no scholarship has *ever* been accomplished alone—while it avoids any consideration of the wider communal relations required for "digitally savvy" work, which would be more fairly called labor relations. Upon thought, one might conclude that it is not communal scholarly effort as such or in general that Cohen was holding up to praise as unprecedented in "Digital

Keys for Unlocking the Humanities' Riches"/"Humanities Scholars Embrace Digital Technology," but a single, discipline-specific form of working together: that of the laboratory model of the applied technical sciences, in which the principal investigator and his postdoctoral researchers pool their efforts to serve industry.

• • • •

SURELY, YOU MAY OBJECT, one might also conclude otherwise. Speculation belongs to the domain of theory, to Cohen's "isms," those grand cathedralic obstacles to getting things done. Have we not just suggested that the era of "isms" has come to a close? In the view of Tom Scheinfeldt, then managing director of the Center for History and New Media at George Mason University, Cohen told her readers, "academia has moved into 'a post-theoretical age.'"

More specifically, it was a new era of and for philology. "This 'methodological moment,'" opined Scheinfeldt in Cohen's paraphrase, "is similar to the late 19th and early 20th centuries, when scholars were preoccupied with collating and cataloging the flood of information brought about by revolutions in communication, transportation and science. The practical issues of discipline building, of assembling an annotated bibliography, of defining the research agenda and what it means to be a historian 'were the main work of a great number of scholars.'"[5]

The second of Cohen's four articles was published on December 3, 2010, with the print title "Analyzing Literature by Words and Numbers" and the web title "Victorian Literature, Statistically Analyzed with New Process." It was followed by "In 500 Billion Words, New Window on Culture," on December 16, and "Giving Literature Virtual Life" (web title "Digital Humanities Boots Up on Some Campuses") on March 21, 2011. In "Analyzing Literature by Words and Numbers," Cohen profiled Dan Cohen and Fred Gibbs, identified as "two historians of science at George Mason University," and their study "Reframing the Victorians," which examined the relative frequency of occurrence of "more than two dozen words" in British book titles from 1789 to 1914.[6] "In 500 Billion Words, New Window on Culture" reported on the launch of the Google Books Ngram Viewer and Erez Lieberman Aiden and Jean-Baptiste Michel et al.'s paper "Quantitative Analysis of Culture Using Millions of

Digitized Books."[7] Finally, "Giving Literature Virtual Life"/"Digital Humanities Boots Up on Some Campuses" profiled Katherine Rowe, professor of English at Bryn Mawr, and undergraduate students in Rowe's introductory Shakespeare course.[8]

At one point in "Digital Keys for Unlocking the Humanities' Riches"/"Humanities Scholars Embrace Digital Technology," Cohen speculated that the main obstacle for impresarios of a new "digital humanities" was the indifference of "most humanities professors" when it came to the novelty of the new approaches. But the reception narrative that Cohen otherwise favored was explicitly affective. For Cohen, humanities scholars belonged to one of two categories: those "exhilirated" by the exotic and unprecedented "alliance of geeks and poets," on the one hand, and those made "anxious" by it on the other. Alice Jenkins of the University of Glasgow, Cohen told her readers, spoke of the "sheer exhiliration" produced by an encounter with the new methods at a scholarly conference, while Matthew Bevis of the University of York stated of the same encounter, "I was excited and terrified."[9] Erez Lieberman Aiden and Jean-Baptiste Michel, the authors of the paper described in "In 500 Billion Words, New Window on Culture," were "exhausted" by the "total Hail Mary pass" of their work, while their collaborator Steven Pinker of Harvard was "energized" by it. Katherine Rowe of Bryn Mawr described "a very exciting generation gap in the classroom."[10] And when it came to describing research results, rather than the affective dispositions of researchers themselves, Cohen's favorite word was "surprise" and its variations. "Digital humanities," she exclaimed, "is so new that its practitioners are frequently surprised by what develops."[11]

· · · · ·

EXHILIRATION, ANXIETY, SURPRISE. Was there room for indifference after all? Such sensationalism was, to be sure, routine: what one expects from a journalist in the United States, no more and no less. It was more interesting to find such affective discourse mirrored by the scholars themselves. A year before Cohen's first article appeared, William Pannapacker, professor of English at Hope College in Holland, Michigan, published the second in what would become a series of columns on the "digital" in the *Chronicle of Higher Education,* the most widely read source of news and commentary on college- and university-level education in the United States.

Pannapacker's first column, titled "Summer Camp for Digital Humanists" and published under the pseudonym Thomas H. Benton on June 27, 2008, had described his experience attending the Digital Humanities Summer Institute at the University of Victoria that summer, which was "informal" and "friendly" and left him "as excited about the future as someone might have felt leaving the Columbian Exposition in 1893." Of the presentation at the Digital Humanities Summer Institute of a virtualized recreation of the latter event by the Urban Simulation Team at UCLA, Pannapacker informed his readers that it "was punctuated by something I had never heard before in an academic context: gasps of astonishment."

What had provoked these gasps of astonishment? "Instead of listening to a paper," Pannapacker explained, "we flew over Lake Michigan past a detailed rendering of the Exposition's vast Manufactures and Liberal Arts Building, into the Court of Honor, up to the animated Columbian Fountain, and, from there, underground to see the workers operating the fountain's plumbing system. Along the way, pop-up images and texts provided the footnotes for the project and portals to more traditional sources of information."[12]

Published December 28, 2009, with the title "The MLA and the Digital Humanities," Pannapacker's second column recounted his impressions of the annual convention of the Modern Language Association (MLA) of America, the largest professional organization of U.S.-based scholars in the literary humanities, whose convention facilitates faculty hiring in English and comparative language and literature studies. "Amid all the doom and gloom of the 2009 MLA Convention," Pannapacker began, "one field seems to be alive and well: the digital humanities. More than that: Among all the contending subfields, the digital humanities seem like the first 'next big thing' in a long time, because the implications of digital technology affect every field. I think we are now realizing that resistance is futile. One convention attendee complained that this MLA seems more like a conference on technology than one on literature. I saw the complaint on Twitter."[13]

In this and the columns that followed, Pannapacker returned to this distinction between "doom and gloom" and "alive and well," as well as other implicitly or explicitly affective distinctions—though the terrain they demarcated seemed already be to shifting. Commenting on how the new digital humanists responded to indifference to their work (that of their professional colleagues as much as the public), Pannapacker observed that MLA conference "panelists speak in a tone of urgency with the expectation of skepticism."[14] ("I used this tone myself," he confided, "when explaining the field to administrators.") Graduate students and recent doctoral awardees struggling with the academic job market crash were the carriers of an "enthusiasm" lost to U.S. academe "at the very moment when our profession needs revitalization and willingness to embrace chance." By the January 2011 MLA convention one year later, the digital humanities could be understood as "triumphant" in its position or its disposition, albeit with a qualifying question mark.[15] Digital humanists, Pannapacker disclosed in "Pannapacker at MLA: Digital Humanities Triumphant?" (January 8, 2011), had waxed indignant at his proclamation of a "next big thing" in his column of the previous year, if only because they wanted it known that they had been at their work for twenty years or more. At the MLA 2011 convention, Pannapacker added, in a more substantive hint that all was not well, they were also defensive, preoccupied by the perceived disrespect and disdain of colleagues who, they believed, regarded them as "disturbingly outré and dangerous."[16]

Onto the domain that Cohen had imagined, divided between exuberant early adopters and anxious, even terrified foot-draggers, Pannapacker projected the anxiety of the early adopters themselves and their self-understanding as persecuted, a self-understanding that he accepted. At the same time, Pannapacker suggested the existence of a problem possibly rooted in such self-understanding, though he seemed willing to imagine it only as a behavioral weakness in response to persecution (rather, for example, than mistaken self-understanding as persecuted): "The field, as a whole, seems to be developing an in-group, out-group dynamic that threatens to replicate the culture of Big Theory back in the 80s and 90s, which was alienating to so many people. It's perceptible in the universe of Twitter: We read it, but we do not participate. It's the cool-kids' table. So, the digital humanities seem more exclusive, more cliquish, than they did even one year ago."[17]

Exuberant early adopters here, anxious and terrified foot-draggers there. Indignant and defensive victims of persecution here, alienated spectators there. It seemed hard to argue with the characterizations supplying the first term in each of these schisms, since Pannapacker, like Cohen, supported them with direct quotations from his interviewees. The second term (anxious, terrified, alienated . . .) was another matter. Was there anything to consider here apart from exhilaration, anxiety, gasps of astonishment, persecution complexes?

One wondered if the readiness to hand of psychologizing commentary reflected a discomfort with more explicitly structural questions of institutional governance, resource allocation, and relationships among institutions, especially in the case of the university as an institution under attack. After all, in "Analyzing Literature by Words and Numbers"/"Victorian Literature, Statistically Analyzed with New Process," Cohen had described Dan Cohen's and Fred Gibbs's study "Reframing the Victorians" as "one of 12 university projects to win a new digital humanities award created by Google that provides money along with access to the company's powerful computers and databases."[18] "Some scholars," Cohen noted more or less immediately, upon introducing this information only halfway through her article, "are wary of the control an enterprise like Google can exert over digital information."[19]

Wary: that seemed not quite anxious, and not quite terrified, either. Of what, one wondered, were "some scholars" *wary?* To judge by the words she published under her name in the *New York Times,* Cohen was simply not curious. Still, we might want to say that it was here, for the first time, perhaps the only time during the period in question, that the words chosen permitted a reader to imagine the publicity enjoyed by the digital humanities movement not as a register of willed affects and personal and professional dispositions, but as both a carrier and a vehicle of something like political conflict.

• • • •

TIME PASSED. IN THE END, Cohen's "Humanities 2.0" series published only the four articles I have mentioned, while Google's ballyhooed "commitment to the digital humanities" lasted one funding cycle.[20] Pannapacker wrote little about the digital humanities in the *Chronicle of Higher Education* after 2013, and as of this writing has published nothing at all in the *Chronicle* since May 2014. His "The MLA and the Digital Humanities" vanished from the *Chronicle*'s website some time after September 8, 2015, and has not been restored. Five years after the publication of Pannapacker's most hyperbolic column, published July 22, 2012, with the title " 'No DH, No Interview,' "[21] job advertisements containing the phrase "digital humanities" have yet to reach 6 percent of the total published annually in the MLA's Job Information List.[22]

All this might suggest that "digital humanities," the latest wave of what I have been calling cryptophilology, have had their moment, that it was little more than a moment, in the end, and that that moment might now be historicized as a moment in the historical present and the recent past. An early hint that times were changing came in one of Pannapacker's final columns, published January 5, 2013, with the title "On 'The Dark Side of the Digital Humanities.' " In this column Pannapacker reported on a session titled "The Dark Side of the Digital Humanities" at that year's MLA convention in Boston, Massachusetts.

"Like all the DH sessions I've attended this year," Pannapacker began, "it was packed. Amid the surge of Twitter conversations (like drinking from a bundle of firehoses), I was able to absorb some points in the larger bill of indictment:"

> That DH is insufficiently diverse. That it falsely presents itself as a fast-track to academic jobs (when most of the positions are funded on soft money). That it suffers from "techno-utopianism" and "claims to be the solution for every problem." That DH is "a blind and vapid embrace of the digital"; it insists upon coding and gamification to the exclusion of more humanistic practices. That it detaches itself from the rest of the humanities (regarding itself as not just "the next big thing," but "the only thing"). That it allows everyone else in the humanities to sink as long as the DH'ers [*sic*] stay afloat. That DH is complicit with the neoliberal transformation of higher education; it "capitulates to bureaucratic and

technocratic logic"; and its strongest support comes from administrators who see DH'ers [*sic*] as successful fundraisers and allies in the "creative destruction" of humanities education. And—most damning—that DH'ers [*sic*] are affiliated with a specter that is haunting the humanities—the specter of MOOCs.

In short, DH is an opportunistic, instrumentalist, mechanized response to the economic crisis—it represents "the dark side of capitalism"—and, as such, it is the enemy of good, organic humanists everywhere: cue the "Imperial March" from *Star Wars.*

The reaction of the DH'ers [*sic*] in the audience was captured immediately by Amanda French, [*sic*] "I didn't recognize the digital humanities in what the panel was discussing."[23]

Pannapacker's defiant sarcasm alone made it clear how unsettled he and the "baffled DH'ers" whose reactions he went on to feature, in the remainder of the column, actually were. To his credit, he did also briefly entertain the possibility that "DH'ers" had come to deserve some unfriendly scrutiny. "Perhaps it is inevitable," he concluded, "that—in our work with administrators, foundations, the general public—we talk about DH in ways that might trouble our colleagues in the humanities." More than anything else, it was Pannapacker's anxiously scornful paraphrase of the arguments made by presenters in "The Dark Side of the Digital Humanities" that confirmed their power and potential for persuasion. By the time that Matthew Kirschenbaum, affecting similarly world-weary impatience, reviewed the same arguments in an essay titled "What Is 'Digital Humanities,' and Why Are They Saying Such Terrible Things about It?" the following year, the die had been cast.[24] Henceforth, digital humanities boosters would be on the defensive, increasingly frustrated as neither defiance and denial, nor half-hearted concession seemed sufficient to redirect attention or to rebuff actually existing, partly imagined, or entirely imagined accusations.

In 2011, while still graduate students, a group of younger scholars who associated using the social media hashtag "#transformDH" had begun publishing critiques that were urgent and pointed, if understandably rarely as uncompromising as the approach of Richard Grusin, a tenured full professor of English, in his contribution to "The Dark Side of the Digital Humanities"—which bluntly, and with no attempt whatsoever to soothe bruised egos, described digital humanities projects as "gateway drugs for administrators addicted to quick fixes and bottomline approaches to the structural problems facing higher education today."[25] Initially broached in blog posts and Twitter conversations by the #transformDH scholars and others, and now significantly amplified by the session at the MLA convention of 2013, questions about both the occasion of emergence and the value of the new cryptophilology were emerging from the slow pipelines of scholarly journals including *American Literature, College Composition and Communication, Culture Machine, differences: A Journal of Feminist Cultural Studies, English Language Notes, J19: The Journal of Nineteenth-Century Americanists, Modern Language Quarterly,* and *Postmodern Culture,* as well as venues for scholarship in domains outside the literary humanities, including *American Historical Review, Cultural Sociology, Dialogues in Human Geography, JiTP: Journal of Interactive Technology & Pedagogy,* and *New Left Review.*[26]

Though they were generally restrained (and even so, frequently challenged by digital humanities enthusiasts), the critiques published in these journals would become increasingly firm, often returning to an identifiably central set of issues, including the ideological weight carried by the word "digital" in an era of aggressive and extreme wealth creation in Silicon Valley and austerity policy nearly everywhere else; the attribution of historical and other contextual novelty to the use of "digital" methods and means; the obfuscation by the phrase "digital humanities" of a much longer history of computer-assisted humanities research, as well as humanities-based research on computing; the explicit or implicit expectation that humanities disciplines adopt the working methods of disciplines in the social sciences, the natural sciences, or the professions, rather than maintaining their own; and the presumptive and preemptive characterization of so-called traditional scholars as objectionably old-fashioned, intransigently conservative obstacles to progress.

Where treatment of the topic in the domains of general and popular journalism picked up where Cohen had left off, in 2011, it was with a markedly negative turn. "Humanities aren't a science," wrote Maria

Konnikova in *Scientific American*. "Stop treating them like one."[27] Stanley Fish published two columns in the *New York Times* describing the discourse of digital humanities scholars as fundamentally "theological," promising "to liberate us from the confines of the linear, temporal medium in the context of which knowledge is discrete, partial and situated . . . and deliver us into a spatial universe where knowledge is everywhere available in a full and immediate presence to which everyone has access as a node or relay in the meaning-producing system."[28]

"Literature," Stephen Marché wrote in a widely circulated essay in the *Los Angeles Review of Books*, "cannot meaningfully be treated as data. The problem is essential rather than superficial: literature is not data. Literature is the opposite of data."[29] "We will wait forever," wrote the editors of *The Point* magazine, introducing a symposium on the topic "What Is Science For?" "to taste the milk and honey promised by . . . 'digital humanities.'"[30] In a widely circulated feature essay in *New Republic*, Adam Kirsch characterized the enthusiasm for digital humanities as carrying an "undertone of menace, the threat of historical illegitimacy and obsolescence. Here is the future, we are made to understand: we can either get on board or stand athwart it and get run over."[31] Writing in *The Baffler*, Catherine Tumber likened it to the confidence of General Motors's Futurama exhibit at the 1939 New York World's Fair, preceding by a mere six months the eruption of yet another worldwide orgy of technologically facilitated self-destruction.[32]

Coverage in the *Chronicle of Higher Education* and *Inside Higher Ed*, its main competitor, soon followed suit. "What now matters, what legitimizes the humanities in the eyes of many 'stakeholders,'" Kathryn Conrad wrote in the former, "is that modifier: digital. Too many of us, beaten down by the relentless insistence on the supposed practicality of STEM degrees—and, thus, in an argumentative leap, the greater value of the STEM fields—are willing to accept this state of affairs."[33]

"A series of critical articles," noted the lede of Carl Straumsheim's "Digital Humanities Bubble," published in *Inside Higher Ed* in May 2014, "have some digital humanists saying the trend has been oversold, particularly with regard to producing academic jobs."[34] "Don't Capitulate. Advocate," wrote a group of nine tenured faculty and one independent scholar a month later, responding to the MLA's digital humanities-flavored proposals for reforming doctoral education in English and other language and literature studies fields. "With the report's recommendations for collaboration across disciplines, sustained work with professionals in libraries, museums, IT, and administration, as well as significant training in new digital methodologies," they wrote, "we cannot see how time to degree could be reduced without abandoning training in the study of literatures and languages themselves."[35] "For the past decade," digital humanities enthusiast Adam Crymble admitted in July in a mea culpa titled "Digital Hubris, Digital Humility: Essay on the Backlash Against the Digital Humanities Movement," "we've been living in the age of digital hubris, and we can therefore hardly blame people for getting sick of us."[36] "It's time to drop the digital," added David J. Hinson in *eCampus News,* two weeks later.[37]

Elsewhere in the higher ed press and academic news sector, respected scholars in science, technology, and media studies challenged the basic stance of the digital humanities movement in its attachment to the word and concept "digital." Writing in *Communications of the ACM,* the newsletter of the world's largest professional society for scientific and educational computing, the historian of technology Thomas Haigh asked a rhetorical question whose answer was very clearly negative: "Social historians have done a great job examining the history of ideas like 'freedom' and 'progress,' which have been claimed and shaped in different ways by different groups over time. In the history of the past 60 years ideas like 'information' and 'digital' have been similarly powerful, and deserve similar scrutiny. If I was a 'digital historian,' whose own professional identity and career prospects came from evangelizing for 'the digital,' could I still do that work?"[38]

The goal of a humanities scholar who studies the history of information technology, Haigh suggested, "is, in a sense, the opposite of the digital humanists: we seek to apply the tools and methods of the humanities to the subject of computing," rather than apply computing to existing humanities research questions.[39]

Writing in *Educause Review,* meanwhile, David M. Berry observed that "today we live in computational abundance whereby our everyday lives and the environment that surrounds us are suffused with digital technologies. . . . Thus, the historical distinction between the digital and the non-digital becomes increasingly blurred, to the extent that to talk about the digital presupposes an experiential disjuncture that makes less and less sense. Indeed, just as the ideas of 'online' or 'being online' have become anachronistic as a result of our always-on smartphones and tablets and widespread wireless networking technologies, so too the term 'digital' perhaps assumes a world of the past."[40]

Such remarks reproduced the considered tone of critiques of the digital humanities movement then appearing in scholarly journals, while bringing them to a broader professional and semi-professional readership in higher education. Subdued as it was, it was Haigh's and Berry's common suggestion that the professional identifier *digital* served as an active impediment to scholarship that seemed the most potentially damaging of all.

• • • •

EVENTUALLY, IT OCCURRED TO SOME THAT the emergence of a new cryptophilology might owe as much to conditions established by the security crisis of 2001 as to those established by the financial panic of 2008. "The recent revelations about the NSA's massive domestic spying operation that implicates nearly every major USA-based technology company that provides a service in exchange for the voluntary submission of more data about ourselves, our connections to others, and our lives," wrote Michael Widner in 2013, "make an understanding of the politics of the digital more pressing than ever. Yet . . . where," he asked, "are the digital humanists critiquing the growing surveillance state?"[41]

"Today," Jan Christoph Meister wrote a year later from the conference Digital Humanities 2014 at the University of Lausanne,

> I sat in a session that was also attended by a delegate wearing an unconspicuously-conspicous [sic] affiliation badge identifying him as belonging to "US Government." That's a designation commonly known to be long-hand for NSA and the likes. . . .
>
> Did this surprise me? Not really. I have myself been contacted twice (i.e., through US academic colleagues) with an offer to consider participation in projects which are funded by the NSA and

similar intelligence agencies. And let us not be naive: the more attention DH researchers invest in Big Data approaches and anything that might help with the analysis of human behaviour, communication and networking patterns, semantic analysis, topic modeling and related approaches, the more our field becomes interesting to those who can apply our research in order to further their own goals.[42]

"It is high time," Meister concluded, "for us to realize that we are now facing the same moral and ethical dilemma which physicists encountered some 70 years ago when nuclear research lost its innocence. What is happening right now, right here is this: our scholarly motivation is being openly instrumentalized for a purpose that is at its very core anti-humanistic."

Jonathan Wilson was next, writing of the *Washington Post*'s reporting in July 2014 that "I don't intend to comment here on the legality, ethics, or wisdom of the NSA's programs or the Snowden leaks. But I do think this report is fascinating and important. And I think it's worth considering from the standpoint of digital history. It seems to me that the Post report is a description of a cutting-edge form of historical methodology. Rightly or wrongly—and this is an idea I find pretty disquieting—the U.S. intelligence community seems to be engaged in collecting much the same information that a historian with similar tools would be."[43]

In an article titled "Is It Research or Is It Spying? Thinking-Through Ethics in Big Data AI and Other Knowledge Sciences," Bettina Berendt, Marco Büchler, and Geoffrey Rockwell suggested that "'How to be a knowledge scientist after the Snowden revelations?' is a question we all have to ask as it becomes clear that our work and our students could be involved in the building of an unprecedented surveillance society."[44] Referring to the 2013 exposure by CIA and NSA contractor Edward Snowden of classified documents describing the ballooning of electronic surveillance programs beginning promptly in September 2001, Berendt, Büchler, and Rockwell considered the possibility that the opportunities both enjoyed and promoted by the new cryptophilology were inconceivable outside of a newly enlarged network of institutional relationships whose character and context presented the researcher with potential compromises of professional ethics, be it through direct or indirect participation and benefit or outright ignorance:

> Questionable data uses, outright data abuses, and data leaks, by government and other actors such as big companies have been described and challenged for a long time. Research into "Big Data" (formerly known as data mining, machine learning, knowledge discovery, etc.) has been increasing steadily also at computer science departments, business schools, and related institutions throughout the world, and research, business and government agencies have pushed for progress together.... At the same time techniques have also been explored in the social sciences and humanities for the study of large literary, historical, and philosophical corpora ...
>
> All these developments, however, were under the radar of most except for the occasional news story.... These stories were treated as anomalies that didn't merit broad democratic discussion. This changed with the Snowden revelations, which (and this is not meant to be negative!) couldn't have been orchestrated better. The revelations have been staggered in "shock value," and coupled with exciting human drama—in short, made newsworthy. [Edward] Snowden, [Glenn] Greenwald, [Laura] Poitras and others at the core of the revelations have managed to provoke an intense public debate for an extended period of time, at least in certain countries like the USA and Germany. Notably absent in this debate are the disciplines, like ours, who benefit from increased investment in the knowledge sciences.[45]

It seems fair to characterize this as a moment of undramatic but authentic collapse, insofar as the authors disclosing such unease do nothing to prevent us from concluding that they had not considered such a challenge to their values, and to the premises, motives, and value of their work, until the course of history, abruptly exposed by a putative revelation, forced them to do so—and that the new cryptophilology that went by the name "digital humanities" had therefore been flying blind. To be sure, it was too late, insofar as the compromises and complicities that now became such nodes of concern were no matters of choice: what the revelation exposed, if it was a revelation, was a structure and a conjunction many years in the making, if not more.

·   ·   ·   ·

IN FORMULATING WHAT I WANT TO suggest here about the digital humanities movement and U.S. national security interests and imperatives since 2001, I am drawing on two sources, both of them entertainingly speculative, essayistic, and erudite histories of the imagination of language in Western intellectual history: Umberto Eco's *The Search for the Perfect Language in European Culture* and Pieter A. Verburg's *Language and Its Functions: A Historico-Critical Study of Views Concerning the Functions of Language from the Pre-Humanistic Philology of Orleans to the Rationalistic Philology of Bopp*.[46]

Eco suggests two factors that, as he sees it, made the biblical story of the Tower of Babel an object of intensified interest in medieval Europe from the fifth century on and especially after the eleventh century. One was the gradual emergence of vernacular literatures; the other was the encroachment of Arab and then Turkic Islam. (In fact, though this is hardly an original thesis, Eco suggests that the idea of "Europe" itself emerged only at this time.)

Eco also suggests that we imagine a methodological bifurcation in the intellectual culture of late medieval missionary Christianity, a bifurcation presenting two quite distinct responses to the Babel story and the post-Roman allegory of "Europe" that it may have come to suggest. The thirteenth century, Eco noted, has left us the writings of the Franciscan friar Roger Bacon, who as Eco puts it "foresaw that contact with the infidels (not merely Arabs, but also Tartars) would require studying foreign languages . . . in order to convert them."[47] But, Eco continued, the thirteenth century has also left us the writings of another Franciscan, Ramon Llull, a Majorcan who composed his works initially in Arabic and Catalan, then went on to formulate, in his *Ars Magna* of 1305, what Eco calls "a system for a perfect language with which to convert the infidels . . . articulated at the level of expression in a universal mathematics of combination."[48]

Over the last two decades, responding to world-historical transitions like those of 1989–1991 and 2001, the discipline of comparative literature has reexamined some of its key concepts (world, comparison, translation) as well as what is probably the most distinctive aspect of its method, acquired professional multilingualism. The contact zone between philology as a practice of literary study and area studies as a militarized social science has always been a hot zone for such introspection, and many of us have had heated debates indeed about the ethics of a professional emphasis on language acquisition, among other ethnological practices, that could certainly be traced back at least partly to the missionary imagination of someone like Roger Bacon.

It is only more recently, we might say, that a nominally newer formation based more exclusively in departments of English studies has re-presented us with the different intellectual legacy of Bacon's contemporary Ramon Llull, and with its own intellectual and also ethical challenges. That formation is the digital humanities, understood as what I would call, adapting a phrase from David Golumbia, a culture of computation—and grasped in its emergence after 2001, alongside a surge of U.S. national security legislation and institution building.[49]

Verburg's *Language and Its Functions* is valuable for its dramatically intricate narratives of conflict between two distinct intellectual formations of modern secularization. The first is the historical humanism that gave us philology as a precursor of what we know as literary studies, today. The second is the rationalism whose ideological and practically applied forms, in what we sometimes call technoscience, still very much constitutes humanism's other culture, even—or especially—today. Bacon's philological multilingualism and Llull's combinatorial unilingualism both traveled within the historical humanism that Verburg divides into three stages: emergence in Italy from 1300 onward, with Leonardo Bruni and Lorenzo Valla and, north of the Alps, in Erasmus, Vives, and Ramus; a "second humanism" of Lessing, Herder, Goethe, Schiller, and Humboldt, among others; and a third, possibly final or nascent post-humanism of Nietzsche and his contemporaries. Verburg's narratives trace the evolving conflict of humanism with medieval scholasticism, then with the "axiomatic rationalism" of the seventeenth century, then with the "proto-positivistic neo-rationalism" of the late eighteenth and early nineteenth centuries.[50] Verburg suggested that in all three of its historical stages, humanism was a more or less practically language-oriented or "lingual" movement, not infrequently pitting rhetoric and literary composition against logic and mathematics, as well as philosophy.[51] Often, Verburg also implied, humanism was a polemicism, invested less in the successful reconciliations of such antipodes of intellectual expression than in their productively extended tension.

We can turn to the work of Edward W. Said for a sense of how the rationalist and antirationalist strains of the secular humanism embodied in nineteenth-century philology *both* rendered service to the European imperial project.[52] And as I suggested in Chapter 2, we can turn to historians of cryptology for the story of how philology was integrated into a nascent U.S. security state during the First World War, through the service of literary scholars who applied simple, crudely mechanized statistical methods to text.

Neither the Baconism of "Colonel" George Fabyan's Riverbank Laboratories nor its reactionary political orientation proved insuperable obstacles to collaboration with liberal Stratfordian academics like John Matthews Manly, chair of the Department of English at the University of Chicago and 1920 president of the MLA. Henry Veggian has argued that Manly was drawn to Riverbank by the "literary-formalist allure" of cryptology[53] as a mathematizable and mechanizable science of constraint and by the opportunity it presented for a broadly technocratic reform of academic literary studies, not unlike the one we are being asked to perform today. The platform formulated by Manly as president of the MLA might therefore sound quite familiar to the association's membership today. Explicitly, it rejected the scholarly individualism of "unorganized," "casual, scrappy, scattering" research, recommending the simultaneously more specialized and more collaborative pursuit of "large, unified achievements," a solid record of which would be needed to secure "financial support for some important undertaking" for which "the Association" could take credit.[54] Explicitly, it endorsed the discovery—or invention—of new problems through linked institutional and methodological reform: "there is little doubt," Manly opined, "that if we once begin to consider the possibilities of properly organized coöperation, we shall soon find plenty of problems."[55] Explicitly, in the name of such scalable reorganization, it called for the MLA to establish a "permanent administration" granted "real control of policies," a "body of greater permanence" than that marked by the "useless and purely ornamental" offices of an annually rotating president and vice president.[56] Explicitly, in the name of such scalable reorganization, Manly's proposal emphasized practical productive philological activity—textual criticism, the study of prosody, surveys of linguistic usage—and enjoined literary scholars to persuade the public of the practical utility of their work. Implicitly, in the name of such scholarly organization, it subordinated interpretive and normative critical discourse and debate to scholarly aggregation and documentation. And implicitly, it submerged the critical function of the intellectual in the interest of the security state: three years after Nicholas Murray Butler and the trustees of Columbia University suspended academic freedom and dismissed Henry Wadsworth Longfellow Dana and James McKeen Cattell from their faculty positions for seditious antimilitarism, Manly had nothing to say about the uproar that now figures so prominently in the history of arguments for academic tenure.[57] Indeed, there is nothing in Manly's 1920 presidential address to the MLA, titled "New Bottles," or in *New Methods for the Study of Literature,* a volume published in 1927 by Manly's Chicago colleague and collaborator Edith Rickert, that would seem out of place in the discourse of the digital humanities movement, which is only the latest formation to proclaim, as Manly proclaimed in his preface to Rickert's book, "the sign and the cause of a new era in the study of literature."[58]

· · · ·

THE LEGACY OF THE INTEGRATION OF Riverbank Baconism into First World War military intelligence, and of the institutional reformism it inspired in academic literary studies, might be traced into the postwar era and the emergence of computational philology as such. Indeed, it might be traced all the way to the antiwar and other social movements of the 1960s, which redirected such reformism against the military–industrial-academic complex with which it had been aligned[59]—and to the authentic, if temporary collapse of a cultural logic of computation, in Golumbia's sense of that phrase, along with the symbolic collapse of the social order. As we have seen, the story of the estrangement of academe from the ideas, the practices, and the institutions of U.S. national security during that period has been told by Robin W. Winks.

We can certainly observe that since the 1980s, much of the disaffection between academe and intelligence agencies that Winks describes as following from the difficult 1960s–1970s has gradually worn away, with the National Security Education Act of 1991 creating the National Security Education Program, National Security Education Board, and National Security Education Trust Fund both marking and enacting a change in relations. Taking U.S. academic anthropology as an example, we might well say that in the years since the security crisis of 2001, with a boost from the financial panic of 2008 as well, a great deal of that disaffection has been aggressively reversed—or at least that the opportunities that obtained until the academic humanities and social sciences sealed themselves off in an isolationist "ivory tower," in the late 1960s, have regained their appeal.[60] It would not be unreasonable to suppose that such change in the relations of academe with security and intelligence agencies is itself one of the conditions of emergence for ostensibly new and unprecedented research formations even, or perhaps especially in the humanities. Combining the pre-1945 histories provided by Kahn, Singh, Gruber, and Veggian with the wartime and postwar history provided by Winks, we see that until the 1960s, intimacy between U.S. academe and U.S. security and military intelligence agencies was the rule, not the exception, not *even* but *especially* in literary studies: an insight providing more context for recent calls for a new "public," as much as digital humanities, along with the castigations of ivory tower isolation that so often support such acts of edupreneurship.[61]

· · · ·

IN PROPOSING THAT THE DIGITAL HUMANITIES movement maintains a latent relation to U.S. national security, I draw on two senses of that term. One is the sense used in communications engineering and human-computer interface or interaction design, where it denotes a measure of systemic temporal delay (for example, the network latency we must often accept when using low-cost or no-cost VOIP telephony). The other is the sense familiar to Freudian psychoanalytic thought, associated with the psychic processes of condensation (*Verdichtung*) and displacement (*Verschiebung*) in "dream-work" (*Traumarbeit*). Both are useful here: the one for marking digital humanities enthusiasts' rather uncomplicated belatedness, even straightforward reluctance, when it comes to historicizing their own opportunities and the provenance of their ideas and resources; the other in helping us to imagine the digital humanities movement as a kind of translative *Traumarbeit*.

In the production of knowledge in universities in the United States, as much as in the security and military intelligence agencies of the United States, the period since 2001 has been marked by a rapid expansion and dissemination of hardware- and software-based means of data collection, storage, and processing, especially text processing, visual data processing, and the "visualization" or rendering of text data as a meaningful image, a fundamentally cryptanalytic activity. This rapid expansion was facilitated by a new intensity of modularization in military hardware, consumer computing devices, and what we now call social media.[62] All of this yielded new masses and massivenesses of specifically cultural data that, we are told by intelligence analysts and digital humanists alike, conceal "surprising" knowledge that in turn demands labor- and other means-intensive analysis and requires support through the ongoing construction of software tools for assistive automation.[63]

Here are some of the facts provided by Dana Priest and William M. Arkin's reporting for the *Washington Post* in July 2010 under the titles "A Hidden World, Growing beyond Control," "National Security Inc.," and "The Secrets Next Door."[64] By the end of 2001, twenty-four new intelligence organizations had been created, including the Office of Homeland Security and the Foreign Terrorist Asset Tracking Task Force, with thirty-seven more being added in 2002, thirty-six more in 2003, twenty-six in 2004, thirty-one in 2005, thirty-two in 2006, and twenty or more in each of 2007, 2008, and 2009, for a total of 246 new intelligence organizations created from 2001 to 2009. Between September 2001 and 2010, thirty-three new building complexes providing seventeen million square feet of space had been constructed in the Washington DC area for intelligence work. The staff of the Defense Intelligence

Agency had doubled, from 7,500 employees in 2001 to 16,500 in 2010; the budget of the National Security Agency been had doubled; and the number of FBI Joint Terrorism Task Forces had tripled, from 35 to 106. And this does not include projects that were only recently completed or were still in the planning stages in 2010: the Department of Homeland Security headquarters in Washington, the NSA data-processing center in Salt Lake City, the U.S. Central Command's new headquarters, intelligence and special operations complexes in Tampa, and the Joint Use Intelligence Analysis Facility in Charlottesville. All this growth, Priest and Arkin note pointedly, "began almost as soon as the Sept. 11 attacks ended"; it "has required more people, and those people have required more administrative and logistic support."[65]

Can such dramatic growth in the production and analysis of the knowledge needed for security and military intelligence have failed to produce structured effects within the university system, even in the humanities, and even in literary scholarship? This is an open question, if one to which we can sensibly apply intuition. Military research performed at universities is hardly difficult to document these days: the various coordinating University Affiliated Research Centers operate openly as nonprofit organizations, while the website of a post-2001 Defense Advanced Research Projects Agency (DARPA) touted its "speaking honestly and directly with potential university partners"[66] and its Young Faculty Award, awarded since 2010 to between thirty and fifty researchers per year and supporting work in electronic engineering, robotics, applied biology and bioinformatics, quantum science, materials and manufacturing science, mathematics, neuroscience, and "computational and quantitative social, decision, and behavioral sciences," a category including software engineering, natural language processing, and social computing.[67] The NSA and CIA have been no less enthusiastically public in detailing what both agencies call "student opportunities."[68] Where the social sciences and the humanities are concerned, Department of State, National Security Education Program, and related initiatives like the National Virtual Translation Center, National Security Language Initiative, Critical Language Scholarship Program, and National Language Service Corps were increasingly well-publicized after 2001. Efforts like the Pat Roberts Intelligence Scholars Program and the Intelligence Community Scholars Program were publicly authorized, if less enthusiastically publicized.[69] Meanwhile, undisclosed CIA funding of scholarship in political science and area studies after 2001 has been revealed by at least one financial audit.[70]

What kinds of things did the new post-2001 intelligence organizations and their contractors do, especially in their Sensitive Compartmented Information Facilities? Anthony Tether's expansion of DARPA work into the life sciences, after taking over from Frank Fernandez as director in 2001, is widely acknowledged[71]; but where security, and military intelligence in particular, is concerned, the expansion would seem to reflect the priorities of the DARPA-led Information Awareness Office (IAO), which was congressionally dismembered in 2003 without doing much to inhibit either its ambitions or their active pursuit. IAO projects were overwhelmingly focused on text data analysis and included projects focused on database aggregation, social network analysis, and automated evidence discovery including biometric data processing and predictive event analysis (including the famous FutureMAP or Futures Markets Applied to Prediction), with a special emphasis on text processing including advanced multilingual natural language processing. To this we might add only the investment in applications of geographic information systems to terrain mapping and other terrain visualization, as well as the aggregation and analysis of visual data encompassing terrain, infrastructure, telecommunications activity, and all kinds of animal and human population data.[72]

Can a ballyhooed turn in the humanities, especially in literary scholarship, that promotes a putatively novel computational philology grounded in the cryptanalytic "visualization" of text data, possibly be or remain isolated from the cultural-analytic and specifically textual-analytic activities of the security and military intelligence organizations that are the university's neighbors—especially when such a turn is represented as a historic opportunity made possible by historic advances in information technology? It seems unlikely. Indeed, a recent publication promoting "macroanalysis" in literary scholarship makes the connection entirely casually: "Nor am I original in considering the applications of technology to large textual collections . . . the National Security Agency is in this business as well: the NSA is reported to have been employing text-mining technologies since the Cold War, and the 'classified' ECHELON surveillance system is purported to capture all manner of electronic information, from satellite communications to email correspondences. . . . Similar to ECHELON is the technology developed by Palantir Technologies in Palo Alto, California."[73]

Nothing in Jockers's discussion of this genealogy suggests that it might already be, or might someday come to be seen as, a compromising one for self-identified humanists to claim for themselves.

Contrast Jockers's stormless detachment with the uproar in academic anthropology that followed University of Kansas anthropologist Felix Moos's promotion of the Pat Roberts Intelligence Scholars Program and the introduction of the Human Terrain System embedding social scientists in U.S. Army and Marine combat units deployed in Afghanistan and Iraq. That uproar culminated in the 2009 report of the American Anthropological Association's Commission on the Engagement of Anthropology with the U.S. Security and Intelligence Communities and Marshall Sahlins's resignation from the National Academy of Sciences in 2013 in protest of its election of Napoleon Chagnon and "the military research projects of the Academy" more generally.[74] Contrast it even with the more muted discussion in academic Comparative Literature over the National Security Language Initiative of 2006, another reactivation of the Cold War infrastructure of area studies that offered language scholars and instructors their own road to renewed complicity in military adventurism.[75]

While we have no record of any prominent digital humanities enthusiast performing significant work for a U.S. security or military intelligence agency or contractor or subcontractor, even through indirect arrangements, one would be mistaken to believe that a project for the military service of the digital humanities has never crossed anyone's desk. A brief discussion of the question "Should DHers accept military / defense funding?," conducted during July 2011 on the "Digital Humanities Questions & Answers" forums supported by the Association for Computers and the Humanities and the aforementioned Prof-Hacker blog of the *Chronicle of Higher Education,* was occasioned by the following prompt, here quoted in full: "Should DHers accept funding from military agencies or defense contractors? Should such funding sources be rejected on principle, or should they be evaluated on a case by case basis using criteria such as basic vs. applied research, the exact nature of the deliverables, and open vs. proprietary outcomes? Discussion welcomed."[76]

Over what appears to have been three to four days,[77] eleven brief answers were submitted by six additional forum members plus the member, Matthew Kirschenbaum, who had submitted the original question. Members considered whether such funding should "be rejected on principle," answering in different cases that "it's in the particulars of the project that things get messier, but a categorical refusal seems irrational," that "rejecting defense funding on principle would be on the the [sic] principle the U.S. military (or other funding entity) is an immoral and / or illegitimate enterprise," that "I'm also prepared to accept some moral ambiguity, and maybe even do some negotiating," that "*all* the devils are in the details. The broad concept of 'military funding' doesn't give us enough to argue about," and that "forecasting evil is wretchedly hard unless one is an oracle."

One member, Bethany Nowviskie, added this: "But I thought I'd mention (lest readers see your question as purely academic) how often this has happened to me and to the project teams I've worked with—particularly on tool-building projects of various sorts, even when we assume our aims are so fundamentally humanistic that they'd be of little interest to such groups. In fact, it has happened on *every single* tool-building project I've been involved in. (Yes, even Juxta and Ivanhoe could have been bombing villages.) It'd be nice to think that, as people are ramping up formal grad programs in DH, a course on research ethics would be in the mix."[78]

Two members suggested that accepting funding from private corporations might well be equally or even more compromising than accepting funding from military agencies or defense contractors. Halfway through the discussion, the member who submitted the original question, Matthew Kirschenbaum, confirmed, in response to an implied follow-up question posed within another member's answer, that "yes I have a reason, and in fact I think it's a question we'll be seeing a lot more of." This member then referred the group to "the public debate over academic anthropology's participation in 'human terrain analysis,'" noting that it was "worth tracking as an example of a neighboring field coming to grips with similar issues."[79] Without necessarily rejecting it as mistaken, two subsequent answers from two different members appear to affirm the position that academic anthropologists were "being prescriptive" in their handling of the issue.

Soon thereafter, Kirschenbaum suggested that "at least going by the limited number of responses here (and including a couple on Twitter), it doesn't appear very contentious at all," asking the other members, "Is that all there is to it then? Do we have our DH 'answer'?" While it included an affirmation of "the consensus you just summarized," the discussion that followed also indicates that the matter had not in fact been settled. In response to a follow-up question posed in an answer by another member, "What are DH values that a military connection might threaten?" Kirschenbaum referred other members to the Pledge of Non-Participation in Counter-Insurgency issued by the Network of Concerned Anthropologists in September 2007, suggesting that "for anthropologists, the predicament is that complicity in counter-insurgency operations is perceived as at odds with the field's professional commitment to trust and responsible engagement with indigenous populations." Kirschenbaum then encouraged further discussion, asking if digital humanities enthusiasts had encountered "similar cruxes in DH where our specific professional values (to the extent we can even articulate *those* coherently) are endangered by, say, work that relies on NLP [natural language processing] and IR [information retrieval] to yield analytics of large textual corpora."

Only one, indirect or oblique reply to this final question was submitted, after which the conversation was discontinued.

· · · ·

Two points in preface of a third about this and in conclusion, both of this final chapter and now this book. First, the opportunity that appears to have prompted the question submitted to "Digital Humanities Questions & Answers" in July 2011 could, in theory, have come to any one of us, at any time. All of us—we scholars, we philologists—must both ask ourselves how we might manage such opportunities and their temptations, and admit the contingency of the position of any of our colleagues who actually do serve as our proxies, in that respect.

Second, we need to recognize the effort to begin a conversation about such temptations, here, and the documentation of that conversation in public. That effort was made in good faith, even if we might say that the public evidence, at least, does not suggest it was pursued for long or with much determination, apart from that of the member who submitted the original question (who also encouraged continued discussion). Third: nonetheless, we need also to see the political and ethical quietism here for what it is, and to situate it in a longer history of both complacently passive and actively collaborative relations between U.S. literary scholars and the military and domestic security agencies of the state. If we *were* to recognize a past and present relationship of the "passwords," the projects, and the institutions of twentieth- and twenty-first-century cryptophilology to those of U.S. national security, would there be anything unusual in such a relationship? The answer to that is, quite emphatically: No, not at all. "Though America's participation in the First World War was of relatively short duration," Gruber wrote in 1975 in her conclusion to *Mars and Minerva: World War I and the Uses of the Higher Learning in America,* "the articulation of interest between the higher learning and the world of power that took place during the war's span was not an ephemeral experience; established and exposed then were assumptions, attitudes, and expectations that would flower in the decades to come."[80]

The real question, it seems to me, is if those acts and events of scholarly conscience that marked the 1960s and 1970s, as Winks narrated them (and to which Gruber also alluded), still mean anything to us today—and if we have perhaps arrived at the point of their repetition.

Notes

Preface

1. See Nicholas Carr, *The Shallows: What the Internet Is Doing to Our Brains* (New York: W. W. Norton, 2011); Jaron Lanier, *You Are Not a Gadget: A Manifesto* (New York: Vintage Books, 2011); Eli Pariser, *The Filter Bubble: How the New Personalized Web Is Changing What We Read and How We Think* (New York: Penguin Books, 2012); and Sherry Turkle, *Alone Together: Why We Expect More from Technology and Less from Each Other* (New York: Basic Books, 2012).

2. Gideon Lewis-Kraus, "Bubble Indemnity," *New York Times Magazine,* May 10, 2016.

3. David Streitfeld, "'The Internet Is Broken': @Ev Is Trying to Salvage It," *New York Times,* May 20, 2017.

4. Such dynamics have appeared outside the United States, though seldom in precisely the same form. My focus in this book is on the predicament of the United States because it is where I live as a citizen and where I work as an educator and thus have a specific responsibility to speak as a critic.

5. See Jenna Wortham, "The New Dream Jobs," *New York Times Magazine,* February 25, 2016.

6. See David Graeber, *Debt: The First 5,000 Years* (Brooklyn: Melville House, 2014); Thomas Piketty, *Capital in the Twenty-First Century,* trans. Arthur Goldhammer (Cambridge, MA: Belknap Press of Harvard University Press, 2014); Astra Taylor, *The People's Platform: Taking Back Power and*

Culture in the Digital Age (New York: Picador, 2015); and Annie McClanahan, *Dead Pledges: Debt, Crisis, and Twenty-First-Century Culture* (Stanford, CA: Stanford University Press, 2016). See also Sarah Brouillette, *Literature and the Creative Economy* (Stanford, CA: Stanford University Press, 2014), also relevant in this context if not directly responsive to the events of 2008. In 2016, Palgrave Macmillan and Johns Hopkins University Press each launched separate publication series with the title "Critical University Studies."

7. See Steven E. Jones, *The Emergence of the Digital Humanities* (New York: Routledge, 2014), 8.

8. See Sally C. Curtin, Margaret Warner, and Holly Hedegaard, "Increase in Suicide in the United States, 1999–2014" (U.S. National Center for Health Statistics, Centers for Disease Control and Prevention, April 2016). Along with nearly every other word in this book, these words were first written before the U.S. presidential election that took place on November 8, 2016. Obviously, I am not among those who professed surprise at its outcome. The programming contest (or no-contest) pitting Ada, the Clinton campaign's voter data analytics "algorithm" named for Ada, Countess of Lovelace, against the Mercer family's Cambridge Analytica opens a whole new chapter, in the grander sense of that word, in the genealogy of cryptophilology sketched in this book.

9. See Nicole Nguyen, *A Curriculum of Fear: Homeland Security in US Public Schools* (Minneapolis: University of Minnesota Press, 2016).

10. John T. Hamilton's *Security: Politics, Humanity, and the Philology of Care* (Princeton, NJ: Princeton University Press, 2016) is the first book-length work of scholarship in the literary humanities to define the post-2001 interval as an interval in scholarship itself.

11. See Dan Schiller and ShinJoung Yeo, "Academic Surveillance Complex," *Information Observatory*, May 22, 2017, http://informationobservatory.info/2017/05/22/academic-surveillance-complex/.

12. See Andrew Kopec, "The Digital Humanities, Inc.: Literary Criticism and the Fate of a Profession," *PMLA* 131, no. 2 (2016): 324–339.

13. On the history of cliometrics, see Francesco Boldizzoni, *The Poverty of Clio: Resurrecting Economic History* (Princeton, NJ: Princeton University Press, 2011). On the history of logic programming in law, see Philip Leith, "The Rise and Fall of the Legal Expert System," *European Journal of Law and Technology* 1, no. 1 (2010). For a proposal for "a research field called *juris-informatics*," see Ken Satoh, "Logic Programming and Burden of Proof in Legal Reasoning," *New Generation Computing* 30, no. 4 (2012): 297–326.

14. See Gregory Crane, David Bamman, and Alison Jones, "ePhilology: When the Books Talk to Their Readers," in *A Companion to Digital Literary Studies*, ed. Ray Siemens and Susan Schreibman (Oxford: Blackwell, 2008).

15. When I write in this book of the automation of scholarly analysis, I am *not* imagining the automation of teaching labor, for example, through the replacement of classroom teaching by MOOC instruction. Rather than a labor process in a meaningful sense, the automated analysis of generic or other formal characteristics of a literary text is a displacement of the scholar's reasoning from observation by the magical authority of a human-initiated, but otherwise partly independent computational process—to the outcome of which is imputed knowledge production of a kind or on a scale (or both) exceeding the capacities of human beings. It is not the knowledge thus produced that is valued and is the real goal of such automation; rather, the goal is to argue that such knowledge production is possible and to support it with a putative demonstration. The pursuit of such a goal is not analytic in the secular sense of that term. Rather, it is cryptanalytic, resting on the revelation of a secret message and on its authority *as* revealed by (at least partly) nonhuman means.

16. See Pieter A. Verburg, *Language and Its Functions: A Historico-Critical Study of Views Concerning the Functions of Language from the Pre-Humanistic Philology of Orleans to the Rationalistic Philology of Bopp*, trans. Paul Salmon (Amsterdam: John Benjamins, 1998).

17. See Verburg, *Language and Its Functions*, 434–435.

18. See Gerald Graff, *Professing Literature: An Institutional History* (Chicago: University of Chicago Press, 2007); and James Turner, *Philology: The Forgotten Origins of the Modern Humanities* (Princeton, NJ: Princeton University Press, 2015).

1. Passwords

1. Umberto Eco, *The Search for the Perfect Language,* trans. James Fentress (Oxford, UK: Blackwell, 1995), 5, 9–10.

2. As John T. Hamilton puts it, "security is an urgent philological problem." See *Security: Politics, Humanity, and the Philology of Care* (Princeton, NJ: Princeton University Press, 2016), 12.

3. *Mots de passe* was produced with a documentary, *Mots de passe: Jean Baudrillard,* by Pierre Bourgeois and Leslie Grunberg, portions of which can be viewed on the website of the European Graduate School. "Le mot de passe" is the everyday French equivalent for the technical denotation of the English "password," though of course it can be used figuratively in French just as it can be in English. For the title of their Turkish translation, titled *Anahtar Sözcükler* (Keywords), Oğuz Adanır and Leyla Yıldırım chose the term *anahtar sözcük* "keyword" rather than "şifre," the equivalent for "password" in a technical context. (Savaş Kılıç has translated Raymond Williams's *Keywords*

into Turkish as *Anahtar sözcükler.*) Sławomir Królak appears to have made a similar choice in producing a Polish translation titled *Słowa klucze.*

4. See Ken Hess, "2012: The Year of Security," *ZDNet,* January 2012, http://www .zdnet.com/blog/virtualization/2012-the-year-of-security/4404—little more than a squib, but one that anticipated a truly dramatic year. Since then, malware-based espionage and data theft sponsored by both nation-states and organized crime have escalated so dramatically that any catalog of spectacular exploits would be stale information within months, if not weeks.

5. "Luser" is a portmanteau word combining "user" and "loser," used by IT service providers to describe those whom they serve.

6. Jean Baudrillard, *Passwords,* trans. Chris Turner (London: Verso, 2011), ix; Jean Baudrillard, *Mots de Passe* (Paris: Pauvert, 2000), 9–10.

7. Baudrillard, *Passwords,* 15; Baudrillard, *Mots de Passe,* 25–26.

8. See William Merrin, *Baudrillard and the Media: A Critical Introduction* (Cambridge, UK: Polity, 2005), 16. See also Richard Terdiman, "Taking Time: Temporal Representations and Cultural Politics," in *Given World and Time: Temporalities in Context* (Budapest: CEU Press, 2008), 131–144. Of the intellectual-historical development through which "Western modernity has increasingly seen the world as language," Terdiman observes: "Such systems *take no time.* Through their rule-boundedness, logics repel temporality, and structuralist models aggressively repudiate it. . . . Paradigms based on language have a low aptitude for modeling time in its productivity" (136–137).

9. See Lydia H. Liu, *The Freudian Robot: Digital Media and the Future of the Unconscious* (Chicago: University of Chicago Press, 2010); John Johnston, *The Allure of Machinic Life: Cybernetics, Artificial Life, and the New AI* (Cambridge, MA: MIT Press, 2010); Bernard Dionysius Geoghegan, "Agents of History: Autonomous Agents and Crypto-Intelligence," *Interaction Studies* 9, no. 3 (2008): 403–414; Bernard Dionysius Geoghegan, "From Information Theory to French Theory: Jakobson, Lévi-Strauss, and the Cybernetic Apparatus," *Critical Inquiry* 38, no. 1 (2011): 96–112.

10. Geoghegan, "Agents of History," 405.

11. See J. Frederik M. Arenas, "From Homer to Hobbes and Beyond—Aspects of 'Security' in the European Tradition," in *Globalization and Environmental Challenges,* ed. Hans Günter Brauch et al., vol. 3 (Berlin: Springer Berlin Heidelberg, 2008), 263–277, 265.

12. Arenas, "From Homer to Hobbes and Beyond," 267, 272. For a basically similar and equally comprehensive treatment of the semantic history of *securitas,* see Hamilton, *Security,* 51–67.

13. See Karl de Leeuw, "Introduction," in *The History of Information Security: A Comprehensive Handbook,* ed. Karl de Leeuw and Jan Bergstra (Amsterdam: Elsevier, 2007), 1–25, 4.

14. Leeuw, "Introduction," 24.

15. The word "authentication," too, has both broad and narrow senses here, standing on the one hand for the history of administrative diplomatic and biometric certification that is as long as the history of writing itself (a history in which philology has its place), and on the other for the specific and specifically mundane event that most of us initiate—or are subject to—many times daily, when we type in the passwords accompanying our user login names.

16. Pieter Wisse, "Semiotics of Identity Management," in *The History of Information Security: A Comprehensive Handbook,* ed. Karl de Leeuw and Jan Bergstra (Amsterdam: Elsevier, 2007), 167–196, 191.

17. "Normal conditions" here means normal consumer conditions, in which a user is not actively taking steps to securely erase data after it is created.

18. See Stig F. Mjølsnes, "Introduction," in *A Multidisciplinary Introduction to Information Security,* ed. Stig F. Mjølsnes (Boca Raton, FL: CRC Press, 2012), 1–18, 5–6. Michael Warner notes the conclusion of Bernard Peters, director in 1967 of an NSA project evaluating terminal multiplexing, that "security cannot be obtained in an absolute sense in a multiprogramming system equipped with remote terminals, and that any introduction of sensitive data into the system should consider the likelihood of compromise." See Michael Warner, "Cybersecurity: A Pre-History," *Intelligence and National Security* 27, no. 5 (October 2012): 783, paraphrasing Bernard Peters, "Security Considerations in a Multiprogrammed Computer System," in *AFIPS Proceedings* 30 (1967): 283–286, and Peters, "Security Considerations in a Multiprogrammed Computer System," as cited by Warner. See also Thomas R. Johnson, *American Cryptology During the Cold War, 1945–1989, Book II: Centralization Wins, 1960–1972* (Washington, DC: National Security Agency Center for Cryptologic History, 1995), 368, as cited by Warner. Warner also notes the opinion of Willis H. Ware. In a report published by the RAND Corporation in 1970, Ware noted that "there would be no engineering solution to the problem of computer security. . . . In short, computer security would have to depend more on 'hygiene' than hardware" (Warner, "Cybersecurity," 784–785). See "Security Controls for Computer Systems. Report of the Defense Science Board Task Force on Computer Security" (Santa Monica, CA: RAND Corporation, 1970), as cited by Warner.

19. Mjølsnes, "Introduction," 5–6.

20. Richard E. Smith, *Authentication: From Passwords to Public Keys* (Boston: Addison-Wesley, 2002), 73–77.

21. Jeffrey R. Yost, "A History of Computer Security Standards," in *The History of Information Security: A Comprehensive Handbook,* ed. Karl de Leeuw and Jan Bergstra (Amsterdam: Elsevier, 2007), 595–621, 602. See also Warner, "Cybersecurity," a useful "pre-history" of the "cybersecurity problem" that might seem otherwise to have emerged so abruptly in 2012.

22. Yost, "History of Computer Security Standards," 642. See also David Elliott Bell and Leonard J. LaPadula, "Secure Computer Systems: Mathematical

Foundations" (Bedford, MA: MITRE Corporation, 1973), and "Secure Computer Systems: Unified Exposition and Multics Interpretation" (Bedford, MA: MITRE Corporation, 1976).

23. A hacker who tests systems for their proprietors (almost always as a contracted professional) dons an imagined "white hat," while a "black hat" hacker conducts criminal exploits. One of the many ways to define a "gray hat" hacker is as someone who employs the methods of the latter for the purposes of the former.

24. For the phrase "watershed event for Internet security," see Laura DeNardis, "A History of Internet Security," in *The History of Information Security: A Comprehensive Handbook,* ed. Karl de Leeuw and Jan Bergstra (Amsterdam: Elsevier, 2007), 681–704, 683. For the phrase "contagion period," see Margaret van Biene-Hershey, "IT Security and IT Auditing between 1960 and 2000," in *The History of Information Security: A Comprehensive Handbook,* ed. Karl de Leeuw and Jan Bergstra (Amsterdam: Elsevier, 2007), 655–680, 675–676. See also Susan W. Brenner, "History of Computer Crime," in *The History of Information Security: A Comprehensive Handbook,* ed. Karl de Leeuw and Jan Bergstra (Amsterdam: Elsevier, 2007), 705–721, 709. Organized cybercrime, Brenner notes, emerged only in the 2000s, with new and established criminal syndicates worldwide adapting botnet DDoS attacks for the time-honored practice of extortion.

25. These include not only fingerprints but speech, signature, hand geometry, palm vein, walking gait, iris, and facial recognition, as well as keystroke dynamic (typing) and stylometric (writing style) recognition—many of the latter representing techniques developed more or less gradually throughout the postwar era, then very rapidly brought to maturity following the security crisis of 2001. Facial recognition techniques, to take only one example, are now both more advanced and more widely deployed than most citizens of wealthy countries appear to realize. On the history and current deployment of biometric techniques, see Edward Higgs, "From Frankpledge to Chip and PIN: Identification and Identity in England, 1475–2005," in *The History of Information Security: A Comprehensive Handbook,* ed. Karl de Leeuw and Jan Bergstra (Amsterdam: Elsevier, 2007), 243–262; Karel Johan Schell, "History of Document Security," in *The History of Information Security: A Comprehensive Handbook,* ed. Karl de Leeuw and Jan Bergstra (Amsterdam: Elsevier, 2007), 197–241; James L. Wayman, "The Scientific Development of Biometrics over the Last 40 Years," in *The History of Information Security: A Comprehensive Handbook,* ed. Karl de Leeuw and Jan Bergstra (Amsterdam: Elsevier, 2007), 263–274; Wisse, "Semiotics of Identity Management."

26. Smith, *Authentication,* 11.

27. Ibid., 5, 7.

28. Schell, "History of Document Security," 204. A lock, for example, shifts the security "problem" to control of access to the key, Smith, *Authentication,* 5.

Schell notes that every advance in techniques for reproduction for currency printing has always also marked an advance in techniques of currency forgery (Schell, "History of Document Security," 204).

29. Smith, *Authentication*, 43.

30. This is Smith's way of putting it (perhaps not one that many scholars of Judges would accept; see my further discussion below). See ibid., 45.

31. The Shibboleth system is designed to facilitate the sharing of resources (for example, across university library systems) while preserving a user's individual privacy. A user authenticates with her or his home institution (this being the "cultural" dimension of membership in a particular community), which then passes only as much information about the user as is strictly necessary to the "federalized" resource provider (for example, an electronic publisher). (A "Where Are You From?" service directs visitors to Shibboleth servers back to authentication mechanisms at their own institutions.) See Mark Needleman, "The Shibboleth Authentication / Authorization System," *Serials Review* 30, no. 3 (2004): 252–253.

32. Smith, *Authentication*, 47.

33. Ibid., 39. But one thinks also, for example, of Virgil's *Vuolsi così colà dove si puote* ("It is so willed where will and power are one"), spoken to Charon, or of all the gates on which inscriptions vocalize passage in place of challenge from a guard, from *Lasciate ogne speranza, voi ch'intrate* to *Arbeit macht frei*.

34. Smith, *Authentication*, xvii, 2.

35. Ibid., 88–89, 91–92.

36. The defensive tactic called "salting" responds to this vulnerability. Passwords are hashed using a pseudo-random variable or "salt" added to the original data to ensure that successive hashes of the same password will be nonidentical. See Ibid., 57.

37. See, for example, Mat Honan, "It's Time to Abandon Passwords," *Gizmodo*, June 2011, http://io9.com/5812685/its-time-to-abandon-passwords; Jared Newman, "The Username / Password System Is Broken: Here Are Some Ideas for Fixing It," *Time*, August 8, 2012; Randall Stross, "Goodbye, Passwords. You Aren't a Good Defense," *New York Times*, August 9, 2008.

38. Smith, *Authentication*, 95.

39. Ibid., 98, 162.

40. In Susan Niditch's literal, lineated translation. See *Judges: A Commentary* (Louisville, KY: Westminster John Knox Press, 2008), 136–138, 252.

41. Ralph Marcus, "The Word šibboleth Again," *Bulletin of the American Schools of Oriental Research*, no. 87 (1942): 39; Ronald S. Hendel, "Sibilants and šibbōlet (Judges 12:6)," *Bulletin of the American Schools of Oriental Research*, no. 301 (1996): 69–75, 69.

42. Kaori Nagai, "Dream Shibboleth," *Journal of European Studies* 38, no. 4 (2008): 428. Nagai gives "shibboleth" more literary and philosophical color

than one finds in etymological debates among A. F. L. Beeston, Alice Faber, Ronald S. Hendel, Gary A. Rendsburg, Pierre Swiggers, and Robert Woodhouse. But on this point, see also Hendel, "Sibilants and šibbōlet (Judges 12)," 69; Gary A. Rendsburg, "The Ammonite Phoneme /ṯ/," *Bulletin of the American Schools of Oriental Research*, no. 269 (1988): 73–79, 75; Gary A. Rendsburg, "More on Hebrew šibbōlet," *Journal of Semitic Studies* 33, no. 2 (1988): 255–258, 256; P. Swiggers, "The Word šibbōlet in Jud. Xii.6," *Journal of Semitic Studies* 26, no. 2 (1981): 205–207, 205.

43. Jennifer Michael, "(Ad)Dressing Shibboleths: Costume and Community in the South of France," *Journal of American Folklore* 111, no. 440 (1998): 146–172, 148.

44. Hannes Kniffka, "Shibboleths: Philologische Bestandsaufnahme Und Gesichtspunkte Zu Ihrer Soziolinguistischen Analyse," *Deutsche Sprache* 19, no. 2 (1991): 159–177, 159.

45. Presley A. Ifukor, "Spelling and Simulated Shibboleths in Nigerian Computer-Mediated Communication," *English Today* 27, no. 3 (2011): 35–42, 37.

46. Tim Mcnamara, "21st Century Shibboleth: Language Tests, Identity and Intergroup Conflict," *Language Policy* 4, no. 4 (2005): 351–370, 352–358.

47. See Pack Carnes, "Then Say 'Shibboleth': Language Stereotyping in 'Neck-Legends,'" *Midwestern Folklore*, no. 15 (1989): 15–24; Dorothy Noyes, "Group," *The Journal of American Folklore* 108, no. 430 (1995): 449–478; Michael, "(Ad)Dressing Shibboleths."

48. Michael, "(Ad)Dressing Shibboleths," 151–153.

49. Carnes, "Then Say 'Shibboleth,'" 16–17.

50. Theodor Herzl Gaster, *Myth, Legend, and Custom in the Old Testament: A Comparative Study with Chapters from Sir James G. Frazer's Folklore in the Old Testament* (New York: Harper & Row, 1969), 228, citing Brewer, *Dictionary of Miracles.*

51. George Foot Moore, *A Critical and Exegetical Commentary on Judges* (New York: Scribner, 1895), 308; J. Alberto Soggin, *Judges, a Commentary* (London: SCM Press, 1987), 222; Jean-Charles-Léonard Simonde de Sismondi, *A History of the Italian Republics. Being a View of the Origin, Progress and Fall of Italian Freedom* (London: Longman, Brown, Green, & Longmans, 1832), 103; William H. Peet, "Shibboleth," *Notes and Queries* 10, no. 10 (256) (1908): 408.

52. A. M. Cramer, "Shibboleth," *Notes and Queries* 10, no. 11 (263) (1909): 36.

53. Gaster, *Myth, Legend, and Custom in the Old Testament,* 433; Rockingham, "Shibboleth," *Notes and Queries* 10, no. 11 (273) (1909): 234.

54. M. C. L., "Shibboleth," *Notes and Queries* 10, no. 11 (273) (1909): 233–234.

55. Noyes, "Group," 465.

56. These include "Scheveningen," "rødgrød med fløde," "schaap" or "schaapje," and "beschuit met muisjes," a place-name, name of a dessert, and other words and phrases supposedly used by the Dutch resistance to identify Germans.

See Robert G. Boling, *Judges: Introduction, Translation, and Commentary* (Garden City, NY: Doubleday, 1975), 214; Soggin, *Judges, a Commentary,* 222; Carnes, "Then Say 'Shibboleth'" 19; Mcnamara, "21st Century Shibboleth," 355, 369. They also include "Lalapaloosa," "Say Larue, Larue, Lily Bolero," and "the green grass grows on the glazed glass," supposedly used by U.S. and British soldiers to distinguish Japanese from Chinese, and "Whither went the winged whippoorwill," supposedly used by the British to identify Germans. See Carnes, "Then Say 'Shibboleth,'" 18.

57. Mcnamara, "21st Century Shibboleth," 353.

58. See David Marcus, "Ridiculing the Ephraimites: The Shibboleth Incident (Judg 12:6)," *MAARAV: A Journal for the Study of the Northwest Semitic Languages and Literatures* 8 (1992): 95–105.

59. Marcus, "Ridiculing the Ephraimites," 95.

60. The Ephraimites, it is noted, were challenged to pronounce a word, not asked to produce the name of something they were shown or referred to. See E. A. Speiser, "The Shibboleth Incident (Judges 12:6)," *Bulletin of the American Schools of Oriental Research,* no. 85 (1942): 10; Marcus, "Ridiculing the Ephraimites," 100.

61. Moore, *Critical and Exegetical Commentary on Judges,* 309. See also Soggin, *Judges, a Commentary,* 220–221. Susan Niditch notes that Judges 12:6 is one of the only passages in the Hebrew Bible, apart from the Babel story, that distinguishes between accents or dialects. See Niditch, *Judges,* 138.

62. Hendel, "Sibilants and šibbōlet (Judges 12)," 71.

63. Swiggers, "The Word šibbōlet in Jud. Xii.6," 207.

64. Jacques Derrida, "Schibboleth: For Paul Celan," in *Word Traces: Readings of Paul Celan,* ed. Aris Fioretos, trans. Joshua Wilner (Baltimore: Johns Hopkins University Press, 1994), 3–72, 29–32; Jacques Derrida, *Schibboleth Pour Paul Celan* (Paris: Galilée, 1986), 51–54. Mieke Bal acknowledged the inversion in describing the shibboleth as a "reversed password," a nonsecret "silent word that has no meaning, that is pure force." See Mieke Bal, *Death & Dissymmetry: The Politics of Coherence in the Book of Judges* (Chicago: University of Chicago Press, 1988), 164. Bal reads Judges 12:6 as turning on a riddle in the form, "Who belongs to the fatherline?" By contrast, Susan Stuart describes what she calls "pseudo-communicative" legal-discursive shibboleths like "managerial discretion" (used by the majority in the Supreme Court's decision in *Garcetti v. Ceballos*) as "passwords," securing the political attention of a specific social group—in *Garcetti v. Ceballos,* the business elite—attentive to connotations they carry that may not be recognizable to others. See Susan Stuart, "Shibboleths and Ceballos: Eroding Constitutional Rights Through Pseudocommunication," *Brigham Young University Law Review,* no. 5 (2008): 1545–1601. Kaori Nagai also describes the shibboleth as functioning as a password, albeit in a "dreamy" sense. See Nagai, "Dream Shibboleth," 425.

65. Marcus, "Ridiculing the Ephraimites," 100. Of the locution "Say, pray, 'shibboleth'" (as Niditch translates it), Marcus notes that it includes a grammatical particle that softens the command or makes it more courteous, and that it might thus be translated, "Please say shibboleth." Such "exaggerated solicitude," he observes, is another clue to the author's satiric intention, which he suggests parallels the satire of the Tower of Babel in Genesis 11. See Marcus, "Ridiculing the Ephraimites," 102. For "he could not accomplish to say it thus" (as Niditch translates it), J. Alberto Soggin suggests "he was not prepared" (thus "he was not prepared to pronounce it correctly") rather than "he did not know how"; confusion in interpretation of this point, Soggin suggested, had arisen from confusing written כ *kaph* with ב *bet*. See Soggin, *Judges, a Commentary,* 213. Niditch emphasizes that the verb with the root "to be established" is difficult to translate; the Codex Vaticanus gives "He could not succeed to speak thus," while the Old Latin gives "And their ways of speaking did not agree." See Niditch, *Judges,* 136.

66. Casual references to "Ali Baba's cave" are frequent in technical literature on authentication. For an unusually sophisticated engagement with variations on the story, see, for example, Steve Gibson and Leo Laporte, "Ali Baba's Cave," http://twit.tv/show/security-now/363, which involves a variation on a variation by Jean-Jacques Quisquater, Louis C. Guillou, and Thomas A. Berson. See Quisquater, Guillou, and Berson, "How to Explain Zero-Knowledge Protocols to Your Children," in *Advances in Cryptology* (New York: Springer-Verlag, 1990), 628–631. See also Alfonso de Gregorio, "Ali Baba, Waldo and the Dining Cryptographers," *Plaintext: Information That Makes Security Stakeholders Better Off* (blog), November 2010, http://plaintext.crypto.lo.gy/en/article/354/ali-baba-waldo-and-the-dining-cryptographers.

67. See Nabia Abbott, "A Ninth-Century Fragment of the 'Thousand Nights': New Light on the Early History of the Arabian Nights," in *The Arabian Nights Reader,* ed. Ulrich Marzolph (Detroit, MI: Wayne State University Press, 2006), 21–82. Jonathan Bloom mentions Abbott's dating of the manuscript to the first quarter of the ninth century, adding that "the oldest dated complete book in Arabic copied on paper that we know is a manuscript dating to 848, recently discovered by accident in the regional library of Alexandria, Egypt; it awaits complete publication." See Jonathan Bloom, *Paper before Print: The History and Impact of Paper in the Islamic World* (New Haven, CT: Yale University Press, 2001), 58.

68. Tzvetan Todorov, "Narrative-Men," in *The Arabian Nights Reader,* ed. Ulrich Marzolph (Detroit, MI: Wayne State University Press, 2006), 122–136, 229.

69. F. E. Peiser, "'Sesam,' Thue Dich Auf," *Orientalistische Litteratur-Zeitung,* no. 5 (1902): 282–285, 282, 284–285.

70. Paul Haupt, "Open Sesame," *Beiträge Zur Assyriologie Und Semitischen Sprachwissenschaft* 10, no. 2 (1927): 165–174, 165–167, 170–172.

71. The Grimms recorded a tale titled "Simeliberg," possibly referring to a mountain in Grabfeld and containing the locutions "Open Simsi!" and "Open Simeli."

72. On recent returns to philology, see especially Paul De Man, "The Return to Philology," in *The Times Literary Supplement* (December 1982), 1355–1356; Edward W. Said, "The Return to Philology," in *Humanism and Democratic Criticism* (New York: Columbia University Press, 2004), 57–84; Paul A. Bové, "Philology and Poetry: The Case against Descartes," *Law and Literature* 21, no. 2 (2009): 149–168; Jonathan Culler, "Anti-Foundational Philology," *Comparative Literature Studies* 27, no. 1 (1990): 49–52; Jonathan Culler, "The Return to Philology," *Journal of Aesthetic Education* 36, no. 3 (2002): 12–16; Michael Holquist, "Erich Auerbach and the Fate of Philology Today," *Poetics Today* 20, no. 1 (1999): 77–91; Michael Holquist, "The Place of Philology in an Age of World Literature," *Neohelicon* 38, no. 2 (2011): 267–287; Michael Holquist, "Why We Should Remember Philology," *Profession*, no. 1 (2002): 72–79; Aamir R Mufti, "Orientalism and the Institution of World Literatures," *Critical Inquiry* 36, no. 3 (2010): 458–493. On the non-Orientalist "project of revitalizing philology," see Edward W. Said, *Orientalism,* 25th anniversary edition (New York: Vintage Books, 2003), 258ff. On the "new eccentricity in Orientalism" introduced by its U.S. Americanization, see Said, *Orientalism,* 261, 290ff. Sheldon Pollock suggests that "Said's demonstration of the noxious colonial epistemology that lay at the core of Orientalism paralyzed a field that, by 1978, was already in jeopardy. The demotion of Oriental philology had started twenty years earlier when the new American security state began to transform non-Western philologies from forms of knowledge with major theoretical claims about the human sciences into a mere content provider for the applied social sciences that went under the name of area studies." See Pollock, "Future Philology? The Fate of a Soft Science in a Hard World," *Critical Inquiry* 35, no. 4 (2009): 946, 931–961.

73. See Said, *Orientalism,* 131–132, and Geoffrey Galt Harpham, "Roots, Races, and the Return to Philology," *Representations* 106, no. 1 (2009): 34–62.

74. See Seth Lerer on Harry Caplan, *Error and the Academic Self: The Scholarly Imagination, Medieval to Modern* (New York: Columbia University Press, 2002), 219; and on Auerback, p. 230. Responding to Lerer's discussion of the work of Harry Caplan, Jan Ziolkowski asks: "What is the point in critiquing Harry Caplan for believing that . . . 'this whole process . . . is not about indeterminacy but about security?' Caplan was not a deconstructionist or even a poststructuralist *avant la lettre* (or *la parole*). So what? Is it not being a trifle totalitarian, to say nothing of being passé, to insist that the only certainty is indeterminacy?" See Jan M. Ziolkowski, "Metaphilology," *Journal of English and Germanic Philology* 104, no. 2 (2005): 239–272, 269.

75. Henry Veggian, "Mercury of the Waves: Modern Cryptology and United States Literature" (PhD diss., University of Pittsburgh, 2005), 38.

2. Cryptophilology, I

1. See Lyle D. Broemeling, "An Account of Early Statistical Inference in Arab Cryptology," *American Statistician* 65, no. 4 (2011): 255–257. Broemeling cites F. N. David, *Games, Gods, and Gambling: A History of Probability and Statistical Ideas* (Ontario, Canada: General Publishing, 1962); Anders Hald, *A History of Probability and Statistics and Their Applications Before 1750* (New York: Wiley, 1990); Hald, *A History of Mathematical Statistics from 1750 to 1930* (New York: Wiley, 1998); Stephen M. Stigler, *The History of Statistics: The Measurement of Uncertainty Before 1900* (Cambridge, MA: Belknap Press of Harvard University Press, 1986); and Stigler, *Statistics on the Table: The History of Statistical Concepts and Methods* (Cambridge, MA: Harvard University Press, 1999), noting that Ibrahim A. Al-Kadi's "Origins of Cryptology: The Arab Contributions" contains "the first reference I found" to Arab contributions. See Al-Kadi, "Origins of Cryptology: The Arab Contributions," *Cryptologia* 16, no. 2 (1992): 97–126, and Broemeling, "Account of Early Statistical Inference," 101, 103–104:

   > Cryptography has been practiced to conceal messages since antiquity by different civilizations, including the ancient Egyptian, Chinese, Indian, Mesopotamian, Greek and Roman. But in none of them was there any cryptanalysis.... Cryptology, the science of both making ciphers (cryptography) and breaking them (cryptanalysis), was born among the Arabs shortly after the rise of the Arab-Islamic empire.... The Arabic foundation of algebra is widely acknowledged, but this is hardly the case with statistics. Historians of mathematics ... attribute the first writings on probability and statistics to correspondence between Pascal and Fermat in 1654. In his recently discovered manuscript, al-Kindi gave the first description of statistical methods in cryptanalysis. He even explicitly required texts to be long enough to allow letter statistics to be meaningful.... This is the world's first known writings [*sic*] in statistics, antedating those of Pascal and Fermat by about 800 years. Statistical techniques were routinely used by Arab cryptologists after al-Kindi.

2. David Kahn, *The Codebreakers: The Comprehensive History of Secret Communication from Ancient Times to the Internet* (New York: Simon and Schuster, 1996), 99.

3. David Kahn, *The Reader of Gentlemen's Mail: Herbert O. Yardley and the Birth of American Codebreaking* (New Haven, CT: Yale University Press, 2004), xvi. See also William F. Friedman, *Elements of Cryptanalysis* (Laguna Hills, CA: Aegean Park Press, 1976). Friedman's modernization of cryptological terminology in the 1920s gave us the distinction between "cryptography," involving the encipherment of plaintext into cryptogram, and cryptanalysis.

Both cryptography and cryptanalysis are subsumed under the term "cryptology." A cipher, which transposes the letters or symbols of a writing system by tabular, mechanical, or electronic means, is also distinguished from a code, which substitutes word units or groups of word units (for example, abbreviations) for each other; likewise, a distinction is made between enciphering and deciphering, on the one hand, and encoding and decoding, on the other. See Kahn, *Reader of Gentlemen's Mail,* xiv, xvi.

4. On Western philology as a "science of reading" established in Arab universities well before its appearance in Christian Europe, see Edward W. Said, "The Return to Philology," in *Humanism and Democratic Criticism* (New York: Columbia University Press, 2004), 57–84, 58. It has been argued that both Arab philologists and Quranic commentators avoided the application of philological methods to Quranic words, to avoid conflict with traditional interpretations, and that for this reason, Arabic-language philology can be decoupled from scriptural exegesis. See L. Kopf, "Religious Influences on Medieval Arabic Philology," *Studia Islamica,* no. 5 (1956): 33–59, 34, 37.

5. See Kopf, "Religious Influences on Medieval Arabic Philology," 40–45.

6. See Al-Kadi, "Origins of Cryptology," 99, and Joseph von Hammer, *Ancient and Hieroglyphic Characters Explained* (London: W. Bulmer & Co., 1806).

7. Kahn, *Codebreakers,* 97.

8. Broemeling, "Account of Early Statistical Inference," 255. Discovered in 1980 in the Süleymaniye Library archives in Istanbul and subsequently edited and published in Arabic, al-Kindi's treatise is also included in the first volume of English translations prepared by Muḥammad Mrāyātī, Yaḥya Mīr 'Alam, and Muḥammad Ḥassān al-Ṭayyān and published as *Arabic Origins of Cryptology* in 2003. The project has recovered, edited, and published in Arabic and translated and published in bilingual Arabic-English editions a range of texts discovered in the Süleymaniye archives, dating from the ninth to the fourteenth century. See Kathryn A. Schwartz, "Charting Arabic Cryptology's Evolution," *Cryptologia* 33, no. 4 (2009): 297–304; Muḥammad Marāyātī, Yaḥyá Mīr 'Alam, and Muḥammad Ḥassān Ṭayyān, eds., *'Ilm at-Ta'miyah Wa Istikhraj Al-Mu'amma Ind Al-Arab,* vol. 1 (Damascus: Arab Academy of Damascus, 1987); Muḥammad Marāyātī, Yaḥyá Mīr 'Alam, and Muḥammad Ḥassān Ṭayyān, eds., *Series on Arabic Origins of Cryptology* (Riyadh: KFCRIS & KACST, 2003); and Muḥammad Marāyātī, Yaḥyá Mīr 'Alam, and Muḥammad Ḥassān Ṭayyān, eds., *Al-Kindi's Treatise on Cryptanalysis* (Riyadh: KFCRIS & KACST, 2003).

9. Marāyātī, Mīr 'Alam, and Tayyān, *'Ilm at-Ta'miyah Wa Istikhraj Al-Mu'amma Ind Al-Arab,* 216; qtd. in Al-Kadi, "Origins of Cryptology," 107–110. For commentary on this passage, see Al-Kadi, "Origins of Cryptology," 107; Simon Singh, *The Code Book: The Science of Secrecy from Ancient Egypt to Quantum Cryptography* (New York: Anchor, 2000), 19; Broemeling, "Account of Early Statistical Inference," 256.

10. Al-Kadi, "Origins of Cryptology," 101; Broemeling, "Account of Early Statistical Inference," 256. See Blaise Pascal, *Oeuvres Complètes,* ed. Jean Mesnard, vol. 2 (Paris: Desclée de Brouwer, 1970); for an English translation, see David, *Games, Gods, and Gambling.*

11. See Marāyātī, Mīr 'Alam, and Tayyān, *'Ilm at-Ta'miyah Wa Istikhraj Al-Mu'amma Ind Al-Arab,* in Arabic, containing three works by al-Kindi, Ibn Adlan, and Ibn ad-Duraihim, and Marāyātī, Mīr 'Alam, and Tayyān, *Series on Arabic Origins of Cryptology,* especially Marāyātī, Mīr 'Alam, and Tayyān, *Al-Kindi's Treatise on Cryptanalysis* and Muḥammad Marāyātī, Yaḥyá Mīr 'Alam, and Muhammad Hassan Tayyān, eds., *Ibn Ad-Durayhim's Treatise on Cryptanalysis* (Riyadh: KFCRIS & KACST, 2004), for accompanying English translations.

12. See Al-Kadi, "Origins of Cryptology," 97; Kahn, *Codebreakers,* 95.

13. Kahn, *Codebreakers,* 96.

14. See ibid., 98; Al-Kadi, "Origins of Cryptology," 120; Schwartz, "Charting Arabic Cryptology's Evolution," 299.

15. Hugh Craig, "Stylistic Analysis and Authorship Studies," in *Companion to Digital Humanities,* ed. Susan Schreibman, Ray Siemens, and John Unsworth, Blackwell Companions to Literature and Culture (Oxford: Blackwell Publishing Professional, 2004), n.p.

16. Craig, "Stylistic Analysis and Authorship Studies."

17. Sarah Stever Gravelle, "Lorenzo Valla's Comparison of Latin and Greek and the Humanist Background," *Bibliothèque d'Humanisme et Renaissance* 44, no. 2 (1982): 269–289, 271. On these points, see also Donald R. Kelley, *Foundations of Modern Historical Scholarship: Language, Law, and History in the French Renaissance* (New York: Columbia University Press, 1970), 4 and 21; Lodi Nauta, "Lorenzo Valla and Quattrocento Scepticism," *Vivarium* 44, nos. 2–3 (2006): 375–395, 377; Harold J. Grimm, "Lorenzo Valla's Christianity," *Church History* 18, no. 2 (1949): 75–88, 79.

18. Djelal Kadir, *Memos from the Besieged City: Lifelines for Cultural Sustainability* (Stanford, CA: Stanford University Press, 2011), 77.

19. On this "war between two cultures," see Kelley, *Foundations of Modern Historical Scholarship,* 6. On the displacement of logic in *studia humanitatis,* see ibid., 19; Christopher S. Celenza, "Lorenzo Valla, 'Paganism,' and Orthodoxy," *MLN* 119, no. 1 (2004): S66–S87, S70.

20. On these points, see Celenza, "Lorenzo Valla," S72, and Christopher S. Celenza, "Lorenzo Valla's Radical Philology: The 'Preface' to the Annotations to the New Testament in Context," *Journal of Medieval and Early Modern Studies* 42, no. 2 (2012): 365–394, 357, 366, 373. Celenza discusses the Carolingian reform of the manuscript editing of sacred texts and the manuscript studies of scholars like Roger Bacon (1214–1294) and Nicholas of Lyra (1270–1349). The characterization of Valla as the *"enfant terrible* of phi-

lology," is Kelley's; see Kelley, *Foundations of Modern Historical Scholarship*, 26.

21. On these points, see Kelley, *Foundations of Modern Historical Scholarship*, 34–37, and Gravelle, "Lorenzo Valla's Comparison," 269.

22. Kelley, *Foundations of Modern Historical Scholarship*, 33; see also Letizia A. Panizza, "Lorenzo Valla's de Vero Falsoque Bono, Lactantius and Oratorical Scepticism," *Journal of the Warburg and Courtauld Institutes* 41 (1978): 76–107, 77.

23. See Lorenzo Valla, *De Falso Credita et Ementita Constantini Donatione*, ed. Wolfram Setz (Weimar: Böhlau, 1976); Lorenzo Valla, *The Treatise of Lorenzo Valla on the Donation of Constantine*, trans. Christopher B. Coleman (New York: Russell & Russell, 1971).

24. On these points, see Celenza, "Lorenzo Valla, 'Paganism,' and Orthodoxy," S76, S82, and William J. Connell, "Lorenzo Valla's Oratio on the Pseudo-Donation of Constantine: Dissent and Innovation in Early Renaissance Humanism," *Journal of the History of Ideas* 57, no. 1 (1996): 1–7, 16.

25. Grimm, "Lorenzo Valla's Christianity," 77.

26. See Kahn, *Codebreakers*, 73, 91–92, 125ff, 140ff. See also Singh, *Code Book*, 26; Gerhard F. Strasser, "The Rise of Cryptology in the European Renaissance," in *The History of Information Security: A Comprehensive Handbook*, ed. Karl de Leeuw and Jan Bergstra (Amsterdam: Elsevier, 2007), 277–325, 281–283.

27. On the "black chambers," see Karl de Leeuw, "Introduction," in de Leeuw and Bergstra, *History of Information Security*, 1–25, 12.

28. Kahn, *Codebreakers*, 163–164, quoted with omissions.

29. See Strasser, "Rise of Cryptology in the European Renaissance"; Leeuw, "Introduction," 329.

30. See Kahn, *Codebreakers*, 108. Singh took a third position, arguing that "revival in the arts, sciences and scholarship during the Renaissance nurtured the capacity for cryptography" and considering the possibility that knowledge of cryptanalysis found its way to Renaissance Europe from Arabic sources, but considering it more likely "independently discovered in Europe." See Singh, *Code Book*, 27.

31. See Umberto Eco, *The Search for the Perfect Language*, trans. James Fentress (Oxford, UK: Blackwell, 1995), 201–203; W. J. Hutchins, *Machine Translation: Past, Present, Future* (Chichester, UK: Ellis Horwood Ltd., 1986), 22.

32. Strasser, "Rise of Cryptology in the European Renaissance," 322.

33. Eco, *Search for the Perfect Language*, 191. The phrases "intellectual disease" and "sense of universal mystery" are Don Cameron Allen's; see Don Cameron Allen, "The Predecessors of Champollion," *Proceedings of the American Philosophical Society* 104, no. 5 (1960): 527–547, 529–530.

34. Eco, *Search for the Perfect Language*, 192.

35. Michel Despland, "Two Types of Scholarship: The Contrast Between Anquetil-Duperron and Champollion," *Historical Reflections/Réflexions Historiques* 20, no. 3 (1994): 413–433, 427.

36. Kahn, *Codebreakers*, 908–909. The phrase "four hundred years of mistakes and illusions" is Don Cameron Allen's; see Allen, "Predecessors of Champollion," 527.

37. Kahn, *Codebreakers*, 181, 194.

38. Ibid., 190.

39. Ibid., 836.

40. Singh, *Code Book*, 66.

41. Kahn, *Codebreakers*, 854.

42. See ibid., 189, 221ff; Singh, *Code Book*, 79–82.

43. Henry Veggian, "Mercury of the Waves: Modern Cryptology and United States Literature" (PhD diss., University of Pittsburgh, 2005), 326–327.

44. See Veggian, "Mercury of the Waves," 36, 327.

45. Kahn, *Codebreakers*, 232–233.

46. See ibid., 348; Singh, *Code Book*, 103–104; Veggian, "Mercury of the Waves," 329.

47. See Veggian, "Mercury of the Waves," 327–329.

48. Singh, *Code Book*, 111.

49. Kahn, *Codebreakers*, 275.

50. Ibid., 274.

51. Ibid., 309–310.

52. See Ibid., 352; Veggian, "Mercury of the Waves," 150, 182, 330.

53. Veggian, "Mercury of the Waves," 332.

54. For the preceding passages, see ibid., 37–38, 333.

55. See James Turner, *Philology: The Forgotten Origins of the Modern Humanities* (Princeton, NJ: Princeton University Press, 2015), 210–229.

56. T. C. Mendenhall, "The Characteristic Curves of Composition," *Science* 9, no. 214S (1887): 238–239.

57. Mendenhall, "Characteristic Curves of Composition," 238.

58. Marjorie Garber, *Shakespeare's Ghost Writers: Literature as Uncanny Causality* (New York: Routledge, 2010), 5; see also Shawn Rosenheim, *The Cryptographic Imagination: Secret Writing from Edgar Poe to the Internet* (Baltimore, MD: Johns Hopkins University Press, 1997), 9–10.

59. See Alfred Harbage, "Shakespeare as Culture Hero," *Huntington Library Quarterly* 27, no. 3 (1964): 217. Susanna Ashton notes that "Bibliographer W. H. Wyman compiled almost 500 titles on the subject by 1890, most of which were periodical articles. Interest in the bibliography alone was such that Wyman published his compilations regularly in *Poet-Lore* and *Shakespeariana*. At the end of the century, and perhaps hoping to close the issue once and for all, John Fiske wrote an exasperated article for the *Atlantic Monthly* titled: 'Forty

Years of Bacon-Shakespeare Folly.'" Susanna Ashton, "Who Brings Home the Bacon? Shakespeare and Turn-of-the-Century American Authorship," *American Periodicals* 6 (1996): 5.

60. For the phrase "anti-Shakespearean bomb," see Harbage, "Shakespeare as Culture Hero," 222–223.

61. See Nancy Glazener, "Print Culture as an Archive of Dissent: Or, Delia Bacon and the Case of the Missing Hamlet," *American Literary History* 19, no. 2 (2007): 329–349, 330 and 339; and Ashton, "Who Brings Home the Bacon?" 12.

62. Glazener, "Print Culture as an Archive of Dissent," 340.

63. See Delia Bacon, "William Shakespeare and His Plays: An Inquiry Concerning Them," *Putnam's Monthly Magazine of American Literature, Science, and Art* 7, no. 37 (1856). On these points, see Ashton, "Who Brings Home the Bacon?" 1, 7–8; Glazener, "Print Culture as an Archive of Dissent," 331–333.

64. Rosenheim, *Cryptographic Imagination*, 10.

65. See W. K. Wimsatt, "What Poe Knew about Cryptography," *PMLA* 58, no. 3 (1943): 754–779, 778.

66. John T. Irwin, "The Symbol of the Hieroglyphics in the American Renaissance," *American Quarterly* 26, no. 2 (1974): 103–126, 106; see also John T. Irwin, *American Hieroglyphics: The Symbol of the Egyptian Hieroglyphics in the American Renaissance* (New Haven, CT: Yale University Press, 1980), 5–6.

67. Irwin, "Symbol of the Hieroglyphics in the American Renaissance," 125–126.

68. The phrase "elitist prejudice" appears in Glazener, "Print Culture as an Archive of Dissent," 333.

69. See Veggian, "Mercury of the Waves," 16, 72. See also Edward H. Abrahams, "Ignatius Donnelly and the Apocalyptic Style," *Minnesota History* 46, no. 3 (1978): 102–111, 107.

70. Abrahams, "Ignatius Donnelly and the Apocalyptic Style," 107.

71. On these points, see Abrahams, "Ignatius Donnelly and the Apocalyptic Style," 103; J. Withayne Baker, "Populist Themes in the Fiction of Ignatius Donnelly," *American Studies* 14, no. 2 (1973): 65–83, 78–79; Kahn, *Codebreakers*, 878.

72. Kahn, *Codebreakers*, 878.

73. Veggian, "Mercury of the Waves," 181.

74. Zachary Lesser, "Mystic Ciphers: Shakespeare and Intelligent Design: A Response to Nancy Glazener," *American Literary History* 19, no. 2 (2007): 350–356, 350, 352.

75. On this point, see Veggian, "Mercury of the Waves," 139–140.

76. Ibid., 144.

77. "One tenacious researcher for the *Popular Science Monthly*," Ashton notes, "thoughtfully created a 'mechanical solution' to the problem in 1901. He assessed the frequency of certain words in all of Bacon's and Shakespeare's

works in order to note the frequency of certain key words and thus make conclusions about the identity of the author." See Ashton, "Who Brings Home the Bacon?" 11.

78. Veggian, "Mercury of the Waves," 75, 151.

79. Rosenheim, *Cryptographic Imagination*, 144; Veggian, "Mercury of the Waves," 146. Veggian cited "archival evidence in the Bacon Cipher Collection" of the New York Public Library "to corroborate this claim that the Riverbank Laboratory was working for the United States government" (147).

80. Veggian, "Mercury of the Waves," 146.

81. See Kahn, *Codebreakers*, 372.

82. Rosenheim, *Cryptographic Imagination*, 144. "NSA" here is the U.S. National Security Agency.

83. See Kahn, *Codebreakers*, 263, 277, 305, and Singh, *Code Book*, 104–106.

84. Kahn, *Codebreakers*, 352.

85. Veggian, "Mercury of the Waves," 146, 150, 152.

86. Ibid., 162.

87. Kahn, *Codebreakers*, 384, 410.

88. Veggian, "Mercury of the Waves," 163.

89. Ibid., 129.

90. See Ibid., 190, 348.

91. Kahn, *Codebreakers*, 973.

92. Ibid., 436.

93. See Singh, *Code Book*, 160.

94. See Kahn, *Codebreakers*, 898.

95. Carol S. Gruber, *Mars and Minerva: World War I and the Uses of the Higher Learning in America* (Baton Rouge: Louisiana State University Press, 1975), 110.

96. Veggian, "Mercury of the Waves," 351.

97. See Ibid., 350.

98. Kahn, *Codebreakers*, 348.

99. John M. Manly, "Introductory Note," in *New Methods for the Study of Literature* (Chicago: University of Chicago Press, 1927), ix–xii, xii.

100. Edith Rickert, *New Methods for the Study of Literature* (Chicago: The University of Chicago press, 1927), v–vi.

101. Robin Winks, *Cloak and Gown: Scholars in the Secret War, 1939–1961* (New York: William Morrow & Co., 1987), 472.

102. Winks, *Cloak and Gown*, 74, 79.

103. Ibid., 131–133, 139.

104. Ibid., 300.

105. Ibid., 255.

106. See Ibid., 307–308.

107. Rosenheim, *Cryptographic Imagination*, 159.

108. Winks mentioned the following as recommended by Pearson in 1948: "Eugene Waith, back in the Yale English department . . . Edward Weissmiller, then teaching English at Pomona College; his old flatmate in London, Calvin Tenney, teaching French at Wesleyan University in Connecticut; H. Donaldson Jordan, the chairman of the Department of History at Clark University, a specialist in British history; and Reginald Phelps, a highly regarded associate Dean of Harvard College" (Winks, *Cloak and Gown*, 315).

109. Ibid., 114–115, 316–317.

110. Ibid., 317; Rosenheim, *Cryptographic Imagination*, 169. "As if it were the CIA" are the words of Robert Dallzell, a 1966 Yale PhD in American Studies, which Rosenheim cites from a personal communication.

111. See Kahn, *Codebreakers*, 563.

112. Ibid., 576.

113. Ibid., 149.

114. Ibid., 744, citing a telephone interview with Shannon conducted November 27, 1961.

115. Ibid., 111, 111n.

116. Ibid., 739.

117. Ibid., 739, 111.

3. Machine Translation

1. As a product of modernity in this sense, MT research also represents a narrowing or focalization of the more amphibolous (or tenebrous) cultural legacy of the earliest known constructed languages, such as Hildegard of Bingen's Lingua Ignota, recorded in the twelfth century, and Bâleybelen (Balaibalan), created by Faẓlullāh of Asterābād in the fourteenth century or by Muhyî-i Gülşenî in the sixteenth century. As John Hutchins tells it, the demise of Latin and the rise of Cartesian thought led to the first modern proposals for universal languages and for mechanical translation methods, in seventeenth-century rationalism. Descartes proposed a cipher language in his correspondence, and Leibniz in his *characteristica universalis*, while mechanical dictionaries were published by Beck, Kircher, and Joachim Becher between 1657 and 1661 and Wilkins's *Essay towards a Real Character and a Philosophical Language* (1668) imagined a logical interlingua in the form of a "universal classification of concepts and entities." Both the concept of a universal language and the concept of an interlingua, Hutchins suggests, inspired MT research, although no one actually proposed the construction of a *machine* (rather than a mechanical *method*) for translating until Troyanskii in 1933. See W. J. Hutchins, *Machine Translation: Past, Present, Future* (Chichester, UK: Ellis Horwood Ltd., 1986), 22–23.

2. Hutchins, *Machine Translation,* 22.

3. Troyanskii was granted a patent in 1933 for what he described as a new method of typesetting "while translating from one language into another or several other simultaneously," but his subsequent proposals to the Academy of Sciences between 1939 and 1944 apparently garnered no support. See John Hutchins and Evgenii Lovtskii, "Petr Petrovich Troyanskii (1854–1950): A Forgotten Pioneer of Mechanical Translation," *Machine Translation,* no. 15 (2000): 188, 191. Hutchins and Lovtskii provide translations of two texts from a 1959 collection of Troyanskii's papers: the 1933 patent application and the 1947 paper described below.

4. Ibid., 196–198.

5. Ibid., 204. For the Russian original of Troyanskii's paper, see I. K. Bel'skaya, L. N. Korolev, and D. Yu. Panov, eds., *Perevodnaja mashina P. P. Trojanskogo: sbornik materialov o perevodnoj mashine dlja perevoda s odnogo jazyka na drugie, predlozhennoj P. P. Trojanskim v 1933* (Moscow: Izd. Akad. Nauk SSSR, 1959), 5–27.

6. Hutchins and Lovtskii, "Petr Petrovich Troyanskii (1854–1950)," 204. Hutchins and Lovtskii note the "ideals of internationalism" in Troyanskii's work, and suggest also that in imagining the way his device would work, "like many others he was inspired in part by the description of a somewhat similar machine in Swift's *Gulliver's Travels*" (referring to the "Literary Engine" described in the third section, "Voyage to Laputa"), which they note was popular in Russia, including in the form of a film version made in the 1930s (198). Hutchins and Lovtskii also observe that "what was perhaps most important" about Troyanskii's proposal "was the monolingual aspect of his method, the fact that translation and communication could be achieved without knowledge of source or target languages" (214).

7. Warren Weaver, "Translation," in *Machine Translation of Languages: Fourteen Essays,* ed. William N. Locke and A. Donald Booth (Cambridge, MA: MIT Press, 1955), 15–23, 18.

8. A. M. Turing, "Intelligent Machinery" (London, UK: National Physical Laboratory, Mathematics Division, 1948), 9. While it may strike us as naive today, Weaver's imagination of Russian as "encoded English" was echoed—if in far less deliberately speculative form—in the presumptions of many early studies. Describing results of a preliminary study of Russian-to-English MT, Kenneth E. Harper asserted "that a word-for-word translation of Russian is adequate for understanding," while admitting that "it is desirable for certain idiomatic constructions to be rearranged in the English translation." Stating that his study concerns only the translation of scientific writing in Russian, as a purposefully "limited sphere" within which "our mechanistic and perhaps naïve approach is valid," Harper justified such circumscription by asserting that sentence structure in scientific Russian was much

closer to English than were other forms of Russian prose, as scientific Russian took less advantage of the normally flexible word order that an inflected language permits. See Kenneth E. Harper, "A Preliminary Study of Russian," in *Machine Translation of Languages: Fourteen Essays,* ed. William N. Locke and A. Donald Booth (Cambridge, MA: MIT Press, 1955), 66–67. The "basic sentence structure of scientific Russian" was in fact "quite similar to that of English," and while this offered no guarantee of intelligibility, "the prerequisites of intelligibility exist," and it can be surmised, Harper suggested, that "Russian text will be intelligible in English when the word order is left undisturbed" (68). Scientists writing in Russian tended to avoid the imperative verb form, Harper claimed, or the first or second person present tense; nouns in the dative case were also quite rare, as were homographs, the problem of which was "not serious in specialized scientific discourse, where it is unlikely that more than one meaning is applicable" (74).

9. Weaver, "Translation," 16.

10. See C. P. Snow, *The Two Cultures and the Scientific Revolution* (New York: Cambridge University Press, 1961).

11. As Wiener put it: "There were two converging streams of ideas that brought me into cybernetics. One of them was the fact that in the last war . . . I tried to see if I could find some niche in the war effort. In that particular problem, I looked for something to do, and found it in connection with automatic computing machines. . . . The other thing which led me to this work was the problem that I actually got put into a war work. It turned out that at that time Professor [Vannevar] Bush did not feel that this contribution was immediate enough to have been effective in the last war. So I looked around for another thing, and the great question that was being discussed at that time was antiaircraft defense." See Norbert Wiener, "Men, Machines, and the World About: The Linsly R. Williams Memorial Lecture," in *Medicine and Science,* ed. Iago Galdston, Lectures to the Laity 16 (New York: International Universities Press, 1954), 13.

12. Andrew D. Booth, Leonard Brandwood, and J. P. Cleave, "Historical Introduction," in *Mechanical Resolution of Linguistic Problems* (New York: Academic Press, 1958), 1–7, 1.

13. For the passages quoted here, see Weaver, "Translation," 15–17.

14. Ibid., 18.

15. For this and the preceding passages quoted, see ibid., 20–23.

16. Hutchins, *Machine Translation,* 30.

17. Victor H. Yngve, "Syntax and the Problem of Multiple Meaning," in *Machine Translation of Languages: Fourteen Essays,* ed. William N. Locke and A. Donald Booth (Cambridge, MA: MIT Press, 1955), 208–226, 208.

18. Hutchins, *Machine Translation,* 38, 61–62. Lew R. Micklesen recalls that work for which Reifler obtained grants in 1952 and 1953 "apparently . . . did not

materialize. I never saw it or heard Reifler mention it." See Lew R. Micklesen, "Erwin Reifler and Machine Translation at the University of Washington," in *Early Years in Machine Translation: Memoirs and Biographies of Pioneers,* ed. W. John Hutchins (Amsterdam: John Benjamins, 2000), 26–27.

19. Micklesen, "Erwin Reifler and Machine Translation," 24.

20. For the passages quoted, see Erwin Reifler, "The Mechanical Determination of Meaning," in *Machine Translation of Languages: Fourteen Essays,* ed. William N. Locke and A. Donald Booth (Cambridge, MA: MIT Press, 1955), 136–164, 136–144.

21. For the quoted passages, see William N. Locke and A. Donald Booth, "Historical Introduction," in *Machine Translation of Languages: Fourteen Essays,* ed. William N. Locke and A. Donald Booth (Cambridge, MA: MIT Press, 1955), 1–14, 9–14.

22. For the quoted passages, see ibid., 11–14.

23. Léon E. Dostert, "The Georgetown-I.B.M. Experiment," in *Machine Translation of Languages: Fourteen Essays,* ed. William N. Locke and A. Donald Booth (Cambridge, MA: MIT Press, 1955), 124–135, 126.

24. For the quoted passages, see ibid., 129–134.

25. Muriel Vasconcellos, "The Georgetown Project and Léon Dostert: Recollections of a Young Assistant," in *Early Years in Machine Translation: Memoirs and Biographies of Pioneers,* ed. W. John Hutchins (Amsterdam: John Benjamins, 2000), 87–96, 94–95.

26. Anthony G. Oettinger, "Machine Translation at Harvard," in *Early Years in Machine Translation: Memoirs and Biographies of Pioneers,* ed. W. John Hutchins (Amsterdam: John Benjamins, 2000), 73–86, 79. Vasconcellos was hired as Dostert's assistant at Georgetown upon enrolling as an undergraduate in the Institute of Languages and Linguistics and held the position for five years. She recounts Dostert's emigration from Longwy, France, to the United States in 1920 and his career as a student of philosophy and languages and a professor of French at Georgetown until 1939, his enlistment as a major in the U.S. Army, and service as personal interpreter to Eisenhower and liaison officer to De Gaulle, and his organization of languages services for the Nuremberg trials. See Vasconcellos, "The Georgetown Project and Léon Dostert," 90. She closes by reflecting that "In recalling my years on the project, I am impressed by how little has changed in the last four decades," noting that she now realizes how complex the problems of MT are, and that the "chaotic and antagonistic" atmosphere of Georgetown in the 1950s was "a blueprint for the future" (95).

27. For the quoted passages, see Yehoshua Bar-Hillel, "Idioms," in *Machine Translation of Languages: Fourteen Essays,* ed. William N. Locke and A. Donald Booth (Cambridge, MA: MIT Press, 1955), 183–193, 185, 191.

28. For the quoted passages, see William E. Bull, Charles Africa, and Daniel Teichroew, "Some Problems of the 'Word,'" in *Machine Translation of Languages: Fourteen Essays,* ed. William N. Locke and A. Donald Booth (Cambridge, MA: MIT Press, 1955), 76–103, 98–101.

29. For the quoted passages, see ibid., 95–98.

30. Hutchins, *Machine Translation,* 58–59.

31. Ibid., 89, 181.

32. James W. Perry, "A Practical Development Problem," in *Machine Translation of Languages: Fourteen Essays,* ed. William N. Locke and A. Donald Booth (Cambridge, MA: MIT Press, 1955), 174–182, 182.

33. For the quoted passages, see Anthony G. Oettinger, "The Design of an Automatic Russian-English Technical Dictionary," in *Machine Translation of Languages: Fourteen Essays,* ed. William N. Locke and A. Donald Booth (Cambridge, MA: MIT Press, 1955), 47–75, 50–51.

34. Hutchins, *Machine Translation,* 16.

35. A. D. Booth and R. H. Richens, "Some Methods of Mechanized Translation," in *Machine Translation of Languages: Fourteen Essays,* ed. William N. Locke and A. Donald Booth (Cambridge, MA: MIT Press, 1955), 24–46, 35.

36. Booth, Brandwood, and Cleave, "Historical Introduction," v.

37. Michael Levison, "The Computer in Literary Studies," in *Machine Translation,* ed. A. D. Booth (Amsterdam: North-Holland, 1967), 173–194, 193.

38. Hutchins, *Machine Translation,* 151.

39. Émile Delavenay, *An Introduction to Machine Translation* (New York: Frederick A. Praeger, 1960). For the French original, see Émile Delavenay, *La Machine à Traduire* (Paris: Presses Universitaires de France, 1959). Because Delavenay produced the English translation himself, supplementing it with additional materials, I refer here exclusively to the English edition.

40. For the quoted passages, see Delavenay, *Introduction to Machine Translation,* 12, 18, 102.

41. For the quoted passages, see ibid., 106, 108, 109–110, 113, 116–117.

42. For the quoted passages, see Delavenay, *Introduction to Machine Translation,* 1, 3, 4.

43. Ibid., 3.

44. Ibid., 8, 9, 16, 23.

45. Ibid., 32, 36.

46. Ibid., 47, 79, 80.

47. Ibid., 89, 90, 94, 98–101.

48. A. D. Booth, ed., *Machine Translation* (Amsterdam: North-Holland, 1967), vii.

49. Hutchins, *Machine Translation,* 157.

50. See ibid., 157–163; Oettinger, "Machine Translation at Harvard," 82; Vasconcellos, "The Georgetown Project and Léon Dostert," 94–95.

51. Oettinger, "Machine Translation at Harvard," 83.

52. Ibid.," 80.

53. ALPAC, "Language and Machines: Computers in Translations and Linguistics. A Report by the Automatic Language Processing Advisory Committee, Division of Behavioral Sciences, National Academy of Sciences, National Research Council" (Washington, DC: National Academy of Sciences, National Research Council, 1966), 11, 16.

54. Ibid., 19.

55. Ibid., 5.

56. Robert T. Beyer, "Hurdling the Language Barrier," *Physics Today* 18, no. 1 (1965), qtd. in ALPAC, "Language and Machines," 28.

57. Hutchins, *Machine Translation,* 167-169.

58. See John Hutchins, "ALPAC: The (in)famous Report," *MT News International,* no. 14 (1996): 9-12.

59. Ida Rhodes, "The Importance of the Glossary Storage in Machine Translation," in *Machine Translation,* ed. A. D. Booth (Amsterdam: North-Holland, 1967), 429-449, 435.

60. Rhodes, "Importance of Glossary Storage," 437.

61. Victor H. Yngve, "MT at M.I.T. 1965," in *Machine Translation,* ed. A. D. Booth (Amsterdam: North-Holland, 1967), 450-523, 500.

62. O. S. Kulagina and I. A. Mel'cuk, "Automatic Translation: Some Theoretical Aspects and the Design of a Translation System," in *Machine Translation,* ed. A. D. Booth (Amsterdam: North-Holland, 1967), 137-171, 146.

63. Hutchins, *Machine Translation,* 178.

64. D. Arnold et al., *Machine Translation: An Introductory Guide* (Manchester, UK: NCC Blackwell, 1994), 14-15.

65. Hutchins, *Machine Translation,* 12.

66. Makoto Nagao, *Machine Translation: How Far Can It Go?* trans. Norman D. Cook (Oxford, UK: Oxford University Press, 1989), 4.

67. Nagao, *Machine Translation,* 33.

68. See Arnold et al., *Machine Translation.*

69. Ibid., 191.

70. Hutchins, *Machine Translation,* 331.

4. Cryptophilology, II

1. D. M. Burton, "Automated Concordances and Word Indexes: The Fifties," *Computers and the Humanities* 15, no. 1 (1981): 1-14, 5.

2. Joan Smith, "Some Thoughts on Literacy and Linguistic Computing," *Hispania* 68, no. 3 (1985): 676-682, 678.

3. Burton, "Automated Concordances and Word Indexes: The Fifties," 5-6.

4. See William N. Locke and A. Donald Booth, eds., *Machine Translation of Languages: Fourteen Essays* (Cambridge, MA: MIT Press, 1955), and A. D. Booth, ed., *Machine Translation* (Amsterdam: North-Holland, 1967).

5. Andrew D. Booth, Leonard Brandwood, and J. P. Cleave, "Historical Introduction," in *Mechanical Resolution of Linguistic Problems* (New York: Academic Press Inc., 1958), 1–7, v.

6. Booth, Brandwood, and Cleave, "Historical Introduction," 6.

7. Roberto Busa, "Informatics and New Philology," *Computers and the Humanities* 24, no. 5/6 (1990): 339–343, 341.

8. John W. Ellison, "Computers and the Testaments," in *Computers in Humanistic Research: Readings and Perspectives,* ed. Edmund A. Bowles (Englewood Cliffs, NJ: Prentice-Hall, 1967), 160–169, 160, 166.

9. Ellison, "Computers and the Testaments," 163–164. Oettinger describes how Aiken, who had received Warren Weaver's 1949 memo, gave him the keys to a laboratory while he was still an undergraduate at Harvard in 1949, encouraging him to pursue work on MT and introducing him to I. A. Richards and Roman Jakobson, who was then heading the Slavic Department and sent graduate students in Russian linguistics to work on the project. Noam Chomsky's wife Carol Chomsky, Oettinger notes, did research and programming work, as did Sylvia Plath's brother Warren Plath, who would later move on to IBM. See Anthony G. Oettinger, "Machine Translation at Harvard," in *Early Years in Machine Translation: Memoirs and Biographies of Pioneers,* ed. W. John Hutchins (Amsterdam: John Benjamins, 2000), 73–86.

10. See Alberto Melloni, "Church History and the Computer," *Computers and the Humanities* 24, no. 5/6 (1990): 393–395, 393.

11. See Burton, "Automated Concordances and Word Indexes: The Fifties," 1. Burton notes a report that "IBM in New York was skeptical about [Busa's] proposal and that it was IBM Italia who provided Busa with technical assistance, card material, and machines."

12. See Thomas N. Winter, "Roberto Busa, S. J., and the Invention of the Machine-Generated Concordance," *Classical Bulletin* 75, no. 1 (1999): 3–20, 8, 11.

13. Burton, "Automated Concordances and Word Indexes: The Fifties," 2–3.

14. See ibid., 4; Dolores M. Burton, "Automated Concordances and Word Indexes: The Process, the Programs, and the Products," *Computers and the Humanities* 15, no. 3 (1981): 139–154, 143.

15. Burton, "Automated Concordances and Word Indexes: The Fifties," 6–7.

16. Ibid.

17. See ibid., 9–10, and Dolores M. Burton, "Automated Concordances and Word Indexes: The Early Sixties and the Early Centers," *Computers and the Humanities* 15, no. 2 (1981): 83–100, 83.

18. See Burton, "Automated Concordances and Word Indexes: The Process," 146–150.

19. See Ibid., 146, and Burton, "Automated Concordances and Word Indexes: The Early Sixties," 96.

20. Ellison, "Computers and the Testaments," 168.

21. Seeibid., 167.

22. See Burton, "Automated Concordances and Word Indexes: The Process," 143–144.

23. Burton, "Automated Concordances and Word Indexes: The Fifties," 4.

24. Roberto Busa, "Half a Century of Literary Computing: Towards a 'New' Philology," *Historical Social Research* 17, no. 2 (1992): 124–133, 125.

25. Ellison, "Computers and the Testaments," 168.

26. Busa, "Half a Century of Literary Computing," 3. See Norbert Wiener, *God and Golem, Inc.: A Comment on Certain Points Where Cybernetics Impinges on Religion* (Cambridge, MA: MIT Press, 1966).

27. Busa, "Half a Century of Literary Computing," 4.

28. Ibid., 5.

29. Ibid., 10.

30. Ibid., 2.

31. Busa, "Informatics and New Philology," 339.

32. Busa, "Half a Century of Literary Computing," 5.

33. Ibid., 2.

34. See, for example, Efstathios Stamatatos, "A Survey of Modern Authorship Attribution Methods," *Journal of the American Society for Information Science and Technology* 60, no. 3 (2009): 538–556, 538, and Moshe Koppel, Jonathan Schler, and Shlomo Argamon, "Computational Methods in Authorship Attribution," *Journal of the American Society for Information Science and Technology* 60, no. 1 (2009): 9–26, 10.

35. See T. C. Mendenhall, "The Characteristic Curves of Composition," *Science* 9, no. 214S (1887): 237–249, and Koppel, Schler, and Argamon, "Computational Methods in Authorship Attribution," 10.

36. Michael Brennan and Rachel Greenstadt, "Practical Attacks against Authorship Recognition Techniques," in *Proceedings of the Twenty-First Conference on Innovative Applications of Artificial Intelligence (IAAI),* Pasadena, California (2009), 3.

37. See Frederick Mosteller and David L. Wallace, *Inference and Disputed Authorship: The Federalist* (Reading, MA: Addison-Wesley, 1964).

38. Antonio Miranda-García and Javier Calle-Martín, "The Authorship of the Disputed Federalist Papers with an Annotated Corpus," *English Studies* 93, no. 3 (2012): 371–390, 371; Patrick Juola, "Authorship Attribution," *Foundations and Trends in Information Retrieval* 1, no. 3 (2007): 233–334, 242.

39. For this and the previous quotation, see Stamatatos, "A Survey of Modern Authorship Attribution Methods," 538.

40. Juola, "Authorship Attribution," 242.

41. David I. Holmes, "The Evolution of Stylometry in Humanities Scholarship," *Literary and Linguistic Computing* 13, no. 3 (1998): 111–117, 112.

42. Frederick Mosteller, "Who Wrote the Disputed Federalist Papers, Hamilton or Madison?" in *The Pleasures of Statistics,* ed. Stephen E. Fienberg, David C. Hoaglin, and Judith M. Tanur (New York: Springer, 2010), 47–67, 47.

43. Patrick Juola, "Large-Scale Experiments in Authorship Attribution," *English Studies* 93, no. 3 (2012): 275–283, 275.

44. See David I. Holmes, "Authorship Attribution," *Computers and the Humanities* 28, no. 2 (1994): 87–106, 98.

45. Holmes, "Evolution of Stylometry," 114.

46. See ibid., 113; Koppel, Schler, and Argamon, "Computational Methods in Authorship Attribution," 10; David I. Holmes and Elizabeth D. Johnson, "A Stylometric Foray into the Anglo-Zulu War of 1879," *English Studies* 93, no. 3 (2012): 310–323, 317.

47. Holmes, "Evolution of Stylometry," 114.

48. Juola, "Authorship Attribution," 322.

49. Ibid., 235.

50. Booth, Brandwood, and Cleave, "Historical Introduction," 50.

51. Hugh Craig, "Stylistic Analysis and Authorship Studies," in *Companion to Digital Humanities,* ed. Susan Schreibman, Ray Siemens, and John Unsworth, Blackwell Companions to Literature and Culture (Oxford: Blackwell Publishing Professional, 2004), n. p.

52. Juola, "Authorship Attribution," 238.

53. Moshe Koppel et al., "The 'Fundamental Problem' of Authorship Attribution," *English Studies* 93, no. 3 (2012): 284–291, 284.

54. Efstathios Stamatatos and Moshe Koppel, "Plagiarism and Authorship Analysis: Introduction to the Special Issue," *Language Resources and Evaluation* 45, no. 1 (2011): 1–4, 2.

55. See Juola, "Authorship Attribution," 238–239.

56. Craig, "Stylistic Analysis and Authorship Studies."

57. Holmes, "Evolution of Stylometry," 111.

58. Craig, "Stylistic Analysis and Authorship Studies."

59. See Holmes, "Authorship Attribution," 91.

60. See Michael Brennan, Sadia Afroz, and Rachel Greenstadt, "Adversarial Stylometry: Circumventing Authorship Recognition to Preserve Privacy and Anonymity," *ACM Trans. Inf. Syst. Secur.* 15, no. 3 (2012): 12:1–12:22, 12:2.

61. Louis Tonko Milic, *A Quantitative Approach to the Style of Jonathan Swift* (The Hague: Mouton, 1967), 17.

62. Holmes, "Evolution of Stylometry," 116.

63. Ibid., 167–204; see John F. Burrows, "Computers and the Study of Literature," in *Computers and Written Texts,* ed. Christopher Butler (Oxford: Blackwell, 1992), 167–204.

64. Holmes, "Evolution of Stylometry," 87.

65. Craig, "Stylistic Analysis and Authorship Studies."

66. Holmes, "Evolution of Stylometry," 111.

67. Juola echoes Holmes on this point, suggesting that it is owing to confusion over the application of analyses, the type and rate of error in various studies, and the failure to generate "best practices" that "the field has perhaps had less uptake and general acceptance than is its due" (Juola, "Authorship Attribution," 233).

68. Holmes, "Evolution of Stylometry," 113.

69. Ibid., 112–113.

70. Louis Milic, "Progress in Stylistics: Theory, Statistics, Computers," *Computers and the Humanities* 25, no. 6 (1991): 393–400, 393–394.

71. Ibid., 394.

72. See Stanley E. Fish, *Is There a Text in This Class?: The Authority of Interpretive Communities* (Cambridge, MA: Harvard University Press, 1980).

73. Craig, "Stylistic Analysis and Authorship Studies," 3–4.

74. See Fish, *Is There a Text in This Class,* 69–70.

75. See ibid., 71–72; Craig, "Stylistic Analysis and Authorship Studies," 3; J. F. Burrows, "'An Ocean Where Each Kind . . .': Statistical Analysis and Some Major Determinants of Literary Style," *Computers and the Humanities* 23, no. 4 / 5 (1989): 309–321, 309.

76. Fish, *Is There a Text in This Class,* 73.

77. See Brian Vickers, "Shakespeare and Authorship Studies," *Shakespeare Quarterly* 62, no. 1 (2011): 106–142, 116–118.

78. See, for example, Burrows's rebuttal of Vickers: John Burrows, "A Second Opinion on 'Shakespeare and Authorship Studies in the Twenty-First Century,'" *Shakespeare Quarterly* 63, no. 3 (2012): 355–392, 379.

79. Craig, "Stylistic Analysis and Authorship Studies," 7–8.

80. Ibid., 10–11.

81. Ibid.

82. Milic, "Progress in Stylistics," 399.

83. Joseph Rudman, "The State of Non-Traditional Authorship Attribution Studies—2012: Some Problems and Solutions," *English Studies* 93, no. 3 (2012): 259–274, 262.

84. Juola, "Large-Scale Experiments," 275–276, quoted with omissions.

85. Ibid., 277.

86. See Vickers, "Shakespeare and Authorship Studies," 114–115.

87. See Juola, "Authorship Attribution," 252–253.

88. Craig, "Stylistic Analysis and Authorship Studies," 4.

89. Juola, "Authorship Attribution," 248.

90. Burrows, "'An Ocean Where Each Kind . . . ,'" 309.

91. Juola, "Authorship Attribution," 258.

92. See Ahmed Abbasi and Hsinchun Chen, "Applying Authorship Analysis to Extremist-Group Web Forum Messages," *IEEE Intelligent Systems* 20, no. 5 (2005): 67–75, 68.

93. David Mimno, "Computational Historiography," *Journal on Computing and Cultural Heritage* 5, no. 1 (2012): 1–19, 2.

94. See Graeme Hirst and Vanessa Wei Feng, "Changes in Style in Authors with Alzheimer's Disease," *English Studies* 93, no. 3 (2012): 357–370, 3, 11–12.

95. Melloni, "Church History and the Computer," 394.

96. Rudman, "State of Non-Traditional Authorship Attribution," 262–263, 267.

97. Ibid., 269–270, quoted with omissions.

98. Rudman, "State of Non-Traditional Authorship Attribution," 264–265, 267–270.

99. Juola, "Authorship Attribution," 246, 248; Rudman, "State of Non-Traditional Authorship Attribution," 265.

100. Juola, "Authorship Attribution," 243–244.

101. Ibid., 245.

102. Ibid., 249.

103. Craig, "Stylistic Analysis and Authorship Studies," 4.

104. See Juola, "Authorship Attribution," 250.

105. Anthony Kenny, *The Computation of Style: An Introduction to Statistics for Students of Literature and Humanities* (New York: Pergamon, 1982), 13.

106. Hans Van Halteren et al., "New Machine Learning Methods Demonstrate the Existence of a Human Stylome," *Journal of Quantitative Linguistics* 12, no. 1 (2005): 65–77, 66.

107. Juola, "Authorship Attribution," 239.

108. Holmes, "Authorship Attribution," 99.

109. Hirst and Wei Feng, "Changes in Style," 3.

110. Rudman, "State of Non-Traditional Authorship Attribution," 263.

111. Brennan, Afroz, and Greenstadt, "Adversarial Stylometry," 12:2.

112. The familiar linguistic concept of a word is entirely incongruent with what "word" designates in computing: a unit of data whose size is determined by processor architecture.

113. Mimno, "Computational Historiography," 4.

114. Juola, "Authorship Attribution," 240; see also Holmes, "Authorship Attribution," 88–89.

115. See Vickers, "Shakespeare and Authorship Studies," 116–117.

116. John Burrows and Hugh Craig, "Authors and Characters," *English Studies* 93, no. 3 (2012): 292–309, 307–308.

117. Booth, Brandwood, and Cleave, "Historical Introduction," 51.

118. Juola, "Authorship Attribution," 322.
119. Rudman, "State of Non-Traditional Authorship Attribution," 264.
120. Craig, "Stylistic Analysis and Authorship Studies," 1.
121. Mosteller and Wallace, *Inference and Disputed Authorship*, vii.
122. Craig, "Stylistic Analysis and Authorship Studies," 5.
123. Alvar Ellegård, *A Statistical Method for Determining Authorship: The Junius Letters, 1769–1772* (Göteborg: Acta Universitatis Gothoburgensis, 1962), 79.
124. J. F. Burrows, *Computation into Criticism: A Study of Jane Austen's Novels and an Experiment in Method* (Oxford: Clarendon Press, 1986), 3.
125. Busa, "Informatics and New Philology," 339.
126. Mimno, "Computational Historiography," 1.
127. See ibid., 16–17.
128. Ibid., 16.
129. David Bamman and David Smith, "Extracting Two Thousand Years of Latin from a Million Book Library," *Journal on Computing and Cultural Heritage* 5, no. 1 (2012): 1–13, 2.
130. Robin Winks, *Cloak and Gown: Scholars in the Secret War, 1939–1961* (New York: William Morrow & Co., 1987), 441.
131. Winks, *Cloak and Gown*, 448–449.
132. Stamatatos, "Survey of Modern Authorship Attribution Methods," 539.
133. Abbasi and Chen, "Applying Authorship Analysiss," 67.
134. See David Freed, "The Wrong Man," *Atlantic*, May 2010.
135. Donald W. Foster, *Author Unknown: On the Trail of Anonymous* (New York: Henry Holt, 2000), 3–5, quoted with omissions.
136. See Winks, *Cloak and Gown*, 472.
137. See Shlomo Argamon et al., "Automatically Profiling the Author of an Anonymous Text," *Commun. ACM* 52, no. 2 (2009): 119–123, 119.
138. Juola, "Authorship Attribution," 234; see also Michael Scheuer, *Imperial Hubris: Why the West is Losing the War on Terror* (Washington, DC Brassey's, 2004).
139. Juola, "Authorship Attribution," 323.
140. See Moshe Koppel, Jonathan Schler, and Elisheva Bonchek-Dokow, "Measuring Differentiability: Unmasking Pseudonymous Authors," *Journal of Machine Learning Research* 8 (December 2007): 1261–1276, 1274.
141. For examples of such elision, see Benno Stein, Nedim Lipka, and Peter Prettenhofer, "Intrinsic Plagiarism Analysis," *Language Resources and Evaluation* 45, no. 1 (2011): 63–82, 79, and Ahmed Abbasi and Hsinchun Chen, "Writeprints: A Stylometric Approach to Identity-Level Identification and Similarity Detection in Cyberspace," *ACM Trans. Inf. Syst.* 26, no. 2 (2008): 7:1–7:29, 7:1–7:2. See also Mike Kestemont et al., "Cross-Genre Authorship Verification Using Unmasking," *English Studies* 93, no. 3 (2012): 340–356, 345.

142. Hagen Hirschmann, Anke Lüdeling, and Amir Zeldes, "Measuring and Coding Language Change," *Journal on Computing and Cultural Heritage* 5, no. 1 (2012): 1–16, 1–2.

143. Juola, "Authorship Attribution," 315.

144. Gary Kacmarcik and Michael Gamon, "Obfuscating Document Stylometry to Preserve Author Anonymity," in *Proceedings of the COLING/ACL on Main Conference Poster Sessions,* COLING-ACL '06 (Stroudsburg, PA: Association for Computational Linguistics, 2006), 444–451, 444.

145. Brennan and Greenstadt, "Practical Attacks," 2.

146. Brennan, Afroz, and Greenstadt, "Adversarial Stylometry," 12:21.

147. Burrows and Craig, "Authors and Characters," 356.

148. C. B. Williams, *Style and Vocabulary: Numerical Studies* (London: Griffin, 1970), x–xi.

149. Williams, *Style and Vocabulary,* vii.

150. Gregory Crane and Anke Lüdeling, "Introduction to the Special Issue on Corpus and Computational Linguistics, Philology, and the Linguistic Heritage of Humanity," *Journal of Computing and Cultural Heritage* 5, no. 1 (2012): 1:1–1:5, 1:3; see also Busa, "Informatics and New Philology," and Carlos G. Diuk et al., "A Quantitative Philology of Introspection," *Frontiers in Integrative Neuroscience* 6 (2012).

5. The Digital Humanities and National Security

1. Patricia Cohen, "Digital Keys for Unlocking the Humanities' Riches," *New York Times,* November 17, 2010, http://www.nytimes.com/2010/11/17/arts/17digital.html.

2. Jason B. Jones, "Weekend Reading: Electoral Hangover Edition," *Chronicle of Higher Education, ProfHacker* (November 2010), http://chronicle.com/blogs/profhacker/weekend-reading-electoral-hangover-edition/28467.

3. See Moshe Z. Marvit, "How Crowdworkers Became the Ghosts in the Digital Machine," *Nation,* February 2014.

4. For this and the previous quoted passages, see Cohen, "Digital Keys for Unlocking the Humanities' Riches."

5. Ibid.

6. Patricia Cohen, "Analyzing Literature by Words and Numbers," *New York Times,* December 4, 2010, http://www.nytimes.com/2010/12/04/books/04victorian.html.

7. See Patricia Cohen, "In 500 Billion Words, New Window on Culture," *New York Times,* December 17, 2010, http://www.nytimes.com/2010/12/17/books/17words.html, and Jean-Baptiste Michel et al., "Quantitative Analysis of Culture Using Millions of Digitized Books," *Science* 331, no. 6014 (2011): 176–182.

8. Patricia Cohen, "Giving Literature Virtual Life," *New York Times,* March 22, 2011, http://www.nytimes.com/2011/03/22/books/digital-humanities-boots-up -on-some-campuses.html.

9. Cohen, "Digital Keys for Unlocking the Humanities' Riches."

10. Cohen, "Giving Literature Virtual Life."

11. Cohen, "Digital Keys for Unlocking the Humanities' Riches."

12. William Pannapacker, "Summer Camp for Digital Humanists," *Chronicle of Higher Education* (June 2008), http://chronicle.com/article/Summer-Camp -for-Digital/45865.

13. See William Pannapacker, "The MLA and the Digital Humanities," *Chronicle of Higher Education, Brainstorm* (December 2009), http://chronicle.com /blogPost/The-MLAthe-Digital/19468/. Sometime after September 8, 2015, "The MLA and the Digital Humanities" was permanently removed from the website of *Chronicle of Higher Education.* An Internet Archive Wayback Machine capture of the web page can be viewed at https://web.archive.org /web/20150908020431/http://chronicle.com/blogPost/The-MLAthe-Digital /19468/.

14. Pannapacker, "The MLA and the Digital Humanities."

15. See William Pannapacker, "Pannapacker at MLA: Digital Humanities Triumphant?" *Chronicle of Higher Education, Brainstorm* (January 2011), https:// chronicle.com/blogs/brainstorm/pannapacker-at-mla-digital-humanities -triumphant/30915. The 126th MLA convention was held in Los Angeles on January 6–9, 2011, and was the first convention to be held in January instead of December. As a consequence, no convention was held in 2010.

16. Ibid.

17. Ibid.

18. See Cohen, "Analyzing Literature by Words and Numbers." See also Google Inc., "Our Commitment to the Digital Humanities," *Official Google Blog,* July 2010, http://googleblog.blogspot.com.tr/2010/07/our-commitment-to -digital-humanities.html.

19. Cohen, "Analyzing Literature by Words and Numbers."

20. As of this writing, the URL https://research.google.com/university/relations/, which once provided information about Google's Digital Humanities Awards program, redirects to https://research.google.com/research-outreach .html#research-outreach/faculty-engagement. On that page, among the descriptions of "Faculty Research Awards," "Focused Research Awards," and "Visiting Faculty Program," one can find no mention of "digital humanities" or any mention of the digital humanities awards made in 2010. An Internet Archive Wayback Machine capture of that page on May 27, 2012, lists "Digital Humanities Awards" under the heading "Closed Programs." See https://web .archive.org/web/20120527083017/http://research.google.com/university /relations/.

21. William Pannapacker, "'No DH, No Interview,'" *Chronicle of Higher Education*, July 2012, https://chronicle.com/article/No-DH-No-Interview/132959/.

22. See Brian Lennon, "'Digital Humanities' by the Numbers," http://bitfragment.net/dh/.

23. William Pannapacker, "On 'The Dark Side of the Digital Humanities,'" *Chronicle of Higher Education, The Conversation* (January 2013), http://chronicle.com/blogs/conversation/2013/01/05/on-the-dark-side-of-the-digital-humanities/.

24. Matthew Kirschenbaum, "What Is 'Digital Humanities,' and Why are They Saying Such Terrible Things about It?" *Differences* 25, no. 1 (2014): 46–63.

25. Richard Grusin, "The Dark Side of the Digital Humanities—Part 2," *Thinking C21: Center for 21st Century Studies*, January 2013, http://www.c21uwm.com/2013/01/09/dark-side-of-the-digital-humanities-part-2/. On #transformDH and its commitment to "transformative critique" of the digital humanities movement, see in particular Amanda Phillips, "#transformDH—A Call to Action Following ASA 2011," *HASTAC*, October 26, 2011, http://www.hastac.org/blogs/amanda-phillips/2011/10/26/transformdh-call-action-following-asa-2011; Alexis Lothian, "Marked Bodies, Transformative Scholarship, and the Question of Theory in Digital Humanities," *Journal of Digital Humanities* 1, no. 1 (2011), http://journalofdigitalhumanities.org/1-1/marked-bodies-transformative-scholarship-and-the-question-of-theory-in-digital-humanities-by-alexis-lothian/; and Alexis Lothian and Amanda Phillips, "Can Digital Humanities Mean Transformative Critique?" *Journal of E-Media Studies* 3, no. 1 (2013). A sympathetic but slightly different approach was taken by Natalia Cecire around the same time (2011), in essays that also influenced the subsequent conversation; see, for example, Natalia Cecire, "Introduction: Theory and the Virtues of Digital Humanities," *Journal of Digital Humanities* 1, no. 1 (2011), http://journalofdigitalhumanities.org/1-1/introduction-theory-and-the-virtues-of-digital-humanities-by-natalia-cecire/; and Natalia Cecire, "When DH Was in Vogue; or, THATCamp Theory," *Works Cited*, October 2011, http://nataliacecire.blogspot.com/2011/10/when-dh-was-in-vogue-or-thatcamp-theory.html.

26. See Tony Bennett, "Counting and Seeing the Social Action of Literary Form: Franco Moretti and the Sociology of Literature," *Cultural Sociology* 3, no. 2 (2009): 277–297; Federica Frabetti, "Rethinking the Digital Humanities in the Context of Originary Technicity," *Culture Machine* 12 (2011), http://www.culturemachine.net/index.php/cm/article/view/431/461; Gary Hall, "The Digital Humanities Beyond Computing: A Postscript," *Culture Machine* 12 (2011), http://www.culturemachine.net/index.php/cm/article/view/441/471; Kenta Tsuda, "Academicians of Lagado?" *New Left Review*, no. 72 (2011): 80–109; Kimon Keramidas, "Afterword: The DML and the Digital Humanities," *JiTP: Journal of Interactive Technology & Pedagogy*, no. 2 (2012), http://jitp

.commons.gc.cuny.edu/?p=1512; Jessica Enoch and Jean Bessette, "Meaningful Engagements: Feminist Historiography and the Digital Humanities," *College Composition and Communication* 64, no. 4 (2013): 634–660; Gary Hall, "Toward a Postdigital Humanities: Cultural Analytics and the Computational Turn to Data-Driven Scholarship," *American Literature* 85, no. 4 (2013): 781–809; Tom Eyers, "The Perils of the 'Digital Humanities': New Positivisms and the Fate of Literary Theory," *Postmodern Culture* 23, no. 2 (2013); Fiona M. Barnett, "The Brave Side of Digital Humanities," *Differences* 25, no. 1 (2014): 64–78; Brian Connolly, "Against Accumulation," *J19: The Journal of Nineteenth-Century Americanists* 2, no. 1 (2014): 172–179; Tim Cresswell, "Deja Vu All over Again: Spatial Science, Quantitative Revolutions and the Culture of Numbers," *Dialogues in Human Geography* 4, no. 1 (2014): 54–58; Alexander R. Galloway, "The Cybernetic Hypothesis," *Differences* 25, no. 1 (2014): 107–131; David Golumbia, "Death of a Discipline," *Differences* 25, no. 1 (2014): 156–176; Richard Grusin, "The Dark Side of Digital Humanities: Dispatches from Two Recent MLA Conventions," *Differences* 25, no. 1 (2014): 79–92; Djelal Kadir, "Dissent and Digital Transumption in an Age of Insecurity," *English Language Notes* 52, no. 2 (2014): 13–24; Adeline Koh, "Niceness, Building, and Opening the Genealogy of the Digital Humanities: Beyond the Social Contract of Humanities Computing," *Differences* 25, no. 1 (2014): 93–106; Brian Lennon, "The Digital Humanities and National Security," *Differences* 25, no. 1 (2014): 132–155; Tara McPherson, "Designing for Difference," *Differences* 25, no. 1 (2014): 177–188; Rita Raley, "Digital Humanities for the Next Five Minutes," *Differences* 25, no. 1 (2014): 26–45; and Matthew Wickman, "Robert Burns and Big Data; or, Pests of Quantity and Visualization," *Modern Language Quarterly* 75, no. 1 (2014): 1–28—all published between 2009 and 2014 (several in a special issue of the journal *Differences: A Journal of Feminist Cultural Studies* devoted to critique of the digital humanities movement). Relevant publications that appeared after the specific interval I am referring to here (2013–2014) include Deborah N. Cohn and Peter Mandler, "The History Manifesto: A Critique," *American Historical Review,* April 2015, 530–554; Lynn Hunt, "Does History Need a Reset?" *Annales* 2 (2015); and Andrew Kopec, "The Digital Humanities, Inc.: Literary Criticism and the Fate of a Profession," *PMLA* 131, no. 2 (2016): 324–339.

27. See Maria Konnikova, "Humanities Aren't a Science. Stop Treating Them Like One," *Scientific American,* August 2012.

28. Stanley Fish, "The Digital Humanities and the Transcending of Mortality," *New York Times,* January 9, 2012. See also Stanley Fish, "Mind Your P's and B's: The Digital Humanities and Interpretation," *New York Times,* January 23, 2012.

29. Stephen Marche, "Literature Is Not Data: Against Digital Humanities," *Los Angeles Review of Books,* October 2012, http://lareviewofbooks.org/essay/literature-is-not-data-against-digital-humanities.

30. Jon Baskin, Etay Zwick, and Jonny Thakkar, "The New Humanities," *The Point,* no. 8 (2014), http://www.thepointmag.com/2014/culture/the-new -humanities.

31. Adam Kirsch, "Technology is Taking over English Departments: The False Promise of the Digital Humanities," *New Republic,* May 2014, http://www .newrepublic.com/article/117428/limits-digital-humanities-adam-kirsch.

32. Catherine Tumber, "Bulldozing the Humanities," *The Baffler,* August 2014, http://www.thebaffler.com/blog/bulldozing-the-humanities/.

33. Kathryn Conrad, "What the Digital Humanities Can't Do," *Chronicle of Higher Education,* September 2014, http://chronicle.com/article/What-the -Digital-Humanities/148597/.

34. Carl Straumsheim, "Digital Humanities Bubble," *Inside Higher Ed,* May 8, 2014, http://www.insidehighered.com/news/2014/05/08/digital-humanities -wont-save-humanities-digital-humanists-say.

35. Hester Blum et al., "Don't Capitulate. Advocate," *Inside Higher Ed,* June 24, 2014, http://www.insidehighered.com/views/2014/06/24/essay-critiques-mla -report-graduate-education.

36. Adam Crymble, "Digital Hubris, Digital Humility: Essay on the Backlash Against the Digital Humanities Movement," *Inside Higher Ed,* July 15, 2014, http://www.insidehighered.com/views/2014/07/15/essay-backlash-against -digital-humanities-movement.

37. David J. Hinson, "Op-Ed: It's Time to Drop the Digital," *eCampus News,* July 2014, http://www.ecampusnews.com/top-news/please-drop-digital-429/.

38. Thomas Haigh, "We Have Never Been Digital," *Communications of the ACM* 57, no. 9 (2014): 24–28, 28.

39. Ibid, 28.

40. David M. Berry, "Post-Digital Humanities: Computation and Cultural Critique in the Arts and Humanities," *EDUCAUSE Review,* May 2014, 22.

41. See Michael Widner, "The Digital Humanists' (Lack of) Response to the Sur-veillance State," *Manuscripts and Machines,* August 2013, https://people.stan ford.edu/widner/content/digital-humanists-lack-response-surveillance -state.

42. Jan Christoph Meister, "Weaponizing the Digital Humanities," *Audior, Ergo Sum,* July 2014, http://jcmeister.de/english-weaponizing-the-digital -humanities/.

43. Jonathan Wilson, "Digital History in the Surveillance State," *Junto,* July 8, 2014, http://earlyamericanists.com/2014/07/08/digital-history-in-the -surveillance-state/.

44. Bettina Berendt, Marco Büchler, and Geoffrey Rockwell, "Is It Research or Is It Spying? Thinking-Through Ethics in Big Data AI and Other Knowledge Sciences," *Künstliche Intelligenz,* March 2015.

45. Ibid.

46. See Umberto Eco, *The Search for the Perfect Language,* trans. James Fentress (Oxford: Blackwell, 1995); Pieter A. Verburg, *Language and Its Functions: A Historico-Critical Study of Views Concerning the Functions of Language from the Pre-Humanistic Philology of Orleans to the Rationalistic Philology of Bopp,* trans. Paul Salmon (Amsterdam: John Benjamins, 1998).

47. Eco, *The Search for the Perfect Language,* 52.

48. Ibid., 53.

49. See David Golumbia, *The Cultural Logic of Computation* (Cambridge, MA: Harvard University Press, 2009).

50. Verburg, *Language and Its Functions,* 235, 387.

51. Ibid., 192–193.

52. See Edward W. Said, *Orientalism* (New York: Vintage Books, 2003); Said, *Humanism and Democratic Criticism* (New York: Columbia University Press, 2004); Said, "The Return to Philology," in *Humanism and Democratic Criticism* (New York: Columbia University Press, 2004), 57–84.

53. Henry Veggian, "From Philology to Formalism: Edith Rickert, John Matthews Manly, and the Literary/Reformist Beginnings of U.S. Cryptology," *Reader,* no. 54 (2006): 67–90, 75.

54. John M. Manly, "The President's Address: New Bottles," *PMLA* 35 (January 1920): xlvi–lx, xlvii–xlix.

55. Ibid., xlix.

56. Ibid., lviii.

57. See Carol S. Gruber, *Mars and Minerva: World War I and the Uses of the Higher Learning in America* (Baton Rouge: Louisiana State University Press, 1975), 187–206.

58. John M. Manly, "Introductory Note," in *New Methods for the Study of Literature* (Chicago: University of Chicago Press, 1927), ix–xii, xii. See also Manly, "The President's Address"; Edith Rickert, *New Methods for the Study of Literature* (Chicago: The University of Chicago Press, 1927).

59. See Fred Turner, *From Counterculture to Cyberculture: Stewart Brand, the Whole Earth Network, and the Rise of Digital Utopianism* (Chicago: University of Chicago Press, 2008).

60. See Montgomery McFate, "Anthropology and Counterinsurgency: The Strange Story of Their Curious Relationship," *Military Review* 85, no. 2 (2005): 24–38, 28, as cited below.

61. See McFate, "Anthropology and Counterinsurgency": "Over the past 30 years, as a result of anthropologists' individual career choices and the tendency toward reflexive self-criticism contained within the discipline itself, the discipline has become hermetically sealed within its Ivory Tower. . . . The retreat to the Ivory Tower is also a product of the deep isolationist tendencies within the discipline. Following the Vietnam War, it was fashionable among anthropologists to reject the discipline's historic ties to colonialism" (28).

62. I use the term "modularization" in the everyday sense, here, connoting both miniaturization and portability; but I do also have in mind Lev Manovich's identification of modularity as a "principle" of new media, Tara McPherson's analyses of modularity and "lenticular logics," and David Golumbia's critiques of philosophical functionalism. See Lev Manovich, *The Language of New Media* (Cambridge, MA: MIT Press, 2001); Tara McPherson, "Why Are the Digital Humanities So White? Or Thinking the Histories of Race and Computation," in *Debates in the Digital Humanities,* ed. Matthew K. Gold (Minneapolis: University of Minnesota Press, 2012), 139–160; and Golumbia, *The Cultural Logic of Computation,* especially chapter 3, "Genealogies of Philosophical Functionalism."

63. In the working methods of the natural sciences and most of the social sciences, some form of automated data processing was long since routine; this, perhaps, is one reason why we have seen no assertive evangelism for a "Digital Natural Sciences," and comparatively less for a "Digital Social Sciences" as such, after 2001. (That's not to say none of the latter: see, for example, the website of the Computational Social Science Society of the Americas: http://computationalsocialscience.org/.)

64. See Dana Priest and William M. Arkin, "A Hidden World, Growing Beyond Control," *Washington Post,* July 19, 2010, "National Security Inc.," *Washington Post,* July 20, 2010, and "The Secrets Next Door," *Washington Post,* July 21, 2010.

65. Priest and Arkin, "A Hidden World, Growing Beyond Control."

66. Phrasing from section of the DARPA website titled "Opportunities: Universities," http://www.darpa.mil/Opportunities/Universities/.

67. See, for example, Kristina Winbladh, Hadar Ziv, and Debra J. Richardson, "iMuse: Interactive Model-Based Use-Case and Storytelling Environment," in *Proceedings of the Eighteenth ACM SIGSOFT International Symposium on Foundations of Software Engineering,* FSE '10 (New York: ACM, 2010), 383–384, a project supported by a Young Faculty Award in 2011. See also the workshop advertised by DARPA in February 2011 titled "Stories, Neuroscience and Experimental Technologies (STORyNET): Analysis and Decomposition of Narratives in Security Contexts"; Bruce Sterling, "Design Fiction: Special Notice DARPA-SN-11-20: Stories, Neuroscience and Experimental Technologies (STORyNET): Analysis and Decomposition of Narratives in Security Contexts," *Wired Magazine: Beyond the Beyond,* February 2011. I thank both David Golumbia and Michael Holquist for this reference. At least two digital humanities enthusiasts with faculty appointments in a university department of English in the United States have recorded their participation in this workshop in their online curricula vitae.

68. See "Student Opportunities," http://www.cia.gov/careers/student-opportunities/; and "Opportunities for You," http://www.nsa.gov/careers/opportunities_4_u/students/index.shtml.

69. See Dave H. Price, "The CIA's Campus Spies," *Counterpunch,* March 2005, and "Obama's Classroom Spies: Son of PRISP," *Counterpunch,* June 2009.

70. See Will Sommer, "GU Profs Receive Secret CIA Funds," *Georgetown Voice,* April 2009, detailing CIA funding of research performed by Georgetown University faculty members.

71. See Noah Shachtman, "Be More Than You Can Be," *Wired* 15, no. 3 (2007).

72. See "GIS in the Defense and Intelligence Communities" (Redlands, CA: Esri, 2007), http://www.esri.com/library/brochures/pdfs/gis-in-defense.pdf.

73. Matthew L. Jockers, *Macroanalysis: Digital Methods and Literary History,* Topics in the Digital Humanities (Urbana: University of Illinois Press, 2013), 20. Palantir Technologies is the CIA-funded tech startup that denies that its "Prism" data analysis product has any connection to the National Security Agency's program of the same name. See Rebecca Greenfield, "CIA-Funded Startup Palantir Denies Link to NSA—but They Both Make a 'Prism,'" *Atlantic Wire,* June 2013, http://www.theatlanticwire.com/technology/2013/06/palantir-prism-nsa/66013/.

74. See John Gledhill, "On the Moos Controversy," *Association of Social Anthropologists of the UK and Commonwealth,* 2006, http://www.theasa.org/ethics/discussion1.shtml; Hugh Gusterson and David Price, "PRISP: Spies in Our Midst," *American Anthropological Association,* 2007, http://www.aaanet.org/press/an/infocus/prisp/gusterson.htm; Robert Albro et al., "Final Report on the Army's Human Terrain System Proof of Concept Program" (American Anthropological Association Commission on the Engageme nt of Anthropology with the US Security; Intelligence Communities [CEAUSSIC], October 2009), http://www.aaanet.org/cmtes/commissions/CEAUSSIC/upload/CEAUSSIC_HTS_Final_Report.pdf; Serena Golden, "A Protest Resignation: Prominent Anthropologist Resigns in Protest from National Academy of Sciences," *Inside Higher Ed,* February 25, 2013, http://www.insidehighered.com/news/2013/02/25/prominent-anthropologist-resigns-protest-national-academy-sciences.

75. See Scott Jaschik, "Millions for 'Strategic' Languages," *Inside Higher Ed,* January 4, 2006, http://www.insidehighered.com/news/2006/01/04/language; Rob Capriccioso, "Bush Push on 'Critical' Foreign Languages," *Inside Higher Ed,* January 6, 2006, http://www.insidehighered.com/news/2006/01/06/foreign.

76. Matthew G. Kirschenbaum et al., "Should DHers Accept Military / Defense Funding? Digital Humanities Questions & Answers," *Digital Humanities Questions & Answers,* 2011, http://digitalhumanities.org/answers/topic/should-dhers-accept-militarydefense-funding.

77. Because "Digital Humanities Questions & Answers" appears to use only relative time stamps for forum posts, this judgment is based on the time stamps

of Internet Archive captures of the URL address content, along with the relative time stamps for forum postings included in those captures.

78. Kirschenbaum et al., "Should DHers Accept Military / Defense Funding?" (emphasis in original).

79. Ibid.

80. Gruber, *Mars and Minerva,* 259.

Acknowledgments

An earlier version of Chapter 1 appeared with the same title in *diacritics* 43.1 (Johns Hopkins University Press, 2015): 82–104. © 2015 by The Johns Hopkins University Press. An earlier version of Chapter 3 with the same title was included in *A Companion to Translation Studies*, ed. Sandra Bermann and Catherine Porter (Wiley-Blackwell, 2014): 135–146. © 2014 John Wiley & Sons, Ltd. Other material from Chapter 3 appeared as "Can Multilingualism Be Simulated?" in *Critical Multilingualism Studies* 1.1 (University of Arizona, November 2012): 94–106 (CC BY 3.0). An earlier version of Chapter 5 appeared with the same title in *differences: A Journal of Feminist Cultural Studies,* 25.1 (Duke University Press, 2014): 132–155. © 2014 by Brown University and *differences: A Journal of Feminist Cultural Studies.* I thank Johns Hopkins University Press, Wiley-Blackwell, and Duke University Press for permission to incorporate this material.

Index